1, 2, & 3 JOHN
A Commentary in the Wesleyan Tradition

*New Beacon Bible Commentary

1, 2, & 3 JOHN
A Commentary in the Wesleyan Tradition

Rick Williamson

BEACON HILL PRESS
OF KANSAS CITY

Copyright 2010
by Beacon Hill Press of Kansas City

ISBN 978-0-8341-2395-3

Cover Design: J.R. Caines
Interior Design: Sharon Page

Unless otherwise indicated all Scripture quotations are from the *Holy Bible, New International Version*® (NIV®). Copyright © 1973, 1978, 1984 by Biblica, Inc.™ Used by permission of Zondervan. All rights reserved worldwide. www.zondervan.com.

American Standard Version (ASV).

King James Version (KJV).

The following copyrighted versions of the Bible are used by permission.

The Holy Bible, English Standard Version (ESV), copyright © 2001 by Crossway Bibles, a division of Good News Publishers. All rights reserved.

The *New American Bible* (NAB). Copyright © 1970 by the Confraternity of Christian Doctrine, 3211 4th St. N.E., Washington, DC 20017-1194. All rights reserved.

The *New American Standard Bible*® (NASB®), © copyright The Lockman Foundation 1960, 1962, 1963, 1968, 1971, 1972, 1973, 1975, 1977, 1995.

The *New Jerusalem Bible* (NJB), copyright © 1985 by Darton, Longman & Todd, Ltd., and Doubleday, a division of Bantam Doubleday Dell Publishing Group, Inc. Reprinted by permission.

The *New King James Version* (NKJV). Copyright © 1979, 1980, 1982 Thomas Nelson, Inc.

The *Holy Bible, New Living Translation* (NLT), copyright 1996, 2004. Used by permission of Tyndale House Publishers, Inc., Carol Stream, IL 60188. All rights reserved.

The *New Revised Standard Version* (NRSV) of the Bible, copyright 1989 by the Division of Christian Education of the National Council of the Churches of Christ in the USA. All rights reserved.

The *Revised Standard Version* (RSV) of the Bible, copyright 1946, 1952, 1971 by the Division of Christian Education of the National Council of the Churches of Christ in the USA.

Library of Congress Cataloging-in-Publication Data

Williamson, Rick
  1, 2 & 3 John / Rick Williamson.
    p. cm. — (New Beacon Bible commentary)
  Includes bibliographical references.
  ISBN 978-0-8341-2395-3 (pbk.)
  1. Bible. N.T. Epistles of John—Commentaries. I. Title. II. Title: 1, 2, and 3 John.
  BS2805.53.W56 2010
  227'.9407—dc22

2010027185

DEDICATION

To my beloved wife, Gladys,
and our dear children, Melissa and Jared,
for their love, patience, and support.

COMMENTARY EDITORS

General Editors

Alex Varughese
    Ph.D., Drew University
    Professor of Biblical Literature
    Mount Vernon Nazarene University
    Mount Vernon, Ohio

Roger Hahn
    Ph.D., Duke University
    Dean of the Faculty
    Professor of New Testament
    Nazarene Theological Seminary
    Kansas City, Missouri

George Lyons
    Ph.D., Emory University
    Professor of New Testament
    Northwest Nazarene University
    Nampa, Idaho

Section Editors

Joseph Coleson
    Ph.D., Brandeis University
    Professor of Old Testament
    Nazarene Theological Seminary
    Kansas City, Missouri

Robert Branson
    Ph.D., Boston University
    Professor of Biblical Literature
        Emeritus
    Olivet Nazarene University
    Bourbonnais, Illinois

Alex Varughese
    Ph.D., Drew University
    Professor of Biblical Literature
    Mount Vernon Nazarene University
    Mount Vernon, Ohio

Jim Edlin
    Ph.D., Southern Baptist Theological
        Seminary
    Professor of Biblical Literature and
        Languages
    Chair, Division of Religion and
        Philosophy
    MidAmerica Nazarene University
    Olathe, Kansas

Kent Brower
    Ph.D., The University of Manchester
    Vice Principal
    Senior Lecturer in Biblical Studies
    Nazarene Theological College
    Manchester, England

George Lyons
    Ph.D., Emory University
    Professor of New Testament
    Northwest Nazarene University
    Nampa, Idaho

Frank G. Carver
    Ph.D., New College, University of
        Edinburgh
    Professor Emeritus of Religion
    Point Loma Nazarene University
    San Diego, California

CONTENTS

General Editors' Preface	11
Author's Preface	13
Abbreviations	15
Bibliography	21
1 JOHN	29
INTRODUCTION	31
A. Authorship	31
B. Date	33
C. Provenance	34
D. Audience	35
E. Occasion and Purpose	35
F. Sociological and Cultural Issues	36
1. Connections Between First-Century Churches	36
2. Use of Family Language	36
G. Textual Witnesses	37
H. Literary Features	38
1. Letter Forms and 1, 2, and 3 John	38
2. Poetic Forms	39
3. Limited Scriptural Allusions	40
4. 1, 2, and 3 John and the Gospel of John	40
I. Theological Themes	41
1. Christology	41
2. Soteriology	42
3. The Spirit	42
4. Ethics	43
5. The World	44
6. Hospitality	44
7. Ecclesiology	45
8. Eschatology	46
J. Hermeneutical Issues	47
1. Authorship and Reading the Letters	47
2. Perspective of the Author and a Profile of the Opponents	49
3. Relationship of the Letters to the Gospel of John and How That Informs Our Reading	50
COMMENTARY	53
I. Prologue and Premises: 1 John 1:1-10	53
A. The Life Appeared (1:1-4)	53
B. Forgiveness and Cleansing (1:5-10)	63

II. Belonging to God and Resisting the Enemy: 1 John 2:1-29 79
   A. Jesus Our Defender (2:1-6) 79
   B. In the Light or in the Darkness? (2:7-11) 87
   C. Words for All Ages (2:12-14) 91
   D. Love God, Not the World (2:15-17) 95
   E. Antichrists (2:18-23) 98
   F. An Anointing and Abiding (2:24-29) 104

III. Christlike Love Now and When Christ Appears: 1 John 3:1-24 109
   A. When He Appears: A Call to Cleansing (3:1-6) 109
   B. Destroying the Devil's Work (3:7-10) 117
   C. Love and Hate, Life and Death (3:11-15) 121
   D. Love in Action (3:16-24) 124

IV. Testing the Spirits and Trusting God's Love: 1 John 4:1-21 133
   A. Test the Spirits (4:1-6) 133
   B. God's Son an Atoning Sacrifice (4:7-15) 141
   C. Perfect Love Drives Out Fear (4:16-21) 148

V. Life in the Son, Death in Departing: 1 John 5:1-21 155
   A. Overcoming Faith (5:1-5) 155
   B. Witnesses to the Truth (5:6-12) 160
   C. Assurance of Eternal Life (5:13-17) 165
   D. Things We Know (5:18-21) 171

2 JOHN 177

INTRODUCTION 179
   A. Authorship, Date, Provenance, Audience, Occasion, Purpose, Sociological/Cultural Issues, and Textual History 179
   B. Literary Features 179
   C. Theological Themes 180
   D. Hermeneutical Issues 180

COMMENTARY 183

VI. Welcomes and Warnings: 2 John 1-13 183
   A. Greetings and Relationships (1-3) 183
   B. Joy Because of Obedience (4-6) 188
   C. Warnings to Enable Faithful Walking (7-11) 190
   D. Future Plans (12-13) 195

3 JOHN	199
INTRODUCTION	201
A. Authorship, Date, Provenance, Audience, Occasion, Purpose, Sociological/Cultural Issues, and Textual History	201
B. Literary Features	201
C. Theological Themes	202
D. Hermeneutical Issues	203
COMMENTARY	205
VII. Supporting Ministers and Painful Separations: 3 John 1-14	205
A. Greetings and Relationships (1-4)	205
B. Ministry and Hospitality (5-8)	209
C. Dangerous Division (9-10)	213
D. Healing Words and Hope (11-14)	216

GENERAL EDITORS' PREFACE

The purpose of the New Beacon Bible Commentary is to make available to pastors and students in the twenty-first century a biblical commentary that reflects the best scholarship in the Wesleyan theological tradition. The commentary project aims to make this scholarship accessible to a wider audience to assist them in their understanding and proclamation of Scripture as God's Word.

Writers of the volumes in this series not only are scholars within the Wesleyan theological tradition and experts in their field but also have special interest in the books assigned to them. Their task is to communicate clearly the critical consensus and the full range of other credible voices who have commented on the Scriptures. Though scholarship and scholarly contribution to the understanding of the Scriptures are key concerns of this series, it is not intended as an academic dialogue within the scholarly community. Commentators of this series constantly aim to demonstrate in their work the significance of the Bible as the church's book and the contemporary relevance and application of the biblical message. The project's overall goal is to make available to the church and for her service the fruits of the labors of scholars who are committed to their Christian faith.

The *New International Version* (NIV) is the reference version of the Bible used in this series; however, the focus of exegetical study and comments is the biblical text in its original language. When the commentary uses the NIV, it is printed in bold. The text printed in bold italics is the translation of the author. Commentators also refer to other translations where the text may be difficult or ambiguous.

The structure and organization of the commentaries in this series seeks to facilitate the study of the biblical text in a systematic and methodical way. Study of each biblical book begins with an **Introduction** section that gives an overview of authorship, date, provenance, audience, occasion, purpose, sociological/cultural issues, textual history, literary features, hermeneutical issues, and theological themes necessary to understand the book. This section also includes a brief outline of the book and a list of general works and standard commentaries.

The commentary section for each biblical book follows the outline of the book presented in the introduction. In some volumes, readers will find section ***overviews*** of large portions of scripture with general comments on their overall literary structure and other literary features. A consistent feature of the commentary is the paragraph-by-paragraph study of biblical texts. This section has three parts: **Behind the Text**, **In the Text**, and **From the Text**.

The goal of the **Behind the Text** section is to provide the reader with all the relevant information necessary to understand the text. This includes specific historical situations reflected in the text, the literary context of the text, sociological and cultural issues, and literary features of the text.

In the Text explores what the text says, following its verse-by-verse structure. This section includes a discussion of grammatical details, word studies, and the connectedness of the text to other biblical books/passages or other parts of the book being studied (the canonical relationship). This section provides transliterations of key words in Hebrew and Greek and their literal meanings. The goal here is to explain what the author would have meant and/or what the audience would have understood as the meaning of the text. This is the largest section of the commentary.

The **From the Text** section examines the text in relation to the following areas: theological significance, intertextuality, the history of interpretation, use of the Old Testament scriptures in the New Testament, interpretation in later church history, actualization, and application.

The commentary provides **sidebars** on topics of interest that are important but not necessarily part of an explanation of the biblical text. These topics are informational items and may cover archaeological, historical, literary, cultural, and theological matters that have relevance to the biblical text. Occasionally, longer detailed discussions of special topics are included as **excurses**.

We offer this series with our hope and prayer that readers will find it a valuable resource for their understanding of God's Word and an indispensable tool for their critical engagement with the biblical texts.

Roger Hahn, Centennial Initiative General Editor
Alex Varughese, General Editor (Old Testament)
George Lyons, General Editor (New Testament)

AUTHOR'S PREFACE

The letters associated with the name John comprise only seven chapters, but their content is significant beyond their size. Their call to transformed lives has been important for Christians generally and to the holiness tradition especially.

First John presents lofty claims: "I write this to you so that you will not sin" (2:1); "No one who is born of God will continue to sin" (3:9); and "Anyone born of God does not continue to sin" (5:18). These must be understood within their original context, without dismissing their enduring spiritual implications. This commentary attempts to balance the scriptural call to holy living with the pastoral call to treat redemptively those who fail.

The smaller letters of 2 John and 3 John occasioned little attention from most early commentators. John Calvin commented only on 1 John. Martin Luther lectured extensively on 1 John, but ignored the smaller letters. John Wesley's *Explanatory Notes on the New Testament* offer relatively few comments on 2 John and 3 John. These personal letters offer a significant window into the life of these first-century churches. Readers encounter issues of ecclesiology (church leadership, gender issues, and how the churches were interconnected) and social/cultural realities. Here we see especially how hospitality in the early churches was related to itinerant evangelism.

Several people helped shape this volume. Shannon Pavlovic, while a theological studies major at Mount Vernon Nazarene University (MVNU), made numerous improvements in style and in content. Pastors Tracy Ogden Johnson, Bob Morrison, and Merrill Williams reviewed selected chapters for their preaching and pastoral values. Walter Baughman, MVNU librarian, suggested improvements in style and clarity. I am deeply indebted to Frank Carver for his patience and wise editing throughout this process.

Finally, my appreciation goes to students who have engaged this rich material with me in Greek and Johannine literature classes over the past few years. May all who are called to preach, teach, and pastor advance the cause of Jesus Christ and challenge those they lead to "walk in the light, as he is in the light." May we all experience "fellowship with one another, [as] the blood of Jesus, his Son, purifies us from all sin" (1 John 1:7).

ABBREVIATIONS

With a few exceptions, these abbreviations follow those in *The SBL Handbook of Style* (Alexander 1999).

General

ad loc.	*ad locum*, at the place discussed
A.D.	anno Domini (precedes date) (equivalent to C.E.)
B.C.	before Christ (follows date) (equivalent to B.C.E.)
B.C.E.	before the Common Era
C.E.	Common Era
ca.	*circa*, approximate time
cf.	confer, compare
ch	chapter
chs	chapters
e.g.	*exempli gratia*, for example
esp.	especially
etc.	*et cetera*, and the rest
f(f).	and the following one(s)
i.e.	*id est*, that is
ktl.	etc. (in Greek transliteration)
lit.	literally
LXX	Septuagint (Greek translation of the OT)
MS	manuscript
MSS	manuscripts
MT	Masoretic Text (of the OT)
n.	note
n.d.	no date
nn.	notes
n.p.	no place; no publisher; no page
NT	New Testament
OT	Old Testament
s.v.	*sub verbo*, under the word
v	verse
vv	verses
vs.	versus

Modern English Versions

ASV	American Standard Version
ESV	English Standard Version
KJV	King James Version
NAB	New American Bible
NASB	New American Standard Bible
NIV	New International Version
NJB	New Jerusalem Bible
NKJV	New King James Version
NLT	New Living Translation
NRSV	New Revised Standard Version
RSV	Revised Standard Version

Print Conventions for Translations

Bold font	NIV (bold without quotation marks in the text under study; elsewhere in the regular font, with quotation marks and no further identification)
Bold italic font	Author's translation (without quotation marks)

Behind the Text:	Literary or historical background information average readers might not know from reading the biblical text alone
In the Text:	Comments on the biblical text, words, phrases, grammar, and so forth
From the Text:	The use of the text by later interpreters, contemporary relevance, theological and ethical implications of the text, with particular emphasis on Wesleyan concerns.

Old Testament

Gen	Genesis	Dan	Daniel		
Exod	Exodus	Hos	Hosea		
Lev	Leviticus	Joel	Joel		
Num	Numbers	Amos	Amos		
Deut	Deuteronomy	Obad	Obadiah		
Josh	Joshua	Jonah	Jonah		
Judg	Judges	Mic	Micah		
Ruth	Ruth	Nah	Nahum		
1—2 Sam	1—2 Samuel	Hab	Habakkuk		
1—2 Kgs	1—2 Kings	Zeph	Zephaniah		
1—2 Chr	1—2 Chronicles	Hag	Haggai		
Ezra	Ezra	Zech	Zechariah		
Neh	Nehemiah	Mal	Malachi		
Esth	Esther				
Job	Job				
Ps/Pss	Psalm/Psalms				
Prov	Proverbs				
Eccl	Ecclesiastes				
Song	Song of Songs / Song of Solomon				
Isa	Isaiah				
Jer	Jeremiah				
Lam	Lamentations				
Ezek	Ezekiel				

(Note: Chapter and verse numbering in the MT and LXX often differ compared to those in English Bibles. To avoid confusion, all biblical references follow the chapter and verse numbering in English translations, even when the text in the MT and LXX is under discussion.)

New Testament

Matt	Matthew
Mark	Mark
Luke	Luke
John	John
Acts	Acts
Rom	Romans
1—2 Cor	1—2 Corinthians
Gal	Galatians
Eph	Ephesians
Phil	Philippians
Col	Colossians
1—2 Thess	1—2 Thessalonians
1—2 Tim	1—2 Timothy
Titus	Titus
Phlm	Philemon
Heb	Hebrews
Jas	James
1—2 Pet	1—2 Peter
1—2—3 John	1—2—3 John
Jude	Jude
Rev	Revelation

Apocrypha:

APOT	*The Apocrypha and Pseudepigrapha of the Old Testament*. Edited by R. H. Charles. 2 vols. Oxford, 1913.
Bar	Baruch
Add Dan	Additions to Daniel
Pr Azar	Prayer of Azariah
Bel	Bel and the Dragon
Sg Three	Song of the Three Young Men
Sus	Susanna
1—2 Esd	1—2 Esdras
Add Esth	Additions to Esther
Ep Jer	Epistle of Jeremiah
Jdt	Judith
1—2 Macc	1—2 Maccabees
3—4 Macc	3—4 Maccabees
Pr Man	Prayer of Manasseh
Ps 151	Psalm 151
Sir	Sirach/Ecclesiasticus
Tob	Tobit
Wis	Wisdom of Solomon

OT Pseudepigrapha:

Ahiqar	*Ahiqar*
Apoc. Ab.	*Apocalypse of Abraham*
Apoc. Adam	*Apocalypse of Adam*
Apoc. Dan.	*Apocalypse of Daniel*
Apoc. El. (H)	Hebrew *Apocalypse of Elijah*
Apoc. El. (C)	Coptic *Apocalypse of Elijah*
Apoc. Mos.	*Apocalypse of Moses*
Apoc. Sedr.	*Apocalypse of Sedrach*
Apoc. Zeph.	*Apocalypse of Zephaniah*
Apocr. Ezek.	*Apocrypon of Ezekiel*
Aris. Ex.	*Aristeas the Exegete*
Aristob.	*Aristobulus*
Artap.	*Artapanus*
As. Mos.	*Assumption of Moses*
2 Bar.	*2 Baruch (Syriac Apocalypse)*

3 Bar.	3 Baruch (Greek Apocalypse)
4 Bar.	4 Baruch (Paraleipomena Jeremiou)
Bk. Noah	Book of Noah
Cav. Tr.	Cave of Treasures
Cl. Mal.	Cleodemus Malchus
Dem.	Demetrius (the Chronographer)
El. Mod.	Eldad and Modad
1 En.	1 Enoch (Ethiopic Apocalypse)
2 En.	2 Enoch (Slavonic Apocalypse)
3 En.	3 Enoch (Hebrew Apocalypse)
Eup.	Eupolemus
Ezek. Trag.	Ezekiel the Tragedian
4 Ezra	4 Ezra
5 Apoc. Syr. Pss.	Five Apocryphal Syriac Psalms
Gk. Apoc. Ezra	Greek Apocalypse of Ezra
Hec. Ab.	Hecataeus of Abdera
Hel. Syn. Pr.	Hellenistic Synagogal Prayers
Hist. Jos.	History of Joseph
Hist. Rech.	History of the Rechabites
Jan. Jam.	Jannes and Jambres
Jos. Asen.	Joseph and Aseneth
Jub.	Jubilees
L.A.B.	Liber antiquitatum biblicarum
L.A.E.	Life of Adam and Eve
Lad. Jac.	Ladder of Jacob
Let. Aris.	Letter of Aristeas
Liv. Pro.	Lives of the Prophets
Lost Tr.	The Lost Tribes
Ps.-Philo	See L.A.B.
3 Macc.	3 Maccabees
4 Macc.	4 Maccabees
5 Macc.	5 Maccabees (Arabic)
Mart. Ascen. Isa.	Martyrdom and Ascension of Isaiah
Odes Sol.	Odes of Solomon
Ph. E. Poet	Philo the Epic Poet
Pr. Jac.	Prayer of Jacob
Pr. Jos.	Prayer of Joseph
Pr. Man.	Prayer of Manasseh
Pr. Mos.	Prayer of Moses
Ps.-Eup.	Pseudo-Eupolemus
Ps.-Hec.	Pseudo-Hecataeus
Ps.-Orph.	Pseudo-Orpheus
Ps.-Phoc.	Pseudo-Phocylides
Pss. Sol.	Psalms of Solomon
Ques. Ezra	Questions of Ezra
Rev. Ezra	Revelation of Ezra
Sib. Or.	Sibylline Oracles
Syr. Men.	Sentences of the Syriac Menander
T. 12 Patr.	Testaments of the Twelve Patriarchs
T. Ash.	Testament of Asher
T. Benj.	Testament of Benjamin
T. Dan	Testament of Dan
T. Gad	Testament of Gad
T. Iss.	Testament of Issachar
T. Jos.	Testament of Joseph
T. Jud.	Testament of Judah
T. Levi	Testament of Levi
T. Naph.	Testament of Naphtali
T. Reu.	Testament of Reuben
T. Sim.	Testament of Simeon

T. Zeb.	Testament of Zebulun	
T. 3 Patr.	Testaments of the Three Patriarchs	
T. Ab.	Testament of Abraham	
T. Isaac	Testament of Isaac	
T. Jac.	Testament of Jacob	
T. Adam	Testament of Adam	
T. Hez.	Testament of Hezekiah	
T. Job	Testament of Job	
T. Mos.	Testament of Moses	
T. Sol.	Testament of Solomon	
Theod.	Theodotus, *On the Jews*	
Treat. Shem	*Treatise of Shem*	
Vis. Ezra	*Vision of Ezra*	

Dead Sea Scrolls and Related Texts

Q	Qumran
1Qap Gen^{ar}	*Genesis Apocryphon*
1QH^a	*Hodayot^a* or *Thanksgiving Hymns^a*
1QIsa^a	Isaiah^a
1QIsa^b	Isaiah^b
1QM	*Milkamah* or *War Scroll*
1QpHab	*Pesher Habakkuk*
1QS	*Serek Hayakad* or *Rule of the Community*
CD	Cairo Genizah copy of the *Damascus Document*

Josephus

Vita	*Vita*
Life	*The Life*
C. Ap.	*Contra Apionem*
Ag. Ap.	*Against Apion*
A.J.	*Antiquitates judaicae*
Ant.	*Jewish Antiquities*
B.J.	*Bellum judaicum*
J.W.	*Jewish War*

Apostolic Fathers

Barn.	*Barnabas*
1–2 Clem.	*1–2 Clement*
Did.	*Didache*
Diogn.	*Diognetus*
Herm. Mand.	*Shepherd of Hermas, Mandate*
Herm. Sim.	*Shepherd of Hermas, Similitude*
Herm. Vis.	*Shepherd of Hermas, Vision*
Ign. Eph.	Ignatius, *To the Ephesians*
Ign. Magn.	Ignatius, *To the Magnesians*
Ign. Smyrn.	Ignatius, *To the Smyrnaeans*
Ign. Phld.	Ignatius, *To the Philadelphians*
Ign. Rom.	Ignatius, *To the Romans*
Ign. Pol.	Ignatius, *To Polycarp*
Ign. Trall.	Ignatius, *To the Trallians*
Mart. Pol.	*Martyrdom of Polycarp*
Pol. Phil.	Polycarp, *To the Philippians*

Later Fathers

Irenaeus

Epid.	*Epideixis tou apostolikou kērygmatos*	*Demonstration of the Apostolic Preaching*
Haer.	*Adversus haereses*	*Against Heresies*

Greek Transliteration

Greek	Letter	English
α	alpha	a
β	bēta	b
γ	gamma	g
γ	gamma nasal	n (before γ, κ, ξ, χ)
δ	delta	d
ε	epsilon	e
ζ	zēta	z
η	ēta	ē
θ	thēta	th
ι	iōta	i
κ	kappa	k
λ	lambda	l
μ	mu	m
ν	nu	n
ξ	xi	x
ο	omicron	o
π	pi	p
ρ	rhō	r
ρ	initial *rhō*	rh
σ/ς	sigma	s
τ	tau	t
υ	upsilon	y
υ	upsilon	u (in diphthongs: *au, eu, ēu, ou, ui*)
φ	phi	ph
χ	chi	ch
ψ	psi	ps
ω	ōmega	ō
῾	rough breathing	h (before initial vowels or diphthongs)

Hebrew Consonant Transliteration

Hebrew/Aramaic	Letter	English
א	alef	ʾ
ב	bet	b
ג	gimel	g
ד	dalet	d
ה	he	h
ו	vav	v or w
ז	zayin	z
ח	khet	ḥ
ט	tet	ṭ
י	yod	y
כ/ך	kaf	k
ל	lamed	l
מ/ם	mem	m
נ/ן	nun	n
ס	samek	s
ע	ayin	ʿ
פ/ף	pe	p; f (spirant)
צ/ץ	tsade	ṣ
ק	qof	q
ר	resh	r
שׂ	sin	ś
שׁ	shin	š
ת	tav	t; th (spirant)

BIBLIOGRAPHY

Akin, Daniel L. 2001. *1, 2, 3 John.* The New American Commentary 38. Nashville: Broadman and Holman.
Alexander, Patrick H., and others, eds. 1999. *The SBL Handbook of Style for Ancient Near Eastern, Biblical, and Early Christian Studies.* Peabody, Mass.: Hendrickson.
Ashton, John. 1992. *abba.* Pages 7-8 in vol. 1 of *Anchor Bible Dictionary.* See Freedman.
Balz, Horst Robert. 1990. *hagnos, ktl.* Pages 22-23 in vol. 1 of *Exegetical Dictionary of the New Testament.* Edited by Horst Robert Balz and Gerhard Schneider. 3 vols. Grand Rapids: Eerdmans, 1990–93. See Balz and Schneider.
Balz, Horst Robert, and Gerhard Schneider, eds. 1990–93. *Exegetical Dictionary of the New Testament.* 3 vols. Grand Rapids: Eerdmans.
Bauer, Walter, Frederick W. Danker, W. F. Arndt, and F. Wilbur Gingrich. 2000. *A Greek-English Lexicon of the New Testament and Other Early Christian Literature.* 3rd ed. Chicago: University of Chicago Press. Cited as BDAG.
Bauernfeind, Otto. 1967. *nikaō, ktl.* Pages 942-45 in vol. 4 of *Theological Dictionary of the New Testament.* See Kittel and Friedrich.
Becker, Ulrich, and Dietrich Müller. 1978. *angellō* in "Proclamation." Pages 44-48 in vol. 3 of *New International Dictionary of New Testament Theology.* See Brown, editor.
Bertram, Georg, Albert Dihle, Eduard Lohse, and Eduard Schweizer. 1974. *psychē, ktl.* Pages 608-66 in vol. 9 of *Theological Dictionary of the New Testament.* See Kittel and Friedrich.
Bettenson, Henry, ed. 1971. *Documents of the Christian Church.* New York: Oxford University Press.
Beutler, J. 1981. *martyria.* Pages 391-93 in vol. 2 of *Exegetical Dictionary of the New Testament.* Edited by H. Balz and G. Schneider. 3 vols. Grand Rapids: Eerdmans, 1990–93.
Black, Clifton C. 1990. Christian Ministry in Johannine Perspective. *Interpretation* 44, 1:29-41.
Blaney, Harvey J. S. 1967. The First Epistle of John. Pages 341-418 in vol. 10 of *Beacon Bible Commentary.* Kansas City: Beacon Hill Press of Kansas City.
Blass, F., A. Debrunner, and Robert W. Funk. 1961. *A Greek Grammar of the New Testament and Other Early Christian Literature.* Chicago: University of Chicago Press.
Böcher, O. 1993. *planaō, ktl.* Pages 98-100 in vol. 3 of *Exegetical Dictionary of the New Testament.* Seee Balz and Schneider.
Bogart, John. 1977. *Orthodox and Heretical Perfectionism in the Johannine Community as Evident in the First Epistle of John.* Society of Biblical Literature Dissertation Series, 33. Missoula, Mont.: Scholars Press.
Boice, James Montgomery. 1979. *The Epistles of John.* Grand Rapids: Baker.
Boring, M. Eugene. 1991. *The Continuing Voice of Jesus: Christian Prophecy and the Gospel Tradition.* Louisville, Ky.: Westminster/John Knox Press.
Bray, Gerald, ed. 2000. *James, 1-2 Peter, 1-3 John, Jude.* Ancient Christian Commentary on Scripture. New Testament. Vol. 11. Edited by Thomas C. Oden. Downers Grove, Ill.: InterVarsity Press.
Brooke, Alan England. 1912. *A Critical and Exegetical Commentary on the Johannine Epistles.* The International Critical Commentary. Edited by S. R. Driver and others. Edinburgh: T & T Clark.
Brown, Colin, ed. and trans. 1975-78. *New International Dictionary of New Testament Theology. New International Dictionary of New Testament Theology. Theologisches Begriffslexikon zum Neuen Testament.* Ed. Lothar Coenen, Erich Beyreuther *and* Hans Bietenhard. 3 vols. Grand Rapids: Zondervan.
Brown, Colin. 1978. Righteousness. Pages 352-77 in vol. 3 of *New International Dictionary of New Testament Theology.* See Colin Brown, ed.
Brown, Raymond E. 1979. *The Community of the Beloved Disciple.* New York: Paulist Press.
———. 1982. *The Epistles of John.* The Anchor Bible 30. Garden City, N.Y.: Doubleday.
Bruce, F. F. 1970. *The Epistles of John.* Grand Rapids: Eerdmans.
Büchsel, Friedrich. 1965. *thymos.* Pages 167-72 in vol. 3 of *Theological Dictionary of the New Testament.* See Kittel and Friedrich.
———. 1967. *monogenēs.* Pages 737-41 in vol. 4 of *Theological Dictionary of the New Testament.* See Kittel and Friedrich.
Büchsel, Friedrich, and Johannes Herrmann. 1965. *hileōs, ktl.* Pages 300-323 in vol. 3 of *Theological Dictionary of the New Testament.* See Kittel and Friedrich.

Bultmann, Rudolf. 1964. *aphiēmi, ktl.* Pages 509-12 in vol. 1 of *Theological Dictionary of the New Testament*. See Kittel and Friedrich.
———. 1973. *The Johannine Letters*. Translated by R. Philip O'Hara, Lane C. McGaughy, and Robert W. Funk. Hermeneia: A Critical and Historical Commentary on the Bible. Minneapolis: Fortress.
Burge, Gary M. 1996. *Letters of John*. Grand Rapids: Zondervan.
Burge, Gary M., Lynn H. Cohick, and Gene L. Green. 2009. *The New Testament in Antiquity: A Survey of the New Testament Within Its Cultural Contexts*. Grand Rapids: Zondervan.
Buttrick, G. A., ed. 1962. *Interpreter's Dictionary of the Bible*. 4 vols. Nashville: Abingdon.
Calvin, John. 1959. *The Gospel According to St. John 11-21 and The First Epistle of John*. Translated by T. H. L. Parker. Grand Rapids: Eerdmans.
———. 1999. *Commentaries*. 22 vols. Translated by John Owen. Edinburgh, Scotland: Calvin Translation Society. Repr. Grand Rapids: Baker.
Carver, Frank. 1996. *When Jesus Said Good-bye: John's Witness to the Holy Spirit*. Kansas City: Beacon Hill Press of Kansas City.
———. 2009. *2 Corinthians*. New Beacon Bible Commentary. Kansas City: Beacon Hill Press of Kansas City.
Charlesworth, James H., ed. 1983. *The Old Testament Pseudepigrapha*. Vol. 1. Garden City, N.Y.: Doubleday.
Clarke, Adam. n.d. *The New Testament of Our Lord and Saviour Jesus Christ*. Vol. 2. Romans to Revelation. Nashville: Abingdon.
Conzelmann, Hans. 1954. *Die Mitte der Zeit: Studien zur Theologie des Lukas*. Tübingen: Mohr.
———. 1961. *The Theology of Luke*. Translated by Geoffrey Buswell. New York: Harper and Row.
———. 1971. *skotia, ktl.* Pages 423-44 in vol. 7 of *Theological Dictionary of the New Testament*. See Kittel and Friedrich.
———. 1974. *pseudos, ktl.* Pages 594-603 in vol. 9 of *Theological Dictionary of the New Testament*. See Kittel and Friedrich.
Crossan, John Dominic. 1991. *The Historical Jesus: The Life of a Mediterranean Jewish Peasant*. San Francisco: HarperSanFrancisco.
———. 1994. *Jesus: A Revolutionary Biography*. New York: HarperSanFrancisco.
Culpepper, R. A. 1975. *The Johannine School*. Society of Biblical Literature Dissertation Series 26. Missoula, Mont.: Scholars Press.
———. 1998. *The Gospel and Letters of John*. Nashville: Abingdon.
Deissmann, Adolf. 1995. *Light from the Ancient East*. New York: George H. Doran Co., 1927. Translated by L. Strachan. Repr. Peabody, Mass.: Hendrickson.
Dodd, C. H. 1968. *The Interpretation of the Fourth Gospel*. Cambridge: Cambridge University Press.
Earle, Ralph. 1984. *Word Meanings in the New Testament*. Vol. 6. Kansas City: Beacon Hill Press of Kansas City.
Ebel, Günter. 1978. Walk, Run, Way, Conduct. Pages 933-47 in vol. 3 of *New International Dictionary of New Testament Theology*. See Colin Brown, ed.
Ehrman, Bart D. 2008. *The New Testament: A Historical Introduction to the Early Christian Writings*. Oxford: Oxford University Press.
Elwell, Walter A., and Robert W. Yarbrough, eds. 1998. *Readings from the First-Century World*. Grand Rapids: Baker.
Fields, Weston W. 2006. *The Dead Sea Scrolls: A Short History*. Boston: Brill.
Fiorenza, Elisabeth Schüssler. 1998. *The Book of Revelation: Justice and Judgment*. Minneapolis: Fortress Press.
Fleming, Steven Robert. 1999. Between Text and Sermon: 1 John 2:1-11. *Interpretation* 53, 1:65-68.
Flemming, Dean. 2009. *Philippians*. New Beacon Bible Commentary. Kansas City: Beacon Hill Press of Kansas City.
Freedman, David Noel, ed. 1992. *Anchor Bible Dictionary*. 6 vols. New York: Doubleday.
Gilmore, George W., and W. Caspari. 1949. Renunciation of the Devil in the Baptismal Rite. Pages 488-89 in vol. 9 of *The New Schaff-Herzog Encyclopedia of Religious Knowledge*. Edited by Samuel M. Jackson. 10 vols. Grand Rapids: Baker, 1949-50.
Greeven, Hans. 1964. *euchomai, ktl.* Pages 775-808 in vol. 2 of *Theological Dictionary of the New Testament*. See Kittel and Friedrich.
Haas, C., M. DeJonge, J. L. Swellengrebel. 1972. *A Translator's Handbook on the Letters of John*. New York: United Bible Societies.

Hartman, Lars. 1981. *onoma*. Pages 519-22 in vol. 2 of *Evangelical Dictionary of the New Testament*. See Balz and Schneider.

Hauck, Friedrich. 1967. *opheilō, ktl*. Pages 559-66 in vol. 5 of *Theological Dictionary of the New Testament*. See Kittel and Friedrich.

Hiers, Richard H. 1992. Day of Judgment. Pages 79-82 in vol. 2 of *Anchor Bible Dictionary*. See Freedman.

Hills, Julian. 1989. "Little children, keep yourselves from idols": 1 John 5:21 Reconsidered. *Catholic Biblical Quarterly* 51, 2:285-310.

Hofius, Otfried. 1991. *homologeō*. Pages 514-17 in vol. 2 of *Exegetical Dictionary of the New Testament*. See Balz and Schneider.

Houlden, J. L. 1973. *A Commentary on the Johannine Epistles*. Harper's New Testament Commentaries. New York: Harper.

Hübner, Hans. 1981. *menō*. Pages 407-8 in vol. 2 of *Exegetical Dictionary of the New Testament*. See Balz and Schneider.

———. 1993. *plēroō, ktl*. Pages 108-10 in vol. 3 of *Exegetical Dictionary of the New Testament*. See Balz and Schneider.

Jenni, E. 1962. Day of the Lord. Pages 784-85 in vol. 1 of *Interpreter's Dictionary of the Bible*. See Buttrick.

Jeremias, Joachim. 1971. *New Testament Theology*. Translated by J. S. Bowden. New York: Scribner's.

Johnson, Luke T. 1986. *The Writings of the New Testament: An Interpretation*. Philadelphia: Fortress Press.

———. 1996. *The Real Jesus: The Misguided Quest for the Historical Jesus and the Truth of the Traditional Gospels*. San Francisco: HarperSanFrancisco.

Johnson, S. E. 1962. Christ. Pages 563-71 in vol. 1 of *Interpreter's Dictionary of the Bible*. See Buttrick.

Jones, Peter Rhea. 2009. *1, 2 & 3 John*. Macon, Ga.: Smyth and Helwys.

Kimbrough, S. T., Jr. 1987. *Lost in Wonder: Charles Wesley—The Meaning of His Hymns Today*. Nashville: Upper Room.

Kittel, Gerhard, and Gerhard Friedrich, eds. 1964-76. *Theological Dictionary of the New Testament*. 10 vols. Grand Rapids: Eerdmans.

Koenig, John. 1992. Hospitality. Pages 299-301 in vol. 3 of *Anchor Bible Dictionary*. See Freedman. 6 vols.

Koester, Craig. 2006. Antichrist. Pages 175-78 in vol. 1 of the *New Interpreter's Dictionary of the Bible*. See Sakenfeld.

Köstenberger, Andreas J. 2009. *A Theology of John's Gospel and Letters: The Word, the Christ, the Son of God*. Biblical Theology of the New Testament. Grand Rapids: Zondervan.

Kruse, Colin G. 2000. *The Letters of John*. Grand Rapids: Eerdmans.

Liddell, H., 1996. *pros*. Pages 1496-99. *An Intermediate Greek English Lexicon*. 9th ed. Oxford: Oxford University Press.

Lieu, Judith M. 1991. *The Theology of the Johannine Epistles*. Cambridge: Cambridge University Press.

Limbeck, M. 1990. Pages 106-7 in vol. 1 of *Exegetical Dictionary of the New Testament*. See Balz and Schneider.

Link, Hans-Georg. 1976. Life. Pages 474-84 in vol. 2 of *New International Dictionary of New Testament Theology*. See Colin Brown, ed.

Malherbe, Abraham J. 1983. *Social Aspects of Early Christianity*. Philadelphia: Fortress Press.

Marrow, Stanley B. 2002. *kosmos* in John. *Catholic Biblical Quarterly* 64, 1:90-102.

Marshall, I. Howard. 1978. *The Epistles of John*. The New International Commentary on the New Testament 18. Grand Rapids: Eerdmans.

Mayer, B. 1990. *elpizō*. Pages 437-41 in vol. 1 of *Exegetical Dictionary of the New Testament*. See Balz and Schneider.

Mendenhall, G. E. 1962. Election. Pages 76-82 in vol. 2 of *Interpreter's Dictionary of the Bible*. See Buttrick.

Menoud, P. H. 1962. Martyr. Page 288 in vol. 3 of *Interpreter's Dictionary of the Bible*. See Buttrick.

Michaelis, Wilhelm. 1967. *euodoō*. Pages 109-14 in vol. 5 of *Theological Dictionary of the New Testament*. See Kittel and Friedrich.

Michel, Otto. 1971. *sphazō, sphagē*. Pages 925-39 in vol. 7 of *Theological Dictionary of the New Testament*. See Kittel and Friedrich.

Mitchell, Margaret M. 1998. "Diotrephes Does Not Receive Us": The Lexicographical and Social Context of 3 John 9-10. *Journal of Biblical Literature* 117, 2:299-320.

Mitton, C. L. 1962. Atonement. Pages 309-13 in vol. 1 of *Interpreter's Dictionary of the Bible*. See Buttrick.
Mounce, William D. 2003. *Basics of Biblical Greek*. Grand Rapids: Zondervan.
Müller, Paul–Gerd. 1993. *phaneroō*. Pages 413-14 of vol 3 of *Exegetical Dictionary of the New Testament*. See Balz and Schneider.
Nauck, Wolfgang. 1957. *Die Tradition und der Character des ersten Johannesbriefs, 3, wissenschaftliche Untersuchungen zum Neuen Testament*. Edited by J. Jeremias and D. Otto Michel. Tübingen: J. C. B. Mohr (Paul Siebeck).
Painter, John. 2002. *1, 2, and 3 John*. Collegeville, Minn.: Liturgical Press.
Patrick, Dale. 1992. Election—Old Testament. Pages 434-41 in vol. 2 of *Anchor Bible Dictionary*. See Freedman.
Pelikan, Jaroslav, ed. 1967. *The Catholic Epistles*. Vol. 30 of *Luther's Works*. St. Louis: Concordia.
Pesch, Wilhelm. 1991. *misthos*. Pages 432-33 of vol. 2 in *Exegetical Dictionary of the New Testament*. See Balz and Schneider.
Radl, Walter. 1990. *airō*. Page 41 in vol. 1 of *Exegetical Dictionary of the New Testament*. See Balz and Schneider.
Rensberger, David K. 1997. *1 John, 2 John, 3 John*. Abingdon New Testament Commentaries. Nashville: Abingdon.
———. 2006. Conflict and Community in the Johannine Letters. *Interpretation* 60, 3:278-91.
Richardson, Cyril. 1943. Page 178 of *Early Church Fathers*. Vol. 1 of *The Library of Christian Classics*. Edited and translated by C. Richardson. Philadelphia: Westminster.
Rist, Martin. 1962. Antichrist. Pages 140-43 in vol. 1 of *Interpreter's Dictionary of the Bible*. See Buttrick.
Ritt, Hubert. 1993. *phōs*. Pages 447-48 in vol. 3 of *Exegetical Dictionary of the New Testament*. See Balz and Schneider.
Ritz, Hans-Joachim. 1990. *bios, biōtikos*. Page 219 in vol. 1 of *Exegetical Dictionary of the New Testament*. See Balz and Schneider.
Roberts, Alexander, and James Donaldson, eds. 1995. *The Teaching of the Twelve Apostles*. Pages 371-82 in vol. 7 of *The Ante-Nicene Fathers*. N.p.: Christian Literature Publishing Company, 1886. Repr. Peabody, Mass.: Hendrickson.
Rossing, Barbara R. 1999. *The Choice Between Two Cities: Whore, Bride, and Empire in the Apocalypse*. Harrisburg, Pa.: Trinity Press International.
Sakenfeld, Katharine Doob, ed. 2006-9. *New Interpreter's Dictionary of the Bible*. 5 vols. Nashville: Abingdon.
Schaff, Philip, ed. Revised by David S. Schaff, 2007. *The Creeds of Christendom*. 3 vols. New York: Harper and Row, 1931. Repr. Grand Rapids: Baker.
Schnackenburg, Rudolf. 1992. *The Johannine Epistles*. Translated by Reginald and Ilse Fuller. New York: Crossroad.
Schniewind, Julius. 1964. *angelia, ktl*. Pages 56-73 in vol. 1 of *Theological Dictionary of the New Testament*. See Kittel and Friedrich.
Schottroff, L. 1991. *zōē*. Pages 105-9 in vol. 2 of *Exegetical Dictionary of the New Testament*. See Balz and Schneider.
Schweizer, Eduard. 1974. *psychē* in the New Testament. Pages 637-56 in vol. 9 of *Theological Dictionary of the New Testament*. See Kittel and Friedrich.
Seitz, O. J. F. 1962. Letter. Pages 113-15 in vol. 3 of *Interpreter's Dictionary of the Bible*. See Buttrick.
Shogren, Gary S. 1992. Election—New Testament. Pages 441-44 in vol. 2 of *Anchor Bible Dictionary*. See Freedman.
Smith, D. Moody. 1991. *First, Second, and Third John*. Interpretation: A Bible Commentary for Teaching and Preaching. Louisville, Ky.: John Knox.
Soden, Hans F. von. 1964. *adelphos, ktl*. Pages 144-46 in vol. 1 of *Theological Dictionary of the New Testament*. See Kittel and Friedrich.
Stählin, Gustav. 1971. *skandalon, skandalizō*. Pages 339-58 in vol. 7 of *Theological Dictionary of the New Testament*. See Kittel and Friedrich.
Stowers, Stanley K. 1992. Letters (Greek and Latin). Pages 290-93 in vol. 2 of *Anchor Bible Dictionary*. See Freedman.
Strecker, Georg. 1996. *The Johannine Letters*. Translated by Linda M. Maloney. Hermeneia: A Critical and Historical Commentary on the Bible. Minneapolis: Fortress.
Szikszai, S. 1962. Anoint. Pages 138-39 in vol. 1 of *Interpreter's Dictionary of the Bible*. See Buttrick.

Thiselton, Anthony. C. 1978. Truth. Pages 874-902 in vol. 3 of *New International Dictionary of New Testament Theology*. See Colin Brown, ed.
Thomas, John Christopher. 2004. *The Pentecostal Commentary on 1 John, 2 John, 3 John*. Cleveland: Pilgrim Press.
Varughese, Alex, ed. 2005. *Discovering the New Testament: Community and Faith*. Kansas City: Beacon Hill Press of Kansas City.
Vermes, Geza, trans. 2004. *The Complete Dead Sea Scrolls in English*. New York: Penguin Press.
Wahlde, Urban C. von. 2002. The Stereotyped Structure and the Puzzling Pronouns of 1 John 2:28-3:10. *Catholic Biblical Quarterly* 64, 2:319-38.
Wallace, Charles, Jr., ed. 1997. *Susanna Wesley: The Complete Writings*. New York: Oxford University Press.
Wallace, Daniel B. 1996. *Greek Grammar Beyond the Basics*. Grand Rapids: Zondervan.
Watson, Duane F. 1992. Elect Lady. Pages 433-34 in vol. 2 of *Anchor Bible Dictionary*. New York: Doubleday. See Friedman.
Watt, Jan van der. 1999. Ethics in First John: A Literary and Socioscientific Perspective. *Catholic Biblical Quarterly* 61, 3:491-511.
_____. 2007. *An Introduction to the Johannine Gospel and Letters*. London/New York: T & T Clark.
Wesley, John. 1983. *Explanatory Notes upon the New Testament*. Repr. Peabody, Mass.: Hendrickson.
_____. 1978-79. *The Works of John Wesley*. 3rd ed. 14 vols. 1872. Repr. Kansas City: Beacon Hill Press of Kansas City.
Westcott, Brooke Foss. 1952. *The Epistles of John*. Grand Rapids: Eerdmans.
Wright, N. T. 2008. *Surprised by Hope: Rethinking Heaven, the Resurrection, and the Mission of the Church*. New York: Harper One.
Yarbrough, Robert W. 2008. *1-3 John*. Baker Exegetical Commentary on the New Testament. Grand Rapids: Baker.

1, 2, & 3 JOHN

I JOHN

INTRODUCTION

A. Authorship

These writings early came to be identified with John, the disciple of the Lord (Irenaeus, *Against Heresies* 3.16.5; Tertullian, *Against Marcion* 5.16; Bruce 1970, 18). By the twentieth century, some scholars were hesitant to identify the author as John the apostle but could accept the traditional attribution of 1 John and the Gospel of John to the same author (Brooke 1912, xviii).

Other reputable scholars differentiate between the author of the Gospel and the author of the letters, notably Raymond E. Brown (1979, 95). On the basis of language, theme, and situation, most interpreters agree that the letters all come from the same writer (e.g., Smith 1991, 14; Brown 1979, 94; Marshall 1978, 46; Bruce 1970, 13).

The letters are anonymous. In 2 John and 3 John the self-designation "the elder" (*ho presbyteros*, 2 John 1; 3 John 1) occurs; but it offers no real clue as to the author's identity. Elsewhere in the NT whenever "elder" appears it is anarthrous (lacking an article). The term indicates Christian leaders in local churches (ten times in Acts; 1 Tim 4:14; 5:19; Titus 1:6; Jas 5:14; 1 Pet 5:1).

The writer of these letters was eager that his readers heed his advice. So, why not identify himself as that early and powerful "disciple whom Jesus loved" (John 13:23; 19:26; 20:2; 21:7, 20), or even as the "apostle"? It is hard to imagine that members of the Johannine community would have departed from the Apostle John to the degree that the "secessionists" had (1 John 2:18-19). We use the term "secessionists" to refer to the author's opponents, who had seceded from the Johannine community (Brown 1979, 70; see Bruce 1970, 70). Brown doubted that first-century Christians would have resisted the elder's authority, as Diotrephes had, if "the elder" was the Beloved Disciple (1979, 95).

Some early authorities expressed reservations about John the apostle as the author. Eusebius (fourth century) classified 1 John among the "acknowledged" (*homologoumena*) writings. But 2 John and 3 John appeared among the "disputed" (*antilegomena*) books of the emerging canon. Eusebius thought they might be the work of another early author with the same name (*Ecclesiastical History* 3.24.17 and 3.25.2-3; Brown 1979, 19).

This ancient tendency to widen the pool of potential authors continues. Scholars propose candidates based on internal hints and attempted reconstructions of the original situation of the Johannine writings.

Some scholars point to John 21:24 as evidence of a later redactor of the Johannine material. The language seems to suggest someone who wrote after the death of the Beloved Disciple. His death may have caused confusion, even despair, among those who believed Jesus had promised that he would not die before the Lord's return. Ehrman suggests that John 21:22-23 may serve as a clarification of Jesus' words and a reassurance to the faith community (2008, 182-83).

Others identify the author of the letter as neither the disciple John nor the final redactor of the Gospel. They prefer the designation "the elder" (2 John 1; 3 John 1), an anonymous figure within the Johannine school of thought. This "school," a network of like-minded churches and individuals, preserved and perpetuated the Gospel traditions of the Beloved Disciple (on Johannine school see Culpepper 1975, 261-90). These Johannine Christians gave distinctive nuances to the language in 1, 2, and 3 John and the Gospel of John. The vocabulary of these writings bears more similarities to one another than to other parts of the NT (Smith 1991, 36).

The prominent use of first person plural in 1 John 1:1-4 suggests an origin within a clearly defined group: "we have heard . . . we have seen . . . we have looked at and our hands have touched . . . we proclaim . . . we have seen . . . we proclaim . . . appeared to us . . . we proclaim . . . we have seen and heard . . . with us . . . our fellowship . . . we write this." This usage is similar to the closing lines of the Gospel. There the text utilizes an interesting combination of pronouns—*"This is* the disciple who testifies to these things and who wrote them down. *We* know that *his* testimony is true" (John 21:24, emphasis added).

While 1, 2, and 3 John are anonymous, this does not remove them from a Johannine circle of influence. The author (or authors) certainly belonged to a faith community that shared a common theological position and literary style. The matter of authorship remains an open question, "an enigma shrouded in mystery" (Smith 1991, 17).

While we cannot know with certainty the identity of the author of the letters, the question of authorship does not undermine our ability to make sense of their pastoral concerns. Although the authorship of 1, 2, and 3 John is uncertain, to avoid the stilted expression "the author," I will usually refer to the author of 1 John as "John" and of 2 John and 3 John as "the elder."

B. Date

Most scholars date the letters some time later than the Fourth Gospel, but before the time of Ignatius of Antioch (martyred ca. A.D. 110; Bruce 1970, 18). This places them in the last decade of the first century (Thomas 2004, 10; Brown 1979, 96; Bruce 1970, 31). That they are subsequent to the Gospel is suggested by absence of any critique of the Gospel's external adversaries, "the Jews"—the Jewish religious leaders who opposed Jesus (e.g., John 2:18; 5:10, 16, 18; 6:41; 7:1; 8:52).

The Fourth Gospel strongly affirms the divinity of Christ as a core claim against Jewish detractors who were not persuaded to become Christians. The letters, however, respond to critics who once were a part of the Johannine community, but left. These "secessionists" seem to have so emphasized Christ's divinity as to dismiss his authentic humanity. John and the readers of the letters were not distancing themselves from Judaism. That separation had largely already occurred. This new religious community, the Johannine Christians, faced the problem of people separating *from them*. Their opponents were not stubborn outsiders, but former insiders.

Some theological development may also suggest that the letters are later. Consider their soteriology. In the Gospel no clear references to the saving nature of Christ's blood appear. But in 1 John overt language states that "the blood of Jesus, his Son, purifies us from all sin" (1:7) and affirms Jesus as an "atoning sacrifice for our sins" (2:2; 4:10; possibly 5:6).

The eschatology of the Gospel is more "realized" (presently experienced). In John 3:15-18 belief brings eternal life *now*; and Jesus' pronouncement in John 11:25, "I am the resurrection and the life," is in contrast to a future resurrection. In 1 John a futuristic eschatology is prominent: "Now we are children of God, and what we will be has not yet been made known. But we know that when he appears, we shall be like him, for we shall see him as his is" (3:2; van der Watt 2007, 24).

C. Provenance

Where were these letters written? They are traditionally identified with Ephesus, the premier city of ancient Asia Minor. More broadly, the Johannine epistles seem to have originated in proconsular Asia (governed by a Roman proconsul appointed by the senate). Tradition links John the apostle to Ephesus in his later years. Even if the author was not the apostle, the Ephesus area is a probable locale for the letters.

A number of Jewish Christians migrated to Asia Minor in the A.D. 60s due to increasing tensions with the Romans. The Jewish revolt in A.D. 66 and the Roman destruction of the temple in A.D. 70 played major roles in their decision to relocate to Asia Minor. Moreover, Christianity had been established there long before (Paul's missionary activity in the region dates from the early 50s; see Acts 19:10; Bruce 1970, 13).

Pergamum was the initial seat of the proconsular government. But the capital was moved to Ephesus, where it remained during NT times. Ephesus was a center of Greek culture and prominent in early missionary activity (Acts 19:1-41; 20:17-38; note Acts 19:10: "all the Jews and Greeks who lived in the province of Asia heard the word of the Lord").

The church at Ephesus (Rev 2:1) and other nearby churches figure prominently as the target audience of Revelation (probably written in the 90s). One of Paul's richest letters went to Ephesus. Some ancient manuscripts suggest Ephesians was a circular letter intended to be shared among several churches (see Col 4:16). The possibility that 1, 2, and 3 John circulated within a network of Johannine churches near Ephesus is consistent with what we know about Christian encyclical letters.

D. Audience

The three Johannine letters were apparently written to individuals and churches at some distance from the author (2 John 12; 3 John 14). This suggests a metropolitan area with several house churches within a reasonable traveling distance.

The author of the letters gives no geographical data; so we cannot know with certainty the location of those to whom he writes. But an urban center like Ephesus and a network of churches like that of Revelation, seems probable (Brown 1979, 98).

Gaius and Diotrephes (3 John) appear to be in the same area although possibly belonging to different churches. Did the elder attempt to obtain hospitality for his traveling ministers in the church of Gaius, and have them turned away by the house church of Diotrephes (Brown 1979, 98)? First John may have been written to reinforce those in the larger urban center who were loyal to John. The second letter could have gone to a church in one of the outlying towns where secessionists were attempting to draw away some of the Johannine faithful.

Third John implies that Diotrephes had rejected the elder's representatives. So the elder wrote to Gaius requesting the hospitality Diotrephes had refused (Brown 1979, 99). These writings may have been sent as a three-letter packet at the same time to the same locale. This companionship of the small letters with the more substantial 1 John may explain the preservation and eventual canonical status of 2 John and 3 John, despite their limited content (Johnson 1986, 503-10).

The identity of the readers may be plausibly reconstructed, but not confirmed. The significant presence of churches influenced by the Johannine community and the geographical situation fit the data.

The recipients of 2 John and 3 John seem to be at some distance from the elder. In both the author conveys greetings to the recipients from others (2 John 13; 3 John 14). Both express his hope of making a personal visit (2 John 12; 3 John 14). Of course, the mention of visiting could be a veiled warning to the readers. This might increase the likelihood of their compliance with his wishes (compare 2 Cor 13:10; Phlm 22).

E. Occasion and Purpose

While the author, readers, and destination of these writings cannot be conclusively established, the issues are clear. The larger work, 1 John, is more a treatise, or pastoral teaching, than a personal letter. It presents a number of significant issues: Christology, soteriology, the Spirit, ethics, "the world"; ecclesiology, and eschatology (see the theological section below).

F. Sociological and Cultural Issues

Sociological and cultural information about the writings is limited due to the uncertain location, readership, and date. It is worth noting, first, how the churches maintained connection with one another and, second, the use in 1, 2, and 3 John of family language to describe relationships in the churches.

1. Connections Between First-Century Churches

The churches of these letters appear well connected to one another. A certain local autonomy obtains due to the limitations imposed by distance between the churches and the resulting delayed communications. But the congregations are intentionally linked. That they experience their faith in fellowship with others is a recurring theme ("we" appears nearly eighty times in 1 John). Paul similarly maintained his apostolic authority by written contact with a number of congregations and ministers.

The imbedded "letters" of Rev 2—3 demonstrate a link between the churches in the region. What is said to a *particular* church in Revelation (2:1, 8, 12, 18; 3:1, 7, 14) is addressed "to the churches" *plural* (Rev 2:7, 11, 17, 29; 3:6, 13, 22).

That all three Johannine letters are preserved at all is remarkable. Their survival and eventual canonization demonstrate a close relationship of trust between the author and the recipients. Such connections between Christians developed also by personal visits. The elder hoped to visit these churches at some distance (2 John 12; 3 John 14). News was delivered orally from place to place by trusted friends. Itinerant ministers enhanced this faith network.

Such connections could work, however, to the detriment of orthodox faith, as we will see. Yet overall, these were ties that bound believers together, making the author's repeated use of the plural "we" understandable as an expression of their corporate mind-set (a "body"; see 1 Cor 12:27). To belong to Christ was to belong to one another in a community of faith, more specifically, a Johannine community of faith.

2. Use of Family Language

A second sociological matter is the sense of being a spiritual family. Family language abounds in the letters ("children" eighteen times; "brother(s)" eighteen times; "fathers" and God as "Father" seventeen times; "friends" twelve times). This warm family terminology expands in 2 John, where the elder addresses "the chosen lady" (2 John 1; "dear lady" in v 5). Greetings from a neighboring church come from "the children of your chosen sister" (v 13).

These distinctly feminine phrases might refer to women in pastoral leadership. Women certainly play prominent ministry roles throughout the NT. Priscilla was a teacher and visiting minister (Acts 18:24-26). Peter's Pentecost sermon quotes the prophet Joel's prediction: "Your . . . daughters will prophesy" (Acts 2:17) and that the outpouring of the prophetic Spirit of God was intended for "both men and women" (Acts 2:18).

These feminine references in 2 John and 3 John might also indicate women who were providing host homes for the house churches. To provide hospitality was to participate in the ministry.

House Churches

Jewish Christians continued to worship in synagogues and in the Jerusalem temple until its destruction in A.D. 70. Two factors, however, led to the increasing use of private homes for Christian gatherings. First, tensions developing between those Jews who embraced Jesus as Messiah and those who did not put pressure on the followers of Jesus to leave the synagogues. The Gospel of John suggests that some Christians were excommunicated from the synagogue (9:22).

A second reason for increased Christian gatherings outside the synagogues was the growing numbers of Gentile believers. Since Gentiles could not participate fully in Jewish worship, a different location, available to all people, was needed. So a "church that meets in your home" became one answer (Phlm 2; see Rom 16:5; 1 Cor 16:19; Col 4:15; Ehrman 2008, 193).

On the other hand, the feminine references may be entirely figurative, referring to a Christian community as the "chosen" of God (Jones 2009, 251; Ehrman 2008, 186-87). The words "lady" and "sister" could function much like the modern practice of referring to ships, planes, cars, and so forth, with female names. The Greek word for church is a feminine noun. While the matter is debatable (Bruce 1970, 137), the text lends itself to the possibility of female pastors as leaders of the Johannine faith community or prominent spiritually for hosting Christian gatherings (see on 2 John 1).

G. Textual Witnesses

The earliest manuscripts containing 1, 2, and 3 John survive on papyrus. Three come from the third century (papyri 9, 20, and 23). Others originated in the late third or early fourth century (papyri 72 and 78) or from the fourth to the seventh century (papyri 54, 74, and 81).

H. Literary Features

1. Letter Forms and 1, 2, and 3 John

These three writings are often categorized as of the same genre, namely as letters. But important differences exist. Both 2 John and 3 John appear to be genuine letters; 1 John less clearly demonstrates elements of Greco-Roman letters.

Greco-Roman Letters

Letters were a common form of communication in the Greco-Roman world, but with marked variation. Private letters to friends differed from open letters to a wider audience. Formal letters must be distinguished from occasional letters and casual notes. Private letters of recommendation to another individual are not the same as public treatises urging a particular course of action. Despite such variables, there were a number of consistent components of ancient letters.

Unlike modern letters, those of the ancient world began by identifying the sender by name or title. The letter then typically mentioned the intended recipient(s), expressing positive regard, well-wishes, or affirming prayers for the recipient(s). Such introductory remarks were conventional, and should not be taken literally. (Compare the modern practice of addressing people we do not know as "dear." For samples of ancient letters, see Elwell and Yarbrough 1998, 194.)

The body of the letter followed, expressing the sender's wishes and concerns. A closing with conventional features completed the letter. These might include words of encouragement or challenge, expressions of hope that authors and readers might meet in the near future, and again, words of blessing or prayers (Johnson 1986, 252-53).

The length of ancient letters varied, though one sheet of papyrus was typical. The letters of 2 John and 3 John, as well as Philemon and Jude, are about this length. Since there was no postal system for private citizens, letters were often hand-delivered by trusted friends or servants. By this means carriers could clarify the tone of the letter, if questions arose from their recipients. At times, carriers were mentioned in letters (e.g., Tychicus in Eph 6:21-22; Col 4:7; Phoebe in Rom 16:1; Ehrman 2008, 186-88).

First John begins abruptly with no indication of who is writing or to whom. Its several instances of "I write" (2:12, 13, 14; 5:13) offer no help in identifying the author. No benediction concludes the document—only a final word of exhortation: "Dear children, keep yourselves from idols" (5:21).

The work reads more like an open letter or a persuasive essay written to a community (Ehrman 2008, 190). But it lacks the systematic organization we might expect. Johnson considers 1 John "not really a letter at all but a word of exhortation" (1986, 504). Jones calls it an "epistle" with a "pastoral-polemical" function (2009, 1). But the distinction sometimes made between letters and epistles is "too sharp for many NT works" (Brown 1982, 87 n. 191).

First John does express strong pastoral concerns in response to the departure of some from the Johannine community (2:19). The writing arose out of the pastoral heart of one alarmed at negative developments in the churches. The letter was an occasional piece—"a tract aimed at a problem" (Burge, Cohick, and Green 2009, 412), written to counter the threat presented by those who were not only separating from the community but also actively evangelizing others to join them.

Both 2 John and 3 John reflect the conventions of a typical Greco-Roman letter. They begin by identifying the author and the intended readers. Words of greeting follow, with expressions of good wishes and prayers. The body of the letter concludes with a personal greeting and a salutation. These appear to be letters of the period in every sense.

The Johannine letters have often been classified as catholic or universal writings, intended for all Christians everywhere. But they are not, strictly speaking. Brown rejects the notion that 1 John was a catholic letter, arguing that a message to churches everywhere from an unidentified sender would have had little weight (1982, 88). These letters were intended for quite specific locales and circumstances. To identify 2 and 3 John as catholic letters designates them based on their canonicity, not their intent.

Literary features within the writings include the use of "we" (especially 1 John 1:1-4), identifying the author as among a community of believers. This may indicate a formal kind of "school" (Culpepper 1975, 34-38, 261-90) or a looser network of like-minded churches and individuals influenced by John. At the least, this is one aspect of the frequent use of family language in the Johannine letters (see above in Sociological and Cultural Issues). They convey a strong sense of investment in maintaining close relationships between believers in the region.

2. Poetic Forms

Another literary feature, evident in 1 John, is poetic parallelism. John reflects a style similar to Hebrew poetry, in which successive lines repeat or reshape phrases, expressing similar thoughts with different words. The prologue (1:1-4) and much of chapter 1 have a repetitive, parallel structure. In v 1 the verbs create a crescendo of parallel testimony:

"We have heard . . ."
"We have seen . . ."
"We have looked at . . ."

Numerous parallel words ("proclaim" three times in the prologue) and contrasting concepts (light vs. darkness, truth vs. falsehood, sins vs. forgiveness, love vs. hate) all lend themselves to a lyrical sense permeating 1 John. Poetic elements mark 1:6—2:1 with the repeated "if we claim" (vv 6, 8, 10) each followed by similarly worded responses/results—"if we walk" (v 7); "if we confess" (v 9); and "if [we] sin" (2:1).

Even more apparent, and typically indicated as poetry in English translations, are the refrains of 1 John 2:12-14. The sentences and phrases repeat and extend John's thoughts in compact and memorable language. A concise and repetitive phrase ("I write to you . . . because" [six times]) is followed by a specific point of celebration ("been forgiven," "have known," "have overcome").

There is an intensifying of the repeated words as well as a wonderful crescendo of three parallel lines in v 14:

you are strong,
and the word of God lives in you,
and you have overcome the evil one.

The three lines make one affirmation with synonymous parallel lines: spiritual victory derives from the activity of the word of God within one's life. Similar parallel lines appear elsewhere (see on 4:3; 5:12, 13).

3. Limited Scriptural Allusions

One notable aspect of the literary forms in these writings is the absence of quotations. No direct citations of biblical passages appear. Especially noticeable is the absence of any overt appeal to the Gospel of John (Brown 1982, 33).

The lack of quoted reference to writings that eventually were included in the NT is understandable. Considerable time passed before the NT came to be recognized as such. The books that now make up the NT were not recognized as normative when these letters were written, as the books of the OT were. Yet the total absence of any precise quotations from the OT is curious. But the same could be said of Paul's letters to Macedonian Christians—our 1 and 2 Thessalonians and Philippians. Some scholars call attention to the similarities of thought in the Johannine writings to texts from Qumran (the Dead Sea Scrolls). But no clear quotations can be demonstrated.

4. 1, 2, and 3 John and the Gospel of John

There are striking similarities in language shared by the letters and the Fourth Gospel. Substantial points of thematic agreement and even wording appear (van der Watt 2007, 22-25; Brown 1982, 757-59; see the last section of this Introduction). If a disciple of John, or the Johannine "school," penned the letters, the similarities are due to the shared Johannine context; dissimilarities reflect their different authors.

I. Theological Themes

Only a few of the more significant theological emphases of the Johannine letters can be addressed here. More will naturally unfold in the commentary proper. Some of the more prominent themes include: (1) Christology, the person and work of Christ; (2) soteriology, how sin is understood and remedied; (3) the Spirit of God; (4) ethics, the nature of human love for God and for one another; (5) "the world" and opposition to it; (6) hospitality, extending welcome to strangers; (7) ecclesiology, the view of the church; and (8) eschatology, or last things.

1. Christology

A renegade Christian group with a different perspective on the person and work of Jesus generated a strong response from the author of these letters. Clearly at issue is whether or not Jesus had come "in the flesh" (1 John 4:2; see vv 1-3). Some were apparently teaching that Jesus had only seemed to be fully human. Or they taught that if he had been truly human, he did not remain so. The perfect tense verb in 4:2, *elēlythota*, may argue not only that Jesus "has come in the flesh" but that he *remained* human. In substance the secessionists denied the full continuity of the historical Jesus of Nazareth with the exalted Christ.

We know that later Christian groups with gnostic tendencies resisted the idea of a fully incarnate Christ. They identified the spiritual realm as good, and the fleshly, material arena as inherently evil, one that a divine Christ could not inhabit. Such thinking derived from a dualism more at home in Greek philosophy than in biblical thought. Greeks typically distinguished the eternal gods, who were neither born nor died, from demigods. These lower level deities were ordinary humans who were elevated to divine status by apotheosis at their deaths. Thus, the secessionists may have considered their Christology more exalted than that of the Johannine community.

Some gnostic Christians distinguished Jesus the man from the Christ, who descended upon Jesus (perhaps at his baptism). This view, a sort of "adoptionism," claimed that Jesus had been empowered by "the Christ"; but "the Christ" had departed from him prior to his death. Thus, although *Jesus* may have truly suffered and died, the *Christ*, a totally spiritual being, was immune from such earthly experiences (Bruce 1970, 16-17).

John's opponents, by denying the incarnation, renounced Jesus Christ as truly fully God and fully human. For them, the best that might be said was that Christ "seemed" to be human. This view, which came to be called Docetism (from *dokeō*, "seem, appear"), undercut the reality of incarnation. The claim in the Gospel of John that "the Word became flesh" (John 1:14) proved especially problematic for Docetism.

Also, and inevitably, Docetism minimized the centrality of the cross and the resurrection. If the one sent from heaven was not the same one who died, then the cross was emptied of its atoning power. A "savior" who had been whisked away prior to the cross needed no resurrection. Docetism and the dualism that found the body evil also eroded the foundational biblical view of creation as "good" (Gen 1:4, 10, 12, 18, 21, 25), indeed "very good" (Gen 1:31).

2. Soteriology

Soteriology (from *sōtēria*: "salvation") attempts to explain the nature of sin and how humans can be delivered from it. This is obviously a powerful concept throughout Scripture, and certainly here. God is holy and calls people to participate in his holiness. Sin is universally experienced; but it is not normal. Sin is a human departure from the divine plan. Thus, sin is a problem that must be dealt with by God and by humans.

Sin is pervasive (1 John 1:8, 10) and manifests itself as lawlessness (3:4) and "all wrongdoing" (5:17). John presents *not* sinning as the Christian standard (2:1; 3:6, 9). Nevertheless, those who sin can be forgiven and cleansed (1:9). Deliverance from sin, indeed, the ultimate destruction of sin, flows from the gracious activity of Jesus Christ, God's Son. Jesus' blood "purifies us from all sin" (1 John 1:7); Jesus "is the atoning sacrifice for our sins" (2:1; 4:10).

John insists that anyone who "does what is sinful is of the devil, because the devil has been sinning from the beginning." But he is equally insistent that "the reason the Son of God appeared was to destroy the devil's work" (3:8). Consequently, he contends, the person "born of God . . . cannot go on sinning" (3:9). First John concludes with the enigmatic mention of "a sin that does not lead to death" and "a sin that leads to death" (5:16-17), which will be addressed in the commentary.

3. The Spirit

The Holy Spirit is understated in the letters (see on 2 John 7). Brown calls their limited references to the Spirit an "eloquent silence" (1979, 141). First John omits several functions of the Spirit emphasized in the Fourth

Gospel (Brown 1979, 140). Perhaps most striking, Jesus, not the Spirit, is called the Paraclete (1 John 2:1-2; compare John 14—15).

Spirit (*pneuma*) in 1 John refers primarily to God's Spirit and appears in only two sections (Brown 1979, 140). In 3:24—4:6 God's Spirit enables one to "test the spirits." At 5:6-10 faithful testimony is central. The "Spirit . . . testifies" as "the truth" (5:7) in both external ways (along with the "water and blood") and internally by a witness to one's own "heart" (5:10).

The word *pneuma* is used in a negative sense, linked to "false" (4:1) and "of the antichrist" (4:3). God's Spirit demonstrates that one lives in God (3:24; 4:13). More than orthodox confession (4:15) or loving conduct (4:16) is involved. The Spirit gives one the ability to discern the false from the true (4:1) and so confess correctly "Jesus Christ as coming in the flesh" (2 John 7).

Such discernment is a result of the abiding "anointing" (*chrisma*) received "from the Holy One" (2:20, 27; Burge 2009, 418-19). Several references to "Father" and "Son" (vv 22, 23, 24) mingle with "anointing" in a Trinitarian allusion. This provides a divine antidote to antichrist activity (2:18, 22) and false prophets (4:1). As Jesus the Anointed One (*christos*) was "anointed" by the Spirit at the beginning of his messianic mission (Luke 4:18; see Isa 61:1), so Christ's followers are to be "little anointed ones" (Köstenberger 2009, 400-402).

4. Ethics

The love of God for persons and the love manifest in the church between persons is a vital concern of these writings. How does one live a life that exemplifies holy love? What does a life lived in harmony with God's heart look like? For John, the consistent theme for ethical consideration is love (*agapē* and cognates occur more than forty times in the three writings).

"God is love" sets the theme (1 John 4:8, 16) and is the foundation for much of John's theology. Divine love compelled God to act, sending Christ, the Son (4:9), to be "an atoning sacrifice for our sins" (4:10). Because he "laid down his life for us" (3:16), he enabled people to "be called children of God" (3:1). This love that seeks in order to redeem, John urges, must be evidenced in the lives of those who have received it. Authentic love comes from God, flows into the lives of those who will accept it, and then flows outward to others.

The mark of Christians is that they "love one another" (3:11, 23; 4:7, 11, 12; 2 John 5) in tangible ways. This includes material support of the needy (3:16-18). Inward love sets believers free from the fear of coming judgment (4:17-18). The tension between the Christlike love in action

John recommends and the sharp words he uses in the letters directed toward adversaries highlights the kind of challenge every age faces to give both loving and theologically grounded expression to the Christian faith (Black 1990, 39).

5. The World

First John's readers are clearly called to love the "brothers" and sisters of the Johannine community (3:10, 17; 4:20, 21). But they are not to love "the world" (2:15-17). Primarily, "the world" (*kosmos*) is humanity and human systems hostile to God and God's people. However, the term is not exclusively used in this negative sense.

God loves the world according to the Fourth Gospel (3:16). But the letters insist that believers are not to love the world, because to do so would show that God's love is not resident in and among them. The world in 1 John is a place of lust (2:16-17) and wickedness (5:19), where false prophets, antichrists, and deceivers are at work (4:1, 3; 2 John 7). The world does not recognize true believers as children of God. Instead, it hates them (3:13). But God (through Christ and the Spirit), who resides in believers, overcomes the world; and so may all who live in Christ (5:4-5). The world is passing away (2:17). So the world is characteristically viewed in a dualistic sense as the realm of evil.

However, it is to this fallen world that the Father sent the Son (4:9) for the purpose of being its Savior (4:14). Christ's sacrifice of himself is "for the sins of the whole world" (2:2). It is in the present world, not only in some world to come, that believers in Jesus Christ may be like God. "Love is made complete among us so that we will have confidence on the day of judgment, because *in this world we are like him*" (1 John 4:17, emphasis added).

6. Hospitality

Christian hospitality is significant in these writings (Koenig 1992, 299-301; Malherbe 1983, 92-112). John is persuaded that love will manifest itself in tangible acts of goodwill (1 John 3:17). Love comes from God and lives itself out in kindness to others. God's love leads to opened homes, where welcome is practiced through the fellowship of shared meals. The love of God in a household makes it a place where sisters and brothers in the faith can find lodging, prayers, support, and love.

Such open-door hospitality is expected to remove the former barriers of ethnicity, gender, and socioeconomic status (see Gal 3:28). By providing places of respite, those who give hospitality contributed to the evangelizing of those they received (3 John 8).

The early Christian mission clearly depended upon such hospitality (Matt 10:40-42; Acts 16:14-15; Rom 16:1-2; *Did.* 12). There were few safe, clean, and inexpensive accommodations in antiquity. Christian travelers benefited from the lodging and friendship offered by sympathetic homeowners. Host homes derived value from the informal ministry of the itinerant ministers as time was shared around meals. It should come as no surprise that Christians "invented" the hospital as a place for hospitality.

Withholding of hospitality could become necessary when a deep divergence of doctrine and practice made genuine fellowship impossible (2 John 10-11). Sometimes the refusal to welcome "brothers," however, could be wrongly motivated (3 John 10).

7. Ecclesiology

Evidence of church structure and practice is relatively sparse in these letters. The word "church" (*ekklēsia*) occurs three times, only in 3 John (vv 6, 9, and 10). But clearly there was a network of churches in some connectional relationship to one another. John's "we" language in 1 John (nearly seventy times) points toward an in-group his writing represents. Admittedly, "we" is customary in NT letters, as authors sought to identify with the recipients of their letters (or as a modest editorial "we" meaning simply "I"). Since John uses the first person singular, "I," numerous times (2:1, 7-8, 12-14; 5:13; 2 John 5, 12; 3 John 4, 9, 13), the communal "we" must be more than conventional.

Also, there is a close fellowship connecting congregations indicated by the family language. This is especially evident in 2 John. The elder writes to "the chosen lady" (v 1) in behalf of her "chosen sister" (v 13). Both women have "children" (vv 1, 13)—apparently gathered believers (the church)—at each locale.

Likewise, election language in 2 John, "chosen" (*eklektēi*, "the elect"), presumes OT covenantal imagery. There it described the people of God as a faith community (Deut 7:6; 14:2; Ps 33:12; Isa 42:1; 43:4; 44:1; 45:4; 65:22; Ezek 20:5).

The community chosen by God (in God's call of Abraham; see Gen 12) created the first people of God, the nation of Israel. Abraham merely embraced the offer and lived in obedience to God. In the same manner, divine election created the renewed people of God, the Christian church. The idea of election is prominent throughout the NT (Matt 24:22, 24, 31; Mark 13:20, 22, 27; Rom 8:33; 11:7; 16:13; Col 3:12; 2 Thess 2:13; 2 Tim 2:10; Titus 1:1; 1 Pet 1:1-2; 2:9; Rev 17:14). In most cases "the elect" refers to those who have chosen to ally themselves with Jesus by accepting his invitation to be disciples. By using "elect" in reference to his circle of churches, the elder identifies the missionary enterprise within which he works. The church is a NT continuation of the OT chosen people of God.

Referring to churches as a "chosen lady" (2 John 1) and a "chosen sister" (2 John 13) follows the Jewish tradition of referring to the covenant people of God with feminine imagery. The OT refers to Israel and Jerusalem as Yahweh's bride (Isa 54:1-8; 62:4-5; Jer 2:2; Hos 1—3). Both are also described as a mother (Isa 54:1-3; Bar 4:5—5:9). The pattern continues in the NT. The church is depicted as a woman (1 Pet 5:13), the bride of Christ (2 Cor 11:2; Eph 5:21-33; Rev 19:6-8; 21:2), and a mother (1 Pet 5:13; Rev 12:1-2, 17).

One further element of these letters that reflects the author's church-consciousness is the phrase "the elder" (*presbyteros*) in 2 John 1 and 3 John 1. The expression might indicate that the writer held the office of a presbyter in a house church (Acts 14:23; 20:17; 1 Tim 5:17; 1 Pet 5:1). Or, the designation may simply have been a reminder of the kind of respect that was deemed due to elders (older people) in the community of faith (1 Tim 5:2; 1 Pet 5:5).

8. Eschatology

John spends considerable energy warning against "antichrists" (2:18, 22; 4:3; 2 John 7). Anyone who does not acknowledge that Jesus has come from God has "the spirit of the antichrist" (4:3). This is not a reference to some end-times personification of evil. Rather, for John an "antichrist" was anyone in the first century whose Christology fell short of embracing Jesus as having come from God and especially as having come "in the flesh" (2 John 7). Surprising though it is to some, the term "antichrist" appears nowhere else in the Bible other than in these letters.

The eschaton can refer to spiritual death. John writes about "a sin that leads to death" (5:16) and seems to imply not so much physical death as spiritual death. The first letter refers to an eschatological "day of judgment" (4:17). The only adequate preparation for that day, a preparation that will enable one to have "confidence," is to have the love of God "made complete." Such a completion occurs in this life, since by definition "in this world we are like him" (v 17). The letters say little more about a day of judgment, except for a brief remark about being "rewarded fully" (2 John 8), if one is not led astray by "deceivers" (2 John 7).

There is sparse mention of the second coming. This is compatible with the Gospel of John, where no developed teaching about a second advent appears. The only possible reference to a return in the Gospel is in Jesus' promise to "come back and take you to be with me that you also may be where I am" (John 14:3). This is in striking contrast to the Synoptic Gospels, each of which has significant "apocalypses" about the coming of the Son of Man and eschatological signs (Matt 24:1-51; Mark 13:1-36; Luke 21:5-36). Brief allusions to the second coming surface in 1 John (2:28; 3:2—"when he appears").

Certain eschatological expectation is reflected in the phrase "the last hour" (twice in 2:18). John does not expand on the term, save for connecting "the last hour" to the "antichrists." The false Christology of the secessionists that denied the incarnation is offered as evidence that the end times had *already* arrived (4:2-3).

The limited eschatological language in the letters may reflect the more "realized" eschatology of the Gospel of John. There Jesus appears as already in some measure glorified. He acts often from divine prerogatives rather than human. Also, the reality of resurrection is not some future event "at the last day" (John 11:24). It is already realized in the person of Jesus—"I am the resurrection and the life" (John 11:25). The Spirit in some real sense accomplishes the promise of the return of Christ to be with his followers (see chs 14, 15, 16).

J. Hermeneutical Issues

At least three important interpretive issues arise in these letters. First, how does one's view of the authorship of these writings affect the reading of the text? Second, how does our perspective on the historical occasion of these letters shape our perception of the opponents being critiqued? Third, how are we to understand the relationship of the letters to the Gospel of John?

1. Authorship and Reading the Letters

One's view of the author of the letters and when he wrote affects how we read them. If we adopt a traditional view that the author was John the apostle, the opening lines of 1 John are a report of an eyewitness to the events of Jesus' life. The claims of having "heard . . . seen . . . looked at . . . [and] touched" (1 John 1:1) give an immediacy and authority to the text and its message that is hard to exceed. The words used are auditory, visual, and even tactile. Surely, many have suggested, these are the words of an eyewitness.

But what if the "we" language (seven times in 1:1-3), or "our" (four times), and "us" (two times) does not reflect the testimony of an eyewitness? What if the author was not one of the Twelve, but a subsequent, later first-century disciple of John who identified with and had substantial standing among the community of Johannine Christians?

Johannine Christians claimed a direct link to the historical Jesus. But this does not necessarily presume that the author of 1 John was an eyewitness to Jesus' ministry. Their knowledge of Jesus came to them in an unbroken chain of faithful witnessing "from the beginning" (1:1) as the "Word of life" (1:1) was proclaimed (1:1, 2, 3).

The language of ch 1 may be understood as words from second-generation Christians. However, they would think of Jesus not as a figure of the remembered past, but as alive and present among the worshipping community with a "continuing voice." Thus, the author expresses a confidence in the ability of God/Christ/Spirit to keep the experience of the believing community current and fresh. The perfect tense verbs translated "have heard . . . have seen" emphasize that these past events have a continuing effect.

Eugene Boring referred to Jesus as having a "continuing" voice (Boring 1991). The opening verses of 1 John may be an instance of this continuing voice. The voice of Jesus, not silenced by the cross, is experienced in ongoing ways. The first person plural language in 1 John 1:1-4 suggests that the voice of Jesus is to be found in corporate worship. This is captured in vivid imagery in Revelation. There the living, resplendent Christ, who "was dead" but is "alive for ever and ever," stands in the midst of the churches (Rev 1:18; see vv 11-20). There he speaks a present tense message suited to their unique needs (Rev 2:1, 8, 12, 18; 3:1, 7, 14).

The "elder" in the two smaller letters (2 John; 3 John) may be understood as one of the generation of teachers succeeding the eyewitnesses. Such persons taught in a "chain" of authority, because they had received the gospel message from those who had seen and heard Jesus (Brown 1979, 100-103).

If an ongoing experience of the risen Lord is combined with the transmission of received traditions about Jesus, then authority resides in both the *remembered past* (oral traditions and texts) and in *present experience* (often in worship). But allowing religious experience alone to define our understanding of Jesus, without the balancing control of consistently remembered and recorded traditions, could result in an adaptive and ever-changing "tradition." Such a "tradition" would run the risk of morphing into whatever contextual circumstances present themselves in new lands and new times.

The responsible interpreter values both aspects of these claims in 1 John. The message about Jesus who lived in the past, received through reliable testimony of early witnesses, is a precious resource. But so is the message that flows from the living Jesus, who continues to speak as the Lord of the church, must always be kept in view. There is strength in the apostolic memory of Jesus. And there is power in the present experience of Jesus. The two witnesses are complementary, not competitive.

2. Perspective of the Author and a Profile of the Opponents

The Johannine letters represent the view of the canonical author. We know the opponents only through the lens of the author of 1, 2, and 3 John. Whether this view is always fair to the secessionists or not is beyond recovery. But perhaps we can make some observations about the secessionists, the one-time members of the Johannine Christian community who had left. John apparently saw no reason to acknowledge the good points of the secessionists, whom he viewed as dangerous antichrists. His readers knew full well who they were and what they had done. But we must not forget that we are reading another's mail.

Thus, the modern interpreter is wise to exercise some caution in too quickly labeling those against whom the letters speak. That they were of so much concern to John and that they were once part of the faith communities he addressed is beyond doubt (2:19). Theirs was not some adversarial heresy from without. Rather, their views were a tangent, a variant expression of Johannine Christianity that had gone, in John's view, to significant excess. He never suggests that the secessionists were influenced by some outside group, a point he would hardly have omitted if it were so (Brown 1979, 106).

The seceding group may have held an overly high Christology, an exaggeration of the Christology of the Gospel of John (Brown 1982, 54). It was precisely that these were once closely allied with the views of John and his circle that made them particularly dangerous.

Their extremist views, holding only to the deity and renouncing the full humanity, probably arose from the tendency in the Gospel of John to emphasize the deity of Jesus. Because they were so like the community of John, their overemphasis was likely to draw away adherents to their christological position. Although John labels them as "antichrists" (2:18) and writes in sharp adversarial tones, he acknowledges that they were at one time a part of "us"—members of his circle of Christians (2:19).

The secessionists probably thought of themselves as loyal defenders of the full divinity of the Son. They were doing so by separating Christ as a heavenly person from Jesus as an earthly individual. Could Jesus (earthly, human, mortal) also be the Christ (heavenly, divine, eternal)? If so, they might have contended, hasn't one polluted the divine by mingling it with the human? A truly divine God would of necessity always remain such.

Such a resistance to the divine entering into the human came to be identified as Docetism. Docetists believed that the Christ had not become human, but only seemed to do so. To think of elevating Christ into the realm of Hellenistic deities would have been easy to imagine. But to affirm a divinity's entrance into the material world would have been unthinkable (Burge, Cohick, and Green 2009, 416). That Jesus as the Christ truly died could scarcely have been imagined.

But the very heart of John's theology carries a strong missionary passion. Though he writes in sharply dualistic ways, John consistently speaks of God's redeeming love toward sinful humanity. The boundaries are not immovable; God's love has come among us (Köstenberger 2009, 280).

Some of the early struggles in the Christian faith to understand the person of Jesus came at this point. Was he fully God? Was he fully human? Was he some of both and fully neither? Later creedal statements affirm both the full deity and the full humanity of Jesus.

In the fourth century the Nicene Creed would speak of Jesus Christ as "very God of very God, begotten, not made, being of one substance [essence] with the Father." It would also affirm "for us men and for our salvation, he came down from heaven, and was incarnate by the Holy Ghost of the Virgin Mary, and was made man" (Schaff 2007, 2:58-59). Such a creed was not taken for granted when these letters were written.

From these letters and the creedal claims that developed later, it is clear that the earliest christological struggles did not turn on a failure to affirm Jesus' divinity. Rather, error arose in a resistance to embracing his full humanity.

3. Relationship of the Letters to the Gospel of John and How That Informs Our Reading

The Gospel of John gives information enabling a partial reconstruction of the history of the Johannine community from its earlier days to the time of the writing of the Gospel (Brown 1979, 13-24). This is usually thought to be a period when the Johannine community moved from a faith identity within Judaism to that of a group excluded from the synagogue.

The opponents in the Gospel are labeled "the Jews" (referring to the Jewish *leaders* who opposed Jesus, not the Jewish *race*). The Christ followers in the Gospel were pressured to leave the synagogues (John 9:22;

12:42; 16:2). This led Johannine Christians to a more marked separation from Judaism.

In contrast to the Gospel, the opponents in the letters of John are former insiders, who had moved outside the Johannine community. The letters give a sense of what transpired between the production of the Gospel and the writing of the letters. By the time the letters were written, the Johannine community no longer stood within the synagogue but was largely differentiated from it (Ehrman 2008, 179-83; Brown 1979, 33-35).

While the Gospel is not quoted in the letters, a number of similarly worded statements appear in both:
- The phrase "the beginning" (1 John 1:1; also 1 John 2:13, 14) echoes John 1:1, as does "the life" (1 John 1:2; see John 1:4).
- Declaring "the life" as "eternal life" (1 John 1:2; 2:25; 3:15; 5:11, 13, 20) is typical of the Gospel (sixteen times).
- The statement "we have looked at" (*etheasametha*) is the same word and verb form translated "we have seen" in John 1:14.
- The idea of making "joy complete" (1 John 1:4) recalls John 15:11 and John 16:24.
- "The truth" as something one does (1 John 1:6, **we are not doing the truth**) in conjunction with the "light" (1 John 1:5; John 3:19-21).
- The death of Jesus is "for the sins of the whole world" (1 John 2:2; see John 1:29).
- The "new command" language (1 John 2:7, 8) appears in John 13:34 and the specifics of that command, to "love one another," are replicated exactly in 2 John 5.
- Denying or acknowledging "the Son" as something also done at the same time to "the Father" (1 John 2:23) has a certain similarity to John 5:23, "He who does not honor the Son does not honor the Father, who sent him" (see also John 15:23).

More instances of similar language in the Gospel of John and the first letter could be cited (Brown 1982, 757-59). But the above are sufficient to make the point. These examples do not necessarily reflect the direct use of the Gospel by the author of the letters. They do, however, suggest that both shared a common thought-world. They employ the "insider" language of a faith community—in which different authors share a common ideology and the influence by the same spiritual figures. The letters were written about the same time, by the same author, and deal with the implications of the same problems in the Johannine churches (e.g., Ehrman 2008, 186-88; Johnson 1986, 501-4; Brown 1979, 32; Bruce 1970, 13-18).

COMMENTARY

I. PROLOGUE AND PREMISES: 1 JOHN 1:1-10

A. The Life Appeared (1:1-4)

BEHIND THE TEXT

How the author uses language is a part of understanding this small writing. This holds especially for the verbs and pronouns in this section. The characters in the ancient story of the text go unnamed in 1 John, but there are characters, nevertheless.

In vv 1-4 there are ten first person plural Greek verbs ("we") and six related pronouns ("us" twice and "our" four times). These pronouns situate the author among a group of like-minded Christians (**we**), writing to another group of Christians (**you**, vv 2-3, always in the plural). He then shifts from addressing the readers as **you**, choosing rather to *identify with them*, using "we" (vv 6-10). Common themes throughout the Johannine writings, along with small hints in John's use of language, suggest the existence of a "school" of disciples identified with John the apostle (Brown 1979; Culpepper 1975).

The prologue to 1 John (vv 1-4) introduces the apostolic proclamation of the gospel. John does this with declarations that point to what he seeks to emphasize throughout the remainder of the letter.

The prologue of 1 John is reminiscent of the prologue of the Gospel of John (1:1-18). But it falls short of being a commentary on it (Smith 1991, 36). Some knowledge of the prologue of the Gospel helps make sense of the opening verses of 1 John. John 1:1-18 and 1 John 1:1-4 share common vocabulary and concepts (**beginning, word, light, life, witness,** and what has been **seen**).

IN THE TEXT

■ **I** What is frequently called the letter of 1 John lacks most of the formal features of Greco-Roman letters of the period (see Introduction). It fails to identify its sender and recipients. It includes no customary greetings and no assurance of prayers or well-wishes. Its conclusion lacks the expected farewells.

At the same time, 1 John gives evidence of being a letter of some sort. In 2:19 John's wording ("they went out from us") depicts him and his readers as an identifiable community of faith. Also, 1 John employs forms of *graphō* ("I write") thirteen times in ten verses (1:4; 2:1, 7, 8, 12, 13, 14, 21, 26; 5:13). Thus, as a decidedly written document, 1 John addresses specific readers. Its frequent use of affectionate address ("children," fifteen times; "dear friends," six times) has the feel of a personal letter (see Introduction).

The word **beginning** (*archēs*) *somewhat* echoes the prologue of the Gospel, which draws readers back to Gen 1:1. But numerous scholars see **the beginning** in 1 John 1:1 as referring to Jesus (Strecker 1996, 57; Brown 1982, 158, 175), the beginning of the Christian movement (Jones 2009, 19-20; Bruce 1970, 35), or specifically to the incarnation itself (Bultmann 1973, 9). The term may highlight the inauguration of the gospel message especially in Johannine circles (Smith 1991, 36-37).

What was **from the beginning** had been **heard** (also v 3). But this was more than a proclaimed message. Verbs of seeing, hearing, and touching argue for an incarnate and personified *logos*, not merely a preached message. Some translations identify *logos* here as Christ by means of capitalization—**Word** (so also the NASB and KJV, but not NRSV; see Brown 1982, 163-66).

This gospel was both **heard** (*akēkoamen*) and **seen** (*heōrakamen*). The Greek perfect tense of both verbs indicates that John's and the community's past experience of Christ had an "abiding" (Brooke 1912, 2) or "enduring" effect (Strecker 1996, 12). The words of the Gospel reverberated in their ears. What they had seen burned an indelible image in their mind's eyes.

The verbs **we have looked at** (*etheasametha;* see John 1:14) and **have touched** (*epsēlaphēsan*) shift to the aorist (simple past tense). This suggests that John's earlier perfect tense was intentional. Bruce suggests that the *apparent* duplication of visual verbs—**seen** and **looked at**—attempted to echo the language of John 14:9. What was seen went beyond mere outward vision to discern the inward glory (1970, 36). Brooke similarly links the use of the aorist to the *character* of what was seen (1912, 4).

John stresses the visual experience—**with our eyes.** This addition of **eyes** emphasizes and personalizes the account, giving immediacy to the report of the experience of Christ (Marshall 1978, 101; Brooke 1912, 2). In the same way the functionally unnecessary **our hands** stresses the tactile evidence. Christ was experienced in all sensory ways (Brooke 1912, 5).

John's claims in these opening lines are bold, first person *plural* (we) assertions. Some interpreters understand them as the words of an eyewitness of Jesus' life, who speaks with a representative, collective voice. They take "we" to mean "I" and the first generation of believers. They presume that John the apostle was the author. This is certainly possible.

But if the author of 1 John wished to make a strong claim to being a personal eyewitness of the events of Jesus' life, why did he not use the first person *singular?* He could easily have written "that which *I* have heard, which *I* have seen." The first person singular appears often elsewhere in the letter—fourteen times. A first person singular claim would have clearly asserted the apostle's unique authority as an eyewitness. This would seem a natural and persuasive tactic, given his theological and ethical struggle with formidable opponents.

The words of the prologue claim an encounter with Jesus that is a highly personal and present reality. But they need not require that the author was an eyewitness. The language may be a standardized way of expressing confidence that the message of the gospel came faithfully to the readers in an unbroken chain from **the beginning.**

The use of **we** may indicate that the author is a spokesman for a Johannine "school" (see Introduction), which preserved and passed on the traditions about Jesus originating from the Beloved Disciple (Brown 1982, 175). The words—**heard, seen, looked,** and **touched**—underline the importance of personal witness to Jesus (Brown 1982, 163).

Jesus is **the Word of life** (*tou logou tēs zōēs*). Yet John delays specific mention of Jesus until v 3. Whereas the Gospel stresses the person of the **Word,** here the emphasis is upon the salvation **life** he imparted. But this

life, truly **seen, heard,** and **touched,** was inconceivable apart from the incarnate Son through whom it came. The "subject matter," the **life,** is Christ the person (Bultmann 1973, 8). The language *is* strongly experiential. As a fully human incarnation of the invisible God, he became visible, audible, and tangible (Smith 1991, 39). The theological implications of this are at the heart of these letters.

John eagerly advocates a Christology that fully embraces Jesus' humanity. The Gospel of John presupposes the humanity of Jesus and elaborates on his divinity. In 1 John the emphasis is inverted, significantly stressing his humanity (Black 1990, 40; see 1 John 1:1-3; 2:2; 4:2, 10).

This changed emphasis is an apparent response to the docetic claims of one-time members of the Johannine community. The Christian faith was firmly grounded in a *person*, Jesus, and also anchored in *history*—time, place, and event. Therefore, John may give a subtle, layered meaning, of *logos* as *both* incarnation—**Word**—and the written and preached message—word—about Christ (see Phil 2:16; Flemming 2009, 124).

In v 1 the words **this we proclaim** are not in the Greek text but supplied from v 3. Verse 1 is, strictly speaking, an anacoluthon, that is, a broken construction. John does not grammatically complete the sentence he begins. He starts the sentence with a series of direct object phrases—**That which . . . , which . . . , which . . . , which . . .** But he delays stating an explicit subject or verb (see NASB). After a parenthesis in v 2, John finally clarifies his point in v 3, providing the subject and verb he left unexpressed in v 1.

■ **2** Jesus Christ—this person, who was **life** embodied—**appeared**; or "was revealed" (NRSV). The idea of **life** "manifested" (NASB) or embodied has its basis in the Fourth Gospel: "In him was life" (John 1:4) and "I am . . . the life" (John 14:6). The root of the Greek verb *ephanerōthē* influences the English word "epiphany" and can refer to the appearance of a deity. It often conveys the idea of making visible that which is invisible.

Several NT passages use the term "epiphany" to refer to an appearance of the risen Lord (Mark 16:9, 12, 14; Luke 24:34; John 21:1, 14). All five instances of *phaneroō* in 1 John (1:2; 3:5, 8; 4:9) refer to Christ's coming into the world. This appearing was soteriological—to "take away our sin" (3:5); "to destroy the devil's work" (3:8); so "that we might live through him" (4:9). Jesus reveals God's love; and this revelation continues in the living witness of the churches (Müller 1993, 414).

The verb **appeared** is in the passive voice, indicating action done by another. By using the passive, rather than the active voice, biblical writers were able to refer to God as the agent who accomplished an action without mentioning his name. This "divine passive" was one way for the postexilic

Jews to avoid the error of their ancestors. They would not take God's name in vain.

Divine Passive

The divine passive in the NT derives from the Hebraic habit of avoiding the divine name. This extra measure of caution was tied to a reverential posture toward God, who was worthy of honor above all. It also expressed a reverential awe before the fearsome holiness of the divine presence. Those who place the kingdom and righteousness first "will be given" (by God) the things necessary for life (Matt 6:33). Faithful asking in prayer means it "will be given to you"—by God (Matt 7:7).

When believers were in need of words to give faithful witness before authorities, Jesus promises, they "will be given what to say" (Matt 10:19). In Revelation divine passive forms include provision of purity—"each of them was given a white robe" (Rev 6:11) and protection (Rev 12:14). The divine passive affirms God as actively engaged in history but without overtly naming him in the text. It also conveys the idea that all things occur within the permission of God. Nothing will happen that can surprise or derail the divine purpose.

An interpretive paraphrase of v 2 would be: **God fully revealed to us in the person of Jesus the very life of God, which was formerly unknown to us.** The emphasis is not on Jesus as an eyewitness of God. Rather, the incarnation allowed believers to see what his enemies failed to see: "The world did not recognize him. . . . his own did not receive him" (John 1:10-11). They saw him for who and what he truly was.

Thus, the divine **life,** identified as **eternal life,** was placed on display, clearly set before human eyes. By examining him who was **life** incarnate, people could come to know the nature of God. Athanasius explained this as the Christian experience of "becoming by grace what God is by nature" (*On the Incarnation,* I). He highlights the knowledge of God not merely as information but crucially as transformation.

These opening lines are similar in tone to the experience of Thomas in the Gospel (John 20:24-29). He would not believe unless he could see for himself and touch the risen Jesus' wounds. In both instances, hearing, seeing, and touching provide conclusive evidence that Jesus' death was not the end of the story. This truly significant fact made the story of Jesus good news that had to be told. The crucified and risen Jesus was experienced as alive and victorious over death. Otherwise, life was hopeless (see 1 Cor 15:14).

The words **life** and **eternal** are combined frequently into **eternal life** (*tēn zōēn tēn aiōnion*) elsewhere in the NT (eight times in the Synoptic

Gospels; nine times in Paul's letters; twice in Acts). But **eternal life** is especially prominent in the Gospel of John (sixteen times) and in 1 John (six times: 1:2; 2:25; 3:15; 5:11, 13, 20).

John perceives **eternal life** as "life from another eon (*aiōn* . . .) or sphere. Indeed, it is the life of God Himself" (Brown 1982, 168). It is life of a different quality, not merely the life of this present age continued without end. The Word (John 1:1) incarnate as Jesus brings us God's age-to-come **life** (John 6:68; 10:28; 12:50; 17:2). Jesus *is* the true life (1 John 5:20). He reveals the life of God from and for all eternity. Jesus is the past, present, and future of God (Rev 4:8; see 1:4, 8).

John differs importantly from the gnostics here. The gnostics located eternal life in an almost inaccessible realm beyond time and space. But the Johannine view brings **eternal life** into the present and firmly anchors it to the person of Jesus Christ (John 17:3). The life of eternity resides in us (John 4:14; 6:27; 12:25; Link 1976, 482).

Jesus gives life and light (John 8:12); indeed he *is* "the light of the world" (John 8:12). He gives light and life even to the creation itself (John 1:3-5). The **eternal life** that Jesus offers is eschatological—it reveals the end times in kind and duration. The implication is that whoever has this life will not be lost in eternity (John 6:40; 10:28). The eternal life is also, in Johannine understanding, a present reality, something one has now (John 3:36; 5:24; 6:47; Schottroff 1991, 108).

Verse 2 reports in the present tense, **we . . . testify** (*martyroumen*) . . . , **and we proclaim** (*apangellomen*). Apostolic and Christian authority is twofold: personal experience and commission. The translation **we are continually testifying and proclaiming** highlights the continuous emphasis of the present tense. Authentic witness is ongoing, a story that never ends. The Greek word for witness gives us the English word "martyr." Later in Christian circles "witnesses" were those willing to die rather than recant their uncompromising devotion to Christ. Such was not yet the experience of believers in 1 John (Beutler 1981, 2:392-93).

Faithful Witness and Martyrdom

In the book of Revelation, the title "faithful witness" (*ho martys ho pistos*) is ascribed first and foremost to Jesus Christ (Rev 1:5). To the church at Laodicea the risen Lord identifies himself as "the faithful and true witness" (Rev 3:14). Witnessing for one's faith did not initially mean to die for one's faith. But martyrdom eventually became a synonym for faithful witness even unto death. This was due, in part, to the expanding persecution of Christians by the Roman Empire.

The early tendency to associate these ideas appears already in Revelation: "Antipas, my faithful witness, who was put to death in your city" (2:13). The statements "be faithful, even to the point of death, and I will give you a crown of life" (Rev 2:10), and to "those who had been beheaded because of their testimony for Jesus" (Rev 20:4) further accentuate the growing issue of martyrdom in the late first century (adapted from Menoud 1962, 288).

■ **3** Bruce distinguishes between the "exclusive" and "inclusive" use of **we**. He argues that it is exclusive in v 3: "we had this experience and you did not." He insists that the prologue is best understood as the words of a first-generation Christian addressing Christians of a later generation (1970, 38).

Faithful witnessing about Jesus comes from a community of faith. The author speaks with a corporate voice, using the first person plural—**we**—in three verbs in this one verse. This collective testimony indicates that their experience of Jesus was not a solitary religious phenomenon. It was something shared as part of a worshipping community.

The main verb for vv 1-3, **we proclaim** (*apangellomen*), anticipated in v 2, finally become explicit. The word connoting a messenger bearing news was employed in both sacred and secular contexts. The word appears in reports of resurrection (Matt 28:8, 10; Mark 16:10, 13; Luke 24:9); of the message of God (Matt 11:4; Luke 7:22); and declaring Jesus as the Messenger of God (Matt 12:18; Heb 2:12; Schniewind 1964, 56-73).

A number of compound words with *angellō* occur in the NT with essentially the same meaning (see v 5, "declare" [*anangellomen*]). These related words often convey a special technical sense, the proclamation of God's intention to save. This is not a declaration of a new age to come as much as it is a recollection and clarification of something already known (Becker and Müller 1978, 46-47).

John's piling up of experiential verbs of testimony and withholding of the main verb emphasized the *content* of the message rather than the *act* of proclaiming (Marshall 1978, 100). In v 3 the verb order is **seen . . . heard**. This reversed the order of v 1, **heard . . . seen**. Along with **seen** in v 2, this poetic repetition intensifies the impact.

John wanted his readers to embrace the one who was **seen** and **heard** and so enter into the **fellowship** (*koinōnian*). To have **fellowship** was to have something in common. Business partners (Luke 5:10); those who share a "common faith" (Titus 1:4); those who enjoy God's grace along with others (Phil 1:7); those who participate in Christ (1 Cor 1:9); and Gentiles who share the benefits of the "spiritual blessings" of Jews (Rom 15:27) all experience a kind of koinonia.

Following Pentecost, Luke describes the life of the first Christians simply as *tēi koinōniai* (Acts 2:42). In view, no doubt, was their "sharing-together quality of life" in the Holy Spirit now understood afresh in terms of participation in the life, death, and resurrection of Jesus.

The word *koinōnia* occurs only in this chapter in the letters (1 John 1:3, 6, 7) and never in the Fourth Gospel. Nevertheless, the word *menō* ("I remain") in the Gospel conveys much the same concept and appears frequently (Smith 1991, 38; Bruce 1970, 38-39). The **fellowship** of 1 John was made possible and developed on the basis of a faithful proclamation of the gospel.

Such a web of rich relationships—between believers and God, and among fellow believers—was a natural outgrowth of the incarnation (Strecker 1996, 20). Because the life of God was revealed in Christ, authentic, spiritually valuable relationships could develop between persons. The present tense of the verb, *exēte* (**you . . . may have**), suggests that John addresses those who are already Christians, encouraging them to *remain* faithful (Marshall 1978, 105).

To be in fellowship with Christ was to belong to a community of believers—**you** (plural) and **with us** (*methē hēmōn*). Healthy horizontal relationships involve persons rightly relating to other persons. But John also writes of connections between his readers and **the Father and with his Son, Jesus Christ.** In such vertical relationships, worshippers rightly relate to God, the object of worship and author of all right human connections. In a real sense the relationship between Christians, at its deepest level, is simply Jesus!

John was apparently troubled by some readers who were no longer closely tied to him and his message. Consequently, he wrote to call the faithful away from a potentially eroding commitment to the apostolic teaching as he understood it. Further evidence of this may be seen in subsequent sections of the epistle about walking in light vs. darkness (1:5-7) and the labeling as "antichrists" those who "went out from us" (2:18-19). John did not write in a vacuum, but out of real pastoral concerns. Verse 3 expresses the aim of his proclamation: **that you may also have fellowship with us,** as opposed to them. His desire for authentic **fellowship** required them to resist the threat posed to the community by the erring teachers.

■ **4** This verse touches on a vital aspect of the advance of the gospel, namely the importance of writing—**we write.** John stresses this means of pastoral care at a distance an inordinate number of times for such a short letter (**write** appears ten times—1:4; 2:1, 12, 13, 14, 21; 5:13). In the one-chapter letters he minimizes the value of writing (while writing!) and expresses his preference for a personal visit (2 John 12; 3 John 13).

The Bible is available to modern readers because first-century Christian leaders wrote. Authors and countless scribes faithfully copied manuscripts by hand before the invention of the printing press. Prophets put pen to paper in response to divine command (Isa 30:8; Jer 30:2; Hab 2:2). Revelation records the command (from God/Christ/an angel) to "write" twelve times (1:11, 19; 2:1, 8, 12, 18; 3:1, 7, 14; 14:13; 19:9; 21:5).

John writes to enable communal **joy**. The word **joy** (*chara*, related to *charis*, "grace") appears seven times on the lips of Jesus in the Fourth Gospel (3:29; 15:11; 16:20-24; 17:13). The Greek words in 1 John 1:4 are identical to those in John 16:24 (NKJV): "that your joy may be full," except in manuscripts of 1 John that have "our" rather than "your."

The variant reading *your* in 1 John may have been introduced by a scribe attempting to harmonize the epistle with the Gospel. Alternatively, a scribe could have heard incorrectly when a reader in a scriptorium was dictating to a group of scribes making multiple copies of 1 John. In such a setting the words *hēmōn* and *hymōn*, like **our** and "your," could be easily confused.

The NIV (also NASB, NRSV) translators preferred the reading **our** (*hēmōn*) in v 4 based on two important fourth-century uncial manuscripts, Sinaiticus and Vaticanus. As the more unexpected reading, it is probably more likely. A later editor might be expected to smooth out the reading, not make it more difficult.

The word **joy** appears four more times in the Johannine letters (2 John 4, 12; 3 John 3, 4). The mutual joy experienced in their shared commitments led them to preserve their written communications and look forward to face-to-face contact.

The readers of 1 John familiar with the Fourth Gospel would no doubt have heard echoes of the joy emphasized in Jesus' final discourse (John 15:11; 16:24; 17:13; see John 3:29). The pattern in John 15 is similar: A shared relationship—**fellowship**—results in **joy**. The meaning in both Gospel and epistle reaches out to include the joy of salvation.

John writes so the **joy** of the Johannine circle may be made **complete** (*peplērōmenē*, "filled up"), experienced in abundance (see 2 John 12). The perfect tense of the participle suggests a **joy** brought to fullness and sustained. Furthermore, the passive voice reminds the readers that their **joy** is a gift from God. This gift is best experienced when received in a faithful, corporate setting in which the hearers obey what they have been taught by apostolic authority.

In summary, vv 1-4 anticipate in essence the message—the theological witness—of the entire letter. Implied first is the continuity of revelation between the Father and the incarnate Son. Second, John stresses the biblical truth that the life of the Christian is a relationship that comprehends both gospel and ethic. Held together is both "What God has done" and "What we are to do"—the inherent unity of the horizontal and vertical dimensions of Christian life.

It is imperative for our spiritual welfare and the health of the church that these two are kept in balance. The presence and interpenetration of both is necessary. "This life, . . . the eternal life," is "fellowship with us" and " with the Father and with the Son."

FROM THE TEXT

A Challenge to Witness Faithfully

Those who experience **eternal life** (v 2) have an obligation to be faithful examples of and spokespersons for this life. Hearers in every generation tell the story and share the life it offers. From the first Christians, through those who brought the Scriptures to us, and passed it on by our faithful witness, the story never ends.

How do we witness faithfully? By personally embracing the Christian faith and the person of Jesus Christ. Faithful testimony happens as we immerse ourselves in that faith. By studying and living its message, we become confident embodiments and retellers of the story. Our competence as faithful witnesses improves with practice.

A Concern to Maintain the Christological Paradox

The ancient struggle to hold in creative tension both Christ's full divinity and full humanity, evident in this letter, continues today. Jesus was a Jewish man of his times, a rabbinic teacher who lived in first-century Israel. Some see him as a courageous social revolutionary (Crossan 1991), but certainly not a deity (Crossan 1994; for critique of such skepticism see Johnson 1996, 20-27). But the overarching testimony of the NT affirms Jesus as "God" (John 1:1) in whom "God was pleased to have all his fullness dwell" (Col 1:19), "in very nature God" (Phil 2:6), and "the Son [who] is the radiance of God's glory and the exact representation of his being" (Heb 1:3).

On the other hand, some well-intentioned Christians have been fearful of anything that might diminish the divine claims made in Scripture and in early creeds about Jesus. So they end up with a Christ who never became truly incarnate. They conceive of his humanity as an illusion or a disguise he left behind when he returned to the Father. This was precisely the error faced in 1 John. Some denied that Christ had come and remained "in the flesh" (4:2-3).

Maintaining both aspects of Christology, even as they stand in paradoxical tension, reflects historic Christian faith. Both the full divinity and the full humanity of Christ are equally true. The early creedal statement from the Council of Nicea (A.D. 325) that was later adapted at Chalcedon (A.D. 451) declared that Christ was "true God of true God" but also "was made flesh . . . and became man" (Bettenson 1971, 26).

A Call to Joy in Christian Community

In the NT joy is associated especially with Jesus' birth (Matt 2:10; Luke 1:14, 44; 2:10) and his resurrection (Matt 28:8; Luke 24:41, 52). Joy naturally flows from a transformed life (Luke 15:7, 10) and within a community that has experienced spiritual renewal (Acts 8:8). Joy is not dependent on circumstances. That is, joy can be present whether or not all the aspects of our lives are flowing smoothly. Rather, joy consists of an inner and abiding peace, knowing that, whatever comes, one is rightly related to God and others. This already experienced eschatological joy (assured by resurrection faith; John 16:20-22) anticipates a not-yet fulfillment (1 Cor 2:9; see Bultmann 1973, 14 n. 28, who sees an eschatological salvation on the basis of John 17:13).

One may know joy individually, but it is best experienced in the company of others. Our allegiance to Jesus Christ is nurtured by other believers. First John encourages us to experience the richness of human friendships, anchored and enriched by fellowship with God.

B. Forgiveness and Cleansing (1:5-10)

BEHIND THE TEXT

The theological vocabulary of this section strongly resembles the nonbiblical manuscripts known as the Dead Sea Scrolls (DSS). This collection of documents and the Essenes, who probably composed, assembled, and preserved them, espouse a strongly dualistic theology. Those who were properly allied with God and righteousness were "sons of light" and those who were hostile to God and would be judged were "sons of darkness."

The Dead Sea Scrolls

In 1947, near the northwest shore of the Dead Sea, a wealth of ancient manuscripts began to be discovered in the caves of the area. The site, called Qumran, provides significant data for understanding the religious thought-world of a separatist Jewish community as well as some aspects of early Christianity. The DSS include copies of every book of the OT except Esther, as well as a large number of noncanonical writings. For introductory material on the Qumran community, English translations of the scrolls, and extensive bibliography see Vermes (2004); for a short history of the DSS see Fields (2006).

The Qumran community was composed of priests who had totally abandoned the established temple at Jerusalem and relocated some distance away at the Dead Sea. This physical separation, in itself a sharp rejection of temple leaders, was coupled with critical language directed toward Jerusalem (1 QS VIII, 8-9, 14-15; IX, 4-5; see Vermes 2004, 77-84). They understood their function in the Jordan valley as a fulfillment of Isa 40:3: "In the desert prepare the way for the LORD; make straight in the **wilderness** a highway for our God."

This separtist Jewish sect was contemporaneous with the developing Christian movement. Both were Jewish expressions of religious faith with significant overlaps in language and worldview. Both intended to perpetuate the best of Judaism; and both affirmed a coming Messiah. But the Essenes anticipated a messiah (or two; 1QS VIII, 10; Vermes 2004, 86) *to come,* while the Johannine Christians celebrated the messiah who *had already come.*

1:5-10   Both the Essenes and the Johannine Christians embraced a sharply dualistic outlook (e.g., truth/lies, light/darkness). The Essenes' self-identity as true light is much like the language of 1 John (Vermes 2004, 84-85; 1QM I, 1-15). In 1 John 2:8 "the true light is already shining" (see John 1:4-9). Both viewed the future as an approaching apocalyptic face-off between good and evil. The references in 1 John to "the last hour" and "antichrists" (2:18) reflect a religious viewpoint akin to those at Qumran.

Both groups practiced water baptism. But it is debatable whether its meaning was similar. The ritualistic lustrations in Judaism were repeated again and again (e.g., prior to entrance to the temple). In contrast, the baptism associated with John the Baptist, and embraced by followers of Jesus, had a "once for all" transformative character to it.

Essenes were, like Jesus, critical of the Jerusalem temple's leadership. John's account of the clearing of the temple (2:13-22) provides more and harsher censure of temple worship than the Synoptic Gospels. John locates this tension-packed action by Jesus at the beginning of his Gospel, whereas the Synoptics report it near the end of Jesus' life. The event heightens the tension between the temple leadership and Jesus (John 7:32; 8:20, 59). Jesus' statement "destroy this temple" (John 2:19), though spoken in reference to his body, ironically points forward to the actual destruction of the temple by the Romans in A.D. 70.

The preaching of John the Baptist in the Jordan valley also contains themes found in the Johannine and Qumran literature. Like the Essenes, he preached words of warning against the religious leaders ("Pharisees and Sadducees") to flee the "coming wrath" of a certain fiery judgment. The Baptist expected a final separation of "wheat" from "chaff." He also urged Jews not to depend on their descent from Abraham as security against this coming judgment (see Matt 3:7-12). This reflects the kind of dualism found at Qumran and evident in 1 John.

IN THE TEXT

First John 1:1-4 introduces the fundamental fabric of the Christian proclamation. Namely, the comprehensive concern of how Christians relate to God and to each other, woven out of the threads of an adequate ethic and an appropriate Christology. In the content and grammatical structure of 1:5-10, John now moves into a more detailed exploration of the inner or theological structure of his witness to the gospel. This is the first and foundational exposition of his proclamation. As we understand these verses, we understand the message of the entire epistle. In them John utilizes either explicitly or implicitly all of his essential concepts in their inner relation.

■ **5** The Christian **message** (*angelia*) had been **heard** and was still sounding in their ears (*akēkoamen*, perfect tense). But this announcement is ongoing—***we are declaring*** (*anangellomen*). The ultimate source of the announcement is God (or Christ; see v 3). The content of this **message** is that **God is light** and **in him there is no darkness at all**. This is a key announcement for John's interpretation of the gospel to his readers. It is "the theological core of his world picture" (Houlden 1973, 57).

The association between **God** and **light** appears on the opening page of the Bible. Genesis 1:1 reports that "darkness . . . over the surface of the deep" was dispelled by God. He spoke light into existence and declared the light "good" (Gen 1:3). Psalm 104:2 describes God as clothed "in light as with a garment." Psalm 27 equates salvation and light and identifies God as the source of both.

The prologue of the Gospel of John employs the language of the Genesis creation narrative to say of Christ: "In him was life, and that life was the light of men. The light shines in the darkness, but the darkness has not understood it" (1:4-5). The Fourth Gospel speaks of light twenty-three times, and presents Christ as "the light" ("light of the world" in John 8:12; 9:5). But in 1 John, only **God is light.**

Life and **light** express the salvation offered to those who will believe in Christ (John 1:4). But **light** also speaks of God's self-revelation as "the true light that gives light to every man" (John 1:9). Thus the "true light" is both a necessity that belongs to God's moral nature and the source of all moral illumination.

John's language seems to counter a gnostic use of life and light as secret knowledge to a *few*. Instead the terms mean the revelation of God clearly to *all*. In the dualistic images of the literature from Qumran, **light** and **darkness** typified the radical difference between good and evil. The Dead Sea sectarians referred to themselves as "sons of light" (War Scroll 1QM, 1Q33, 4Q491-7, 4Q471; see Vermes 2004, 161-85; Ritt 1993, 3:448). They were ruled by "the Prince of Light" as opposed to the great enemies of God, who were led by "the Angel of Darkness" (1QS III, 13-IV, 1). *T. Levi* 19:1, a Jewish pseudepigraphal document, speaks of the "sons of light" and the "sons of darkness" (see John 12:35-36, 46; also 1 Thess 5:5: "You are all sons of the light and sons of the day").

The imagery of **light** in contrast to **darkness** in 1 John identifies those allied with the Johannine community in contrast to the secessionists. To "walk in the light" (v 7) is to live by the truth (implied in v 6). To journey in the light of God's self-revelation in Jesus is to experience fellowship with God's people and cleansing "from all sin" (v 7). **God is light** and "God is love" (1 John 4:16), and by inference, God is "truth" (1:6). God as light, love, and truth is good; and evil cannot coexist with good (Marshall 1978, 109).

■ **6** A series of false claims begins. The false statements in vv 6, 8, and 10 are matched with truthful antidotes in vv 7, 9, and 2:1. Each set of erroneous assertions is introduced by **if we claim** (*ean eipōmen*). In v 6, **if we claim** is followed by "but if we walk" (v 7). In v 8, "if we claim" is paired with "if we confess" (v 9). In v 10, "if we claim" (v 10) has its corollary in 2:1.

John expresses the heretical false claims in climactic order. That is, the problems he faces move from the general to the specific, and then to the most personally condemning (vv 6, 8, 10). The solutions follow the same pattern, from the general to the specific and then to the down-to-earth life of the disciple (vv 7, 9; 2:1-2).

The structure of each verse in the sequence is nearly identical—condition, consequence, and explanation (1:6, 7, 8, 9, 10; 2:1*b*-2). Verse 6 is typical: **if we claim to have fellowship with him yet walk in darkness** is the condition. It is followed by the consequence: "we lie," and the explanation: we "do not live by the truth" (Nauck 1957, 23-24).

The ethical character of the problem John addresses is stressed primarily in the three "conditions" in vv 6, 8, and 10. Its christological implications are present in the "consequences" and "explanations." The latter two put together balance the verses in a more formal structure. Thus, the problems and the solutions John has set up are both ethical and christological in character.

The verbs in the three pairs of claims are in the subjunctive mood. This suggests a hypothetical probability, but not a certainty (Wallace 1996, 461). A person might or might not make such claims. A professing Christian might choose to walk in darkness, but this is not a certainty. An expanded translation to capture the ideas would be *if* we claim to have fellowship with him *(though one might make such a claim, or one might not)*—and if we . . . walk in the darkness *(though that need not happen)*.

The repeated phrase **if we claim** seems to indicate that some, either outside or within the Johannine churches, have actually made such claims. This is what John seeks to correct (Smith 1991, 43). John considered such aberrant views a serious danger to his readers. Some had perhaps already been swayed to these positions. It is risky to reconstruct the views of a group by reading materials critical of them written by others. But the opponents of John seem to have been close at hand, even people formerly within the Johannine churches (1 John 2:19). John no doubt understood all too well what the opponents were teaching (Bogart 1977, 28-29).

John, by using **we**, may be identifying with the group to whom he writes (Strecker 1996, 29). He stood as one of them in order to dissuade them from the dangers of the secessionists. But the repeated **if we claim** (vv 6, 8, 10) may be merely a stylistic device. Bogart considers the three first person plurals here as equivalent to the three impersonal pronouns in 1 John 2, represented by the substantive participles *ho legōn* (**the one saying**, 2:4, 6, and 9; Bogart 1977, 28).

Both verbs in the first clause, **we claim** and **[we] have**, are in the present tense. So if we claim to be in a continuous, shared (*koinōnia*) relationship with Christ, but live in a way that is inconsistent with our **claim**, we are actually presently living **in the darkness.** To do so is to **walk** at odds with the **truth** (v 6: *we are not doing the truth;* see John 3:21).

This would involve believing a teaching different from that of the Johannine churches (2 John 9-11). At issue also would be not loving the "brother" (1 John 1:7; 2:9-11; 3:23). To so **walk in the darkness** is to engage in blatant self-deception: **we lie** (*pseudometha*) and are failing to **live by the truth.**

Truth

The concept of "truth" (*alētheia*) appears more than two dozen times in the Gospel of John, twice as many as in the Synoptic Gospels combined. Truth is the most frequent key word in the letters (Thomas 2004, 20, 39).

In the Gospel of John truth can refer to *content to be believed*—"If you hold to my teaching, you are really my disciples. Then you will know the truth, and the truth will set you free" (8:31-32; see vv 40-46). God's "word is truth" (17:17).

But truth also assumes *living in right relationship with* "the only true God" (17:3). Jesus is truth incarnate as God's revelation (1:17; 14:6; Bultmann 1973, 97, 99), and the Holy Spirit is "the Spirit of truth" (14:17; 15:26; 16:13). The individual who receives God's truth "lives by" it (3:21), worships "in spirit and truth," and is sanctified by the truth (17:17).

The world, a domain of darkness and falsehood, has been invaded by Christ, "the true light" (1:9). Jesus, active in creation (1:10), comes into the world he helped shape, but "his own did not receive him" (1:11). Ironically, as Jesus is tried and condemned, *the world is on trial* for its rejection of truth (Köstenberger 2009, 288-89, 437-41).

In the letters John assures his readers that they "have an anointing from the Holy One, and . . . know the truth" (1 John 2:20; see 2 John 1; John 8:32). In 3 John 8 believers are to be coworkers in the truth (Jones 2009, 268). The five instances of "truth" in 2 John 1-4, and five more in 3 John, may signal the elder's concern over doctrine as he calls his readers to "walk in the truth" (3 John 3). But his imagery indicates that his concern is not for static creedal orthodoxy (Jones 2009, 268; see Lieu 1991, 94-96). The image of walking presents a picture of truth as a dynamic, ongoing, shared relationship.

Truth can be personified and so give testimony in behalf of another (3 John 12). Believers walk in truth, indeed, may live in truth forever (2 John 2; 3 John 3, 4). For the elder, truth signifies not only the Christian message but also the incarnate Jesus, who by the Spirit can enter into a believer (Marshall 1978, 62 n. 17). Not only is Christ the revealer of truth, but also he himself is the truth (John 14:6). Thus, knowing the truth means more than hearing Christ's words; it involves personal union with him (Dodd 1968, 177-78).

The theme of practicing truth appears also in the Qumran literature—1QS I, 5: "that they may abstain from all evil and hold fast to all good; that they may *practice* truth, righteousness, and justice . . ."; V, 3: "They shall *practice* truth and humility in common, and justice and uprightness and charity and modesty in all their ways"; VIII, 2: "They . . . shall atone for sin by the *practice* of justice" (emphases added; see Vermes 2004, 98, 103, 109).

Truth spurs to action. In 1 John **doing the truth** includes acting in loving ways toward one's fellow believer (2:9-10) and being generous with material support to "his brother [and sister] in need" (3:17; see vv 16-18). This is strikingly similar to James, for whom true faith is always demonstrated by actions (Jas 2:14-26). Also **doing the truth** means not being led astray from what "you have heard from the beginning" (1 John 2:24). The emphasis on **fellowship with** God and the mention of "the blood of Jesus, his Son" in v 7 indicates that Christology as well as ethics is in view.

Walking, having **fellowship**, and doing the **truth** are related, continuous activities. Quitting one reflects cessation of the others. The ancient metaphor of walking naturally became a part of the Christian vocabulary. Jesus said, "Whoever follows me will never walk in darkness, but will have the light of life" (John 8:12; also 11:9-10; 12:35). The Apostle Paul employed the image of walking often (*peripateō* is translated "live" in Rom 6:4; 8:4; Gal 5:16; Eph 4:1; 5:8).

The metaphor appears several times in the Psalms (1:1; 15:2; 86:11; 128:1). To walk with another was to be in agreement with him (Amos 3:3), to keep in pace with another (Gal 5:25). Remaining aligned with the Johannine churches was "walking in the truth" (2 John 4; 3 John 4), and to "walk as Jesus did" (1 John 2:6).

■ **7** God's work in us **purifies** (*katharizei*, present tense) and may be understood as having a continuous aspect—*is continually purifying*. The purifying continues as we walk with God. Cleansing is both *what God does for us* and an unfolding reality as *our obedience enables us to live in a purifying relationship with God*.

The blood of Jesus speaks of his suffering on the cross unto death. John offers it as the sufficient basis to cleanse **from all sin**. This purity, conditioned upon a continuing obedient response to God's grace, means this work of God is not accomplished once-for-all in a moment. As Harvey Blaney rightly stressed:

> It is a mistake to think that all which John implies here can be attained on one occasion or in response to a momentary total surrender to God. Jesus said "Follow me." Only those who begin to follow and walk in the light can experience the results spoken of. (Blaney 1967, 354-55)

We keep walking, and God keeps the purifying efficacy of the merits of Christ's death applied to our lives. We may never presume we are cleansed from sin by our own efforts.

Walking **in the light** enables believers to **have fellowship with one another**. The image of walking in light is found in the Psalms (Pss 56:13;

89:15) and in Isaiah, "Let us walk in the light of the LORD" (2:5). In the Gospel of John the image is of believing and loving discipleship toward Jesus (John 8:12).

The Essene community considered walking in light evidence one was among the sons of righteousness. In contrast, walking in darkness revealed one to be a son of wickedness (1QS III, 20; Vermes 2004, 101). In 1 John walking **in the light** is to live in obedience to God, who "is light" (v 5). It is to experience God's presence and be shaped by God's character as revealed in **Jesus, his Son.**

Previously in v 6 the claim "we . . . have fellowship with him" was negated by walking "in the darkness." So one might now expect to find John saying that walking **in the light** leads to fellowship with God. Instead, John extends the thought a step further (Brooke 1912, 15). The result of walking **in the light** means **we have fellowship with one another.** For the Johannine Christians, fellowship with the Father and the Son was inextricably woven together with fidelity to the community of faith (1:3).

John is careful to stress the fact that it is God, through **Jesus, his Son,** who does the cleansing. Most specifically, it is **the blood** of Jesus that **purifies.** Many modern minds are deeply resistant to the imagery of blood sacrifice. However, John, the collective witness of the NT, and indeed, the entire Bible, all point toward the concept of reconciliation between sinful humanity and the holy, loving God. This was accomplished by a death, which meant the shedding of Christ's blood. His death, conceived as a blood sacrifice, appears in the NT in numerous places (Mark 14:24; Rom 3:25; 1 Cor 11:25; Eph 1:7; Heb 9:11-14) and will soon appear in this letter (see the commentary on 1 John 2:2).

The word **purifies** (*katharizei*, v 9), in a variety of usages in the NT and LXX, suggests making clean. It means to cleanse from sin in Heb 9:22, 23; 10:2. Luke, reporting Peter's words about the outpouring of the Spirit upon Gentiles in Cornelius' household, describes the giving of the Holy Spirit as achieving the *katharisas* of their hearts (Acts 15:9). The primary point in both Hebrews and Acts is the removal of all that hinders relationship to God.

In the Gospel of John forms of *katharizō* appear in 15:2-3 to describe the cleaning away of branches not producing fruit. In John 13:10-11 the idea is applied metaphorically to explain that not all the twelve disciples were *katharoi*, a reference to Judas the betrayer as having a heart alien to Jesus.

In Matthew the term describes one being cleansed from leprosy (8:2, 3; 10:8). This transformation enables ceremonial, ritual acceptance for the one so cleansed. John, here in v 7, asserts that God does more than *view* a person differently due to Christ's death and a person being "in" Christ. God **purifies** so that a person *becomes* morally different when brought into relation to him. What was unclean is made clean. The defilement of sin, the fact and the effects of living contrary to God's will, is cleansed (see on 1:9).

The work of God being stressed in 1 John calls for an ethical ordering of one's life as a natural result of a new relationship. It is a holiness that, though certainly and always derived from Christ, and achieving reconciliation to God through him, becomes a transformative reality in the life of the disciple of Jesus.

How thorough is the cleansing? It is from **all sin.** Brooke understood the phrase **purifies us from all sin** as indicating "the *removal* of sin" from the life of the believer (1912, 15). Brooke further proposes that John envisions sin here as an active power, not a reference to specific acts of sin (Brooke 1912, 16-17). Smith speaks of sin as first a root cause, a condition of alienation from God that leads to expressions that are sinful (Smith 1991, 46). Marshall writes that "purification signifies the removal *not only of the guilt of sin but also of the power of sin* in the human heart" (1978, 114, emphasis added). The idea of an inner condition of sinfulness is readily apparent in other NT passages, notably Paul's treatment of sin in Romans as a power at work in persons (Rom 6:12-14; 7:11, 13).

The phrase **from all sin** thus conveys wonderful promise. God's cleansing activity that flows from Christ's death is a deep and thorough work, attending to "all that is called sin" (Blaney 1967, 355). The Greek word *pas* is rendered "all" in three instances in 1 John when the word is used as an adjective with a singular noun—here in v 7, **all sin** (*pasēs hamartias*); v 9, "all unrighteousness" (*pasēs adikias*); and at 5:17, "all wrongdoing" (*pasa adikia*).

The cleansing addresses **all sin** (or "every sin," NIV margin). Forms of *pas* are translated three times as "every" in 1 John as an adjective with a singular noun—in 4:1 as "every spirit" (*panti pneumati*) and in 4:2-3 as "every spirit" (*pan pneuma*). Whichever translation is used, the implication remains that God's remedy for sin is complete. Sin cannot continue to defile the person, or faith community, that continually walks in the light.

Two instances in 1 John might be taken as approaching a definition of sin. "Sin is lawlessness" (*anomia*, 3:4) and "All wrongdoing [*adikia*] is sin" (5:17). The statement in 3:4 suggests sin as a condition. In 5:17 the obvious sense is of violations. In John 16:9 Jesus speaks of sin as unbelief. The lack of proper belief in Jesus (Christology) is one of the foundational problems faced in the letter.

So in the Johannine writings sin is against God's law, against righteousness, and a failure to believe in Jesus. While "law" occurs only once in the letters, "command" appears twelve times. The commands are twofold: (1) "believe in the name of his Son, Jesus Christ" (3:23; 5:10, 13); and (2) "love one another" (3:11, 23; 4:7, 11, 12). When John writes of a cleansing from all sin and from all unrighteousness, he points toward a divine remedy for all that is anti-God's law, anti-God's character, and anti-Christ.

What we need, God provides. Liberation from sin through the atoning death of Christ is offered to all, for sin is universal (Strecker 1996, 31). John, in this well-structured set of verses (1:5—2:2) brings strong language to bear on the pastoral challenges at hand. Sin is real, personal, serious, and pervasive. But divine correction is all these as well.

■ **8** The **claim to be without sin** creates a challenge for interpretation. The present tense of the verb perhaps indicates a continuous force: *if we are presently claiming we have no sin.* Later, John calls his readers to live no longer under the dominion of sin (2:1). But he does, however, clearly acknowledge that sin may intrude into the lives of Christians.

John obviously does not agree with what his opponents are saying. Two different types of perfectionism appear in 1 John, "heretical" and "orthodox" (Bogart 1977, 47-49). Proponents of the rival "heretical perfectionism" perverted the Johannine understanding. It seems to presume gnostic influences, which viewed the material universe, including the human body, as evil. John vigorously resists this understanding as a theological and practical danger for his churches (vv 6, 8, 10).

John energetically contends for the other, "orthodox perfectionism." This type is that of being "born of God" (3:9), with sins forgiven and God's purifying work a present reality by "the blood of Jesus" (1:7, 9). This orthodox perfectionism is marked by avoiding sin through abiding in Christ—"No one who lives in him keeps on sinning" (3:6). Here in v 8, those who **claim to be without sin** are claiming to have knowledge of a superior kind. As essentially "spiritual" rather than physical beings, sin is of no moral issue to them, sin does not relate as such to their lives.

The use of **sin** (singular) and the contrast that follows in v 9, where "sins" are addressed, might permit *hamartian* here to be thought of as ***sinfulness***, a condition rather than acts of disobedience. Bede understood the term in this way, as inherited sinfulness. He appealed to this passage in opposition to Pelagians, who taught that children were born without such a sinful propensity (Bray 2000, 172).

To **claim to be without sin** is to engage in intentional self-deception. The Greek word order can be emphatically translated as ***ourselves we are deceiving***. John repeatedly warns his readers against this (2:26; 3:7).

Earlier (v 6) John linked walking "in the darkness" with not doing the truth. Similarly here he says **the truth is not in** one who wrongly claims sinlessness.

■ **9** John offers as an alternative to the false claim of sinlessness the confession of sins. He does not state to whom the confession is to be made. The proposal and the promise are urged upon his readers corporately—**we** and **us**. John may be calling, as does James, for mutual confession—"to each another" (Jas 5:16). Ultimately the confession is intended toward God/Christ, who grants forgiveness and purity as a result.

In the *Didache* (14) the confession of **sins** occurred on "the Lord's day." It was also commended as preparation for it—"on the Lord's day assemble and break bread and give thanks, having first confessed your sins, that your sacrifice may be pure" (Bettenson 1971, 66).

Forms of **confess** are relatively infrequent in the NT and only a few (Matt 3:6; Mark 1:5; Jas 5:16) are related to the confessing of sins. Secular Greek texts employ *homologeō* for admission of guilt or error, though not with a religious connotation (Hofius 1991, 515).

In the face of human sinfulness, and especially when **sins** are confessed, God is **faithful** (*pistos*). The word can mean "trustworthy" or "dependable" (BDAG 2000, 820; see Matt 25:21; 2 Tim 2:2) or said of promises that are certain. God's character is **just** (*dikaios*, **righteous**). God's righteousness is manifested as faithfulness in spite of human unfaithfulness (see Heb 10:23).

The divine act, to **forgive** (*aphēi*) . . . **sins**, can mean to send them away, to remit a debt, or to let off from penalty. Brooke understood that forgiveness of sins might be thought of as a symbolic act whereby the barrier that sins had created between God and persons was removed (Brooke 1912, 20).

In vv 6-8, John used present tense verbs to discuss what God does and what persons do. Here, at a strategic point in his argument, he uses the aorist tense to speak of what God purposes to do, namely, **forgive us** and **purify us**. The aorist tense in Greek is the simple past tense. It does not necessarily make a specified statement about when something occurred, but simply views the act as accomplished, not its duration or result (Haas, DeJonge, and Swellengrebel 1972, 38). At times, however, it can carry the sense of a completed action, even a decisive one.

It is intriguing that just here the aorist tense appears in reference to what God does with cleansing **from all unrighteousness** (*adikias*). The Greek alpha (*a*) at the beginning of the word negates the word to which it is attached. Thus, God removes all that is not righteous. The connection between the words used by John to speak of the nature of God and what God can do for persons is seen when it is translated by **he is . . . *righteous*** (*dikaios*) **and . . . will . . . purify us from all unrighteousness** (*adikias*).

Earlier (vv 6-8) John stressed God's continuous, ongoing saving work (and the believer's response to it) with present tense verbs. By using aorist verbs John may be emphasizing an action by God, not as continuous, but as a decisive act. God's work speaks to the universal human need to be pardoned and to be purified for relational restoration and personal healing. John urges his readers to understand and experience both forgiveness and purification.

John Calvin rightly saw that confession occasioned "a twofold fruit . . . That God, who is reconciled by the sacrifice of Christ, forgives us; and that He corrects and reforms us" (1959, 241). Yet Calvin resisted a thorough addressing of sin in the present. He too closely identified sinning with being in the body. He dismisses the clear intent of v 9, insisting, "John is not telling us what God performs in us now" (1959, 241).

Only God can purify. But God does not override the human will to accomplish purification. The verbs (**forgive**—*aphēi;* and **purify**—*katharisēi*), both in the subjunctive mood, are combined with the conditional conjunction *ean*. This "if . . . then" construction is a conditional statement, indicating what may or may not happen (Mounce 2003, 293). God can purify us and wants to do so. The pardon and purity God offers is conditioned upon our response. As moral agents, we can either respond positively toward, or resist, the offer of grace.

■ **10** Some first-century readers (heretical perfectionists) appear to have gone so far as to say they had committed no sins from which they needed to be forgiven or delivered. But John will not allow such false assertions to go unchallenged. Claiming no sins on our record is to call God a **liar**. This gives evidence that God's word is not residing in us. The term **liar** here recalls "we lie" in v 6. These may be something of an *inclusio* (a "packaging" of a text portion with literary bookends, so to speak) for the section (Brown 1982, 225). John disputes any who would say **we have not sinned**.

The perfect tense refers to past sins that have continuing effects in the present. The secessionist apparently claimed that they had not committed sins that needed forgiveness. Or, they claimed that their past sins were of no consequence in the present.

Regardless, John's perfect tense verb undermines both notions. In this he agrees with Paul's assertion: "All have sinned and fall short of the glory of God" (Rom 3:23). All continue to be affected by past sins, forgiven and cleansed or not. We cannot claim a sinless past. And we cannot imagine that past sin does not impact the present.

What a perilous thing to call God a **liar** (*pseustēn*)! John does not suggest that the secessionists say this in so many words. But this is what their beliefs and practices imply. Denial of sin, saying **we have not sinned**, declares God wrong about us.

The word for **liar** appears only eight times in the NT. It occurs twice in the Gospel of John, where Jesus calls the devil and those who listen to him "liar" (John 8:44, 55; see Rom 3:4). Significantly **liar** appears five times in 1 John. Two of these refer to a person's words or beliefs denigrating God as a **liar** (1:10; 5:10). Three times they identify persons who defy God's commands, deny Christ, and dismiss their brothers and sisters (2:4, 22; 4:20).

John says that a denial of having **sinned** means **his word has no place in our lives**. This phrase is virtually identical in Greek to the concluding portion of v 8:

- 1:8: "the truth is not in us" (*hē alētheia ouk estin en hēmin*)
- 1:10: **his word *is not in us*** (*ho logos autou ouk estin en hēmin*)

Further, these two lines sustain the thought from earlier. When "we lie" we obviously "do not [do] the truth" (v 6). When "we deceive ourselves" we demonstrate that "the truth is not in us" (v 8). And when we make God **out to be a liar** then **his word *is not in us*** (v 10).

The parallelism in these verses suggests that "the truth" (vv 6, 8) is to be equated with God's **word** (v 10). This linkage of truth and God's **word** can also be seen in the Fourth Gospel (see John 17:17). The message of the gospel has neither been heard nor responded to, that is, Christ has not been received!

False claims lead to ever increasing delusion. In v 6 claiming to have a close relationship with God while living in disobedience is effectively a "lie" told to others. Then in v 8 a denial that sin affects our lives is to "deceive [lie to] ourselves." Finally, in the most unthinkable of charges, in v 10, to deny having **sinned** is to call God **a liar**!

FROM THE TEXT

The Danger of Hypocrisy

When we conduct ourselves in morally corrupt ways and continue to claim to be Christians, we blatantly live a lie (v 6). But worse, **we deceive**

ourselves (v 8). Eventually, the boundary between lies and truth becomes so blurred that we call God a liar by denying even that we have sinned (v 10). Tragically, we believe ourselves spiritually in need of nothing (see Rev 3:17).

The Necessity of Divine Cleansing

Sometimes, as with the opponents of John, the most significant flaw in us might be the self-deception that we have no flaws! Refusal to acknowledge one's sins (not confessing) means God is blocked, called a **liar,** and God's word is absent **in our lives** (v 10).

God will cleanse **from all sin** (v 7) and **from all unrighteousness** (v 9). John Wesley understood **all sin** in v 7 to refer to "both original and actual, taking away all the guilt and the power" (Wesley 1983, n.p.). Adam Clarke, similarly, spoke of sin in two "modes": in *"guilt,* which requires *forgiveness* or *pardon"* and in *"pollution,* which requires *cleansing"* (Clarke n.d., 904). Martin Luther, citing Augustine, differentiated between sin as condition ("indwelling sin") and sinful acts (Pelikan 1967, 228).

Adam Clarke makes a powerful affirmation:

> And being cleansed from all sin is what every believer should look for, what he has a right to expect, and what he must have *in this life,* in order to be prepared to meet his God. Christ is not a *partial Saviour;* he saves to the uttermost, and he cleanses from ALL *sin.* (Clarke n.d., 904)

God wants to purge us from all that is unlike God. By this cleansing, **all sin** (v 7) and **all unrighteousness** (v 9) are defeated. Over time God works to smooth out the lingering flaws in our lives—to remove all that is inconsistent with the character of God.

The Relational Nature of Holiness

The theme of **fellowship** (vv 4, 6) highlights the critical nature of righteousness as relational. Being cleansed from all sin does not mean that we experience a surgical intervention, as if sin were organic. Rather, being cleansed from sin means entering into a cleansing relationship with God. We are cleansed by being rightly related to the God who is pure and who always cleanses what is surrendered into his possession. Cleansing results from living in Christ.

John's use of **all** (vv 7, 9) expresses his confidence that God does not merely nibble away at sin in our lives. His intention is to defeat sin decisively. Thus **holy** and **righteous** appropriately describe the true character, not simply the position or standing, of God's people.

The Limits of Christian Fellowship

To what degree can we participate with other Christians who have different views and practices? When does fellowship go beyond shared lives and become compromise? What key doctrinal matters or lifestyle practices are nonnegotiable? There is danger in too quickly labeling those with whom we disagree as being **in . . . darkness** (vv 5, 6). But it is also dangerous too quickly to welcome divergent theologies and practices.

John Wesley dealt with the matter in his sermon "Catholic Spirit." He urged steadfastness in what one "believes to be the truth as it is in Jesus" (not having "a muddy understanding"). Settled in one's own theological convictions, and active in a local congregation, the person of a catholic spirit yet has a "heart . . . enlarged toward all" who love Jesus Christ, love others, and seek always to please God (Wesley 1978-79, 5:502-4).

II. BELONGING TO GOD AND RESISTING THE ENEMY: 1 JOHN 2:1-29

A. Jesus Our Defender (2:1-6)

IN THE TEXT

■ 1 The expression of endearment—**My dear children**—is frequent in the letter (2:12, 28; 3:7, 18; 4:4; 5:21). It suggests a warm relationship between the author and his readers. It also may hint that the author was well along in years. The word **children** provides a powerful image of spiritual relationship of a leader with his followers. But both John and his readers are "children of God" (3:1).

John highlights his pastoral concern with the interruption of **my dear children, I write, . . .** into the structure he has employed throughout vv 6-10. That 2:1-2 belongs to the train of thought begun at v 5 is indicated by the continuation of the sequence—condition, consequence, explanation (vv 1*b*, 1*c*, 2; Nauck 1957, 23-24).

Whereas in 1:4 John penned "we write," here for the first of nine times he shifts to a first person singular—**I write** (2:7, 8, 12, 13, 14; 5:13). This apparent change of the "voice" occurs from time to time in the letter. In the opening lines of 1 John, "we" represents the collective and historic testimony of apostolic tradition. Now John speaks a more personal word using **I**, perhaps underscoring his urgent pastoral concern for his audience.

Early in ch 2, John reveals both his pastoral heart and the high calling of being a Christian. He writes to maintain a relationship with his audience. He wants to buffer them from all that might lead them to sin. His goal is clear: **so that you will not sin.** The aorist tense of the Greek verb suggests the total avoidance of sin of any kind. Thus, he implies that Christians are capable of "sinlessness" rightly understood (Brooke 1912, 23). His readers must recognize the all-pervasive nature of sin while living without habitual sinning (Marshall 1978, 116).

A regular practice of sin as the norm for Christians is foreign to 1 John. Yet John is equally insistent that Christians cannot claim to have no sin with which to deal (1:8). Everyone has had sins that needed to be forgiven (1:9-10). So, what does 2:1 mean? Certainly he is not adopting here the position he criticized in 1:8 and 10 (Kruse 2000, 71).

The conditional statement **but if anybody does sin** presents a hypothetical but real case. The verb *hamartēi* is in the subjunctive mood, indicating a possibility, which is not inevitable. John says **anybody** can sin, and what **if** one does? A paraphrase highlighting these might be: ***let us consider the situation when one does sin, although such need never be the practice.***

The verb is in the aorist tense, the simple past tense. The imperfect tense would have served John better had he wanted to stress an ongoing *practice* of sin rather than an *occasion*. The aorist subjunctive suggests a lapse into sin, not a continuing life of sin (Painter 2002, 158).

The text affirms the standard of living above sin. But John realistically acknowledges that some Christians occasionally falter in their walk. To them he affirms the continuing offer of reconciliation to God. These first-century Christians illustrate a timeless tension and challenge. We can be free from the habitual practice of sin through God's gracious help. But at times this ideal is not the reality in our lives. So how do we remain faithful both to God's holy character and to his expectation that holiness should be authentically present in us?

This text, indeed all of Scripture, calls God's people to live holy lives. As v 1 encourages, sin need not be fatal, due to Christ's atoning death (Rensberger 2006, 287). Acts of sin affect not only the one who does them but also the body of believers. **But if anybody** [singular] **does sin, we** [plural] **have one who** helps us (see Brooke 1912, 27).

John affirms the holiness of God and God's call that people be holy. God's holiness works in redemptive ways. Although **sin** is real, we have **one who speaks . . . in our defense.** This phrase translates a single word in Greek (*paraklēton*), composed of two words, "along side of" (*para*) and "to call" (*kalein*).

The image is that of a legal counsel who speaks on behalf of another, as a lawyer represents a client in court. This "advocate" (NRSV, NASB) would stand alongside and offer the support of his presence. The word may have a less technical sense of one called in to help. Frequent in nonbiblical Greek, the term appears in the NT only in the Johannine literature.

In the Gospel, Jesus uses *paraklētos* to describe "the Holy Spirit" (John 14:26), "the Spirit of truth" (John 14:17; 15:26). The four appearances of *paraklētos* in the Gospel (14:16, 26; 15:26; 16:7) are translated as "Counselor" in the NIV. The "Counselor" is sent by the Father at Jesus' request (14:16) and in his "name" (14:26). Or Jesus sends the Spirit (16:7) from the Father (15:26). In 1 John, Jesus, not the Spirit, is the *paraklētos*.

The views of the term are not so different as first appears. The usage in the two writings suggests either some fluidity or development in the use of the term. When Jesus was physically absent after the resurrection, the churches recalled his language about sending "another Counselor" (*allon paraklēton*) (John 14:16). *Allon* would suggest another of the same sort, and they could have adopted the term for the "absent yet present-by-the-Spirit" Jesus.

Jesus is called **the Righteous One** (*dikaion*). Each of the three instances of this title in Acts (3:14; 7:52; 22:14) occurs with the sense of messianic identity within a speech or sermon by significant early Christian leaders—Peter, Stephen, and Paul.

The Prophet Isaiah uses the same image when he speaks of the Lord God—"glory to the LORD" (Isa 24:15) in parallel with "glory to the Righteous One" (Isa 24:16). Jeremiah anticipated "a righteous Branch" (Jer 23:5; 33:15) as "the LORD Our Righteousness" (Jer 23:6) from the line of David. Zechariah saw a "king" coming to "Zion" who was "righteous and having salvation" (Zech 9:9). The passages in the apocryphal book of Enoch that call the Messiah "the Righteous One" (*1 En.* 38:2; 53:6) likely reflect an early use of this term that found its way naturally into early Christian vocabulary.

■**2** "Jesus Christ, the Righteous One" (v 1) is **the atoning sacrifice** (*hilasmos*, also in 4:10) **for our sins.** Christ comes alongside to help and speak for the believer who has succumbed to sin. But he does more than stand beside; he actively becomes the resolution of the dilemma sin has caused. This is the language of sacrifice; it draws on imagery from the temple system and demonstrates the gravity of sinning against God.

Hilasmos

The words *hilasmos* and the related *hilastērion* appear infrequently in the NT (only here and in Rom 3:25, Heb 9:5, and 1 John 4:10). These passages are translated "atoning sacrifice" (1 John 2:2; 4:10), "sacrifice of atonement" (Rom 3:25), or "place of atonement" (Heb 9:5 NLT). Related words and images in the NT seek to explain what transpired in the death of Jesus that enabled reconciliation with God. These often reflect the practices of animal sacrifices within Judaism (Eph 5:2; Heb 10:12). They refer to Christ as Lamb (John 1:29, 36; 1 Cor 5:7; and thirty times in Revelation) and use the language of ransom (Mark 10:45), purchase (1 Cor 6:20; 7:23), and redemption and forgiveness (Gal 3:13-14; 4:5; Eph 1:7; Col 1:14).

The word *hilasmos* in 1 John 2:2 is often translated as "propitiation" (ASV, ESV, KJV, NASB, NKJV) or "expiation" (RSV, NJB). Adam Clarke (n.d., 905) preferred "atoning sacrifice" (NIV, NRSV). In the LXX *hilastērion* was associated with the "mercy seat" (see Heb 9:5), *the place* where reconciliation was accomplished. Both *hilastērion* and *hilasmos* are also connected with *the means by which* reconciliation occurred.

Some understand the transaction as the means by which God is propitiated and sin expiated (Büchsel and Herrmann 1965, 317-18). Such suggests that God, as the offended party, needs to be placated. But the NT repeatedly indicates that God takes the initiative to restore sinful humanity to a right relationship with himself (John 3:16; 2 Cor 5:18-19; 1 John 4:10). "Propitiation" emphasizes the change that occurs in the divine side—God is appeased. "Expiation" focuses more on the human side—offenders are cleansed and restored.

The translation "atoning sacrifice" stresses the saving effect of Christ's death, without indicating whether the change occurs more in the holy God or sinful humanity. God did all that was needed to offer reconciliation to sinful humanity. The statement of Paul in 2 Cor 5:19, "God was reconciling the world to himself in Christ," reflects the controlling perspective for NT writers, who attempted to convey what transpired in the death of Christ (Büchsel and Herrmann 1965, 317; Mitton 1962, 313).

Most translations ignore the emphatic pronoun (*autos*, he). It is grammatically unnecessary, since the subject is implicit within the verb **He is** (*estin*). Yet the pronoun provides a significant emphasis—**He *himself*** (*autos*) **is the atoning sacrifice**. Thus, Christ is at once the High Priest who offers the *hilasmos* and the *hilasmos* that is offered (Marshall 1978, 118-19;

Brooke 1912, 28). In Heb 9:26 Christ offers "the sacrifice of himself." The Father initiates the process, so God cannot be viewed as an unwilling, reluctant judge waiting to be placated. He provides the Son through whom the forgiveness is offered (1 John 4:9).

This redemptive offering by Christ is not narrow in scope. Christ died **for our sins** and **also for the sins of the whole world.** There is no limited atonement here. Calvin admirably affirmed, "Christ suffered sufficiently for the whole world." Yet he also unfortunately held that the reference to **the whole world** meant only those who would believe (1959, 244). But the clear inference of the text is that Christ died for all, not merely for those who believe. Christ held nothing back. All who believe may receive life through the merits of his death.

The word **world** (*kosmos*) occurs twenty-two times in sixteen verses in 1 John. Only here and in 4:9 and 14 does *kosmos* refer to the world as the object of God's redeeming love, as in John 3:16. In all its other instances, **the world** is alienated from God and in opposition to him, a place of false prophets and hatred, and something to be overcome (2:15-17; 3:1, 13; 4:1, 3-5; 5:4, 5, 19). The removal of **the sins of the whole world** recalls John's witness to Jesus in the Fourth Gospel, "Look, the Lamb of God, who takes away the sin of the world" (1:29, 36).

■ **3-11** The theme of the knowledge of God replaces the theme of fellowship with God in these verses. John moves from the reality of sin in human experience (1:5—2:2) to the necessity of obedience in knowing God (vv 2-7). He defines obedience as love (vv 7-11). John expands the thesis in v 3 in vv 4-6, first negatively (v 4), then positively (v 5), and finally more specifically (v 6).

■ **3** The passage affirms a present knowledge of God: **we know** (*ginōskomen*) is present tense. What we know in the present is based on a past experience that is still true. **We have come to know him** (*egnōkamen*) is in the perfect tense. We have come to know God and that reality remains true in that we **obey his commands.** They were demonstrating the knowledge of their earlier Christian experience through its abiding results (Brooke 1912, 30).

John presents obedience not as "the condition" nor as a means of procuring the knowledge of God. Rather, it is "the characteristic of the knowledge of God" (Bultmann 1973, 25). Obedience flows from the knowing. Grace finds us, forgives us, and begins to heal us. Our lives begin to say "thank you" by walking in obedience to God's **commands.**

■ **4** John continues to hold up the difference between what one **says** and what one **does,** or more precisely *what one is.* One's verbal claims (***while***

saying, *legōn,* a present participle) are fraudulent and useless unless they result in a change of lifestyle marked by obedience to God's word (Fleming 1999, 66). Such a person **is not keeping** God's **commands.** The present participle suggests *an ongoing practice* of disobedience. A testimony based only on the past, **I have come to know him** is more than suspect for John. Indeed, it makes one **a liar** (see 1 John 1:6).

The Greek text places *pseustēs* in an emphatic position at the beginning of the clause, **liar he is.** The phrase **is a liar** refers to more than an individual experiencing an occasional lapse (Brooke 1912, 31; see 1 John 1:6, 8). John labels the person **a liar** who habitually disobeys God's **commands.** This label is coupled with the assertion that **truth is not in him** (a few manuscripts read **the truth of God**). John minces no words when authentic Christian faith is challenged (see 2:22; 4:20; 5:10; John 8:44; Rev 22:15).

■ **5** The emphasis shifts to those who do obey, underscoring the required personal response. The phrase **anyone** (lit. ***whoever may***) and the verb **obeys** (lit. ***keeps,*** subjunctive mood) convey the idea that obedience is not automatic. One may choose to obey or not to obey. The life that leads to Christlikeness is reflected in an ongoing response to the **word** of God.

The language of obeying God's commands/word is distinctively Johannine. It occurs in the Gospel twelve times (John 5:24, "hears"; 8:51, 52, 55; 14:15, 21, 23, 24; 15:10, 20; 17:6), in the letters eight times (1 John 2:3, 4, 5; 3:22, 24; 5:2, 3; 2 John 6), and in Revelation six times (3:8, 10; 12:17; 14:12; 22:7, 9). By keeping the commands, and by walking in obedience, **God's love** achieves its purpose.

God's love (lit. ***the love of God***) is "almost certainly" a subjective genitive designating God's love for the Christian, rather than an objective genitive, indicating one's love for God (Jones 2009, 54; Thomas considers both "potentially present," 2004, 98).

Marshall suggests a third option: the grammar supports the idea of a godlike love (Marshall 1978, 124). This seems overly nuanced, since God is at work lovingly completing the divine kind of love in believers (Jones 2009, 54). The working of God's love is in persons—**in him.** Still, we know that the divine love is prior to and enabling the human response of love (Brooke 1912, 31; see 1 John 2:15; 3:17; 4:12; 5:3).

When love attains its goal, it is **made complete** (*teteleiōtai*). The passive voice of the verb implies that God is the active agent (see the sidebar "Divine Passive" at 1 John 1:2). Those who are **made complete** still need further development. But the intent of divine love may be achieved only in those who obey God's words. John will go on to particularize this obedience in vv 7-11 as love of fellow believers (see 4:11-21).

God's love is decidedly prior to, and enables, any human response of love (Brooke 1912, 31; see 1 John 2:15; 3:17; 4:12; 5:3). It is God, not human effort, who brings believers to completeness. The completing, or perfecting, of love is **in him,** and thus decidedly *not in us apart from Christ.*

The Greek word is the same as that in Jesus' statement from the cross—"It is finished" (*tetelestai*, John 19:30). It conveys the idea of bringing something to its intended conclusion, even with a note of triumph. The term appears six times in the Gospel (John 4:34; 5:36; 17:4, 23; 19:28, 30), indicating the completion of the work given to Jesus by God (Thomas 2004, 99).

John presents this completing or perfecting in love as normal for the Christian. John Wesley drew on the words of 1 John (2:5; 4:12, 17) to support his doctrine of "perfect love," characteristic of fully dedicated Christians (Wesley 1978-79, 366-446). This divine love is perfect in that it achieves its intended purpose (Marshall 1978, 125 n. 14).

Both here and in the Fourth Gospel, obeying God's commands means expressing love toward Christ and toward one another. That love then returns to God in worship and settled intimacy (John 14:21, 23; see also 1 John 5:3). This reciprocal movement of love from God and back to God enables the completing, or perfecting, of love's intention. It is **God's love** achieving the divine purpose as it develops in relationships (Brown 1982, 257).

■ **6** A significant moral duty appears in v 6. One **must** (*opheilei*, what one owes) **walk** in a certain way. This call profoundly stretches us to **walk as Jesus did;** that is, *just as that one walked also himself so to walk.*

Making **claims** of an intimate relationship with Christ—**to live in him** (*to remain/dwell in him*)—does not in itself prove one's spiritual faithfulness. The proof is in the **walk,** in an obedient and growing relationship of journeying together with Christ. The image of walking stresses the daily, one-step-at-a-time, regular, lifestyle nature of the **walk.** This walking is so distinctively holy as to be identified with the walk of Jesus himself. It is the language of authentic discipleship, to walk *with,* and so more and more to walk *like* the one with whom we walk.

Walk imagery abounds in the OT. In Deut 5:33 (just before Israel's great confession of faith in the Shema—"Hear, O Israel . . ."), God's people are enjoined to "walk in all the way that the LORD your God has commanded you" (see Deut 10:12; 11:22; 26:17; and Josh 22:5). Psalms promises access to God's sanctuary to the one "whose walk is blameless" (Pss 15:2; 84:11). The great eighth-century prophet Isaiah called the nation to "walk in [God's] paths" (Isa 2:3), "in the light of the LORD" (Isa 2:5), and to "walk uprightly" (Isa 57:2). Micah summed up much of the message of

God's purpose in the majestic words that call people to "walk humbly with your God" (Mic 6:8).

FROM THE TEXT

One Who Stands Beside to Help

What an incredible thought, that the one who died for us sinners represents us before **the Father** (v 1)! The Paraclete Jesus, who comes alongside to help, believes in us so much that he has already endured supreme suffering for sin. We stand before God; but we do not stand alone. Forgiveness is offered. Reconciliation is real. The work of God in our lives is **made complete** (*teteleiōtai*, v 5) at great cost to Christ. Christ's declaration from the cross, "It is finished" (*tetelestai*; John 19:30) highlights the completed work. Christ's full obedience to the Father took him to the cross, where he achieved the divine intent of redemption. Just so, our full obedience to the Father, wherever it leads, achieves the divine purpose in us.

Is Sinning Necessary?

Full obedience to Christ can mean that we **not sin** (v 1). Some would readily dismiss this possibility, arguing that "to err is human" and so, also, is to sin.

Martin Luther found no energy to address the high aim of v 1; instead, he focused on the inevitably of sin. "But even if you fortify yourself to the utmost, yet sin remains, and you sin from day to day" (Pelikan 1967, 235). Luther, however, also paradoxically affirmed concerning 1 John 3:6, "He who is in Him, that is, in Christ, does not sin; for when Christ is present, sin is conquered." He added, "Even if they sin, yet they do not permit sin to reign" (Pelikan 1967, 270).

While "all have sinned" (Rom 3:23), sin need not be the norm for God's people. The matter turns importantly on how sin is defined. If sin is any lack of perfect conformity to the law of God, known or unknown, then freedom from sin surely eludes humans.

But what if sin is a willful violation of a known law of God? Then surely the redeeming work of Christ on the cross and the power of resurrection are sufficient. Christ can so capture our affections that we may be freed from habitual sin. Grace not only reaches but also pardons, and, more importantly, heals. Commenting on v 1, John Wesley wrote: "All the words, institutions, and judgments of God are leveled against sin, either that it may not be committed, or that it may be abolished" (Wesley 1983).

Honesty When Sin Occurs

When Christians fail to act in a holy manner, it challenges their claim to lived-out holiness. Can one claim to be holy and offer a sharply worded criticism or harbor deep resentments, and resist confessing such failures. Some who have testified to sanctifying grace and freedom from sin are resistant to confessing failure of any kind. They mistakenly think that to do so would be to deny their profession and undermine their theology. Others excuse themselves and fail to admit their sin, relabeling it a "mistake." Knowing they have hurt another person, they don't ask for forgiveness from that one or God. They perhaps rationalize, "God knows my heart." The activity of the Spirit of God in us should make us more likely to notice when we have wounded another, more apt to admit our fault and ask for pardon.

Christ Died for All

A further emphasis that affects both preaching and pastoral care turns on the extent of Christ's atoning death. He died for all—"the sins of the whole world" (v 2; see also 2 Cor 5:14-15). Christ's death is sufficient ground for anyone's salvation, but it does not presuppose that result in everyone. Paul similarly distinguished the all-sufficient offer of universal salvation and the limited embrace applying only to believers. He spoke both of the "all" for whom Christ died (2 Cor 5:14) and yet of "those who live" as a more restricted number (2 Cor 5:15).

God comes in grace and invites—drawing and enabling, but he does not coerce anyone. Christ's death does not lead to a limited atonement theory. That is, he did not die for "the elect" only and not for all. First John 2:2 and 2 Cor 5 argue forcefully for an understanding of Christ's death as truly for all. Yet they maintain that a person makes a grace-enabled response to the salvation offered through that death, for good or for ill and for eternity.

B. In the Light or in the Darkness? (2:7-11)

BEHIND THE TEXT

The dualistic imagery calls to mind the theology of some of the scrolls found near the Dead Sea at Qumran. Themes of light and darkness, love and hate, and truth and lies, all were at home in the sectarian Jewish circles of Qumran. The early Christians were mostly Jews and thoroughly a part of their cultural heritage (see Behind the Text at 1 John 1:5-10).

It is important as this section unfolds to keep in view how the language of **command** (vv 7, 8) would have been heard by Jewish ears. The Ten Commandments (Exod 20:1-17) would have come quickly to mind. While John did not present himself as a latter-day Moses, the use of **command** is prominent in the Johannine writings (see discussion at 2:5). Also the **new command** to love others (vv 7, 8; see John 13:34; 2 John 5) draws on the OT call to "love your neighbor as yourself" (Lev 19:18) as a tangible expression of one's supreme love for God (Deut 6:5).

Thus John's ethical concern continues in 1 John 2:7-11 as he repeats the **command** language from vv 3-4 and further develops it in a fresh and powerful way. He does this using three contrasts—new and old, darkness and light, hatred and love.

IN THE TEXT

■ **7** Endearing family language continues to weave its way through the epistle. John addresses his readers as **dear friends** (*agapētoi*, **beloved ones**, from *agapē*, "love"). This warm language is common in the letters (*agapētoi*, 1 John 3:2, 21; 4:1, 7, 11; and *agapēte*, 3 John 2, 5, and 11).

John says he is **writing** them **not . . . a new command** (see 2 John 5) but **an old *command*** that dates back to **the beginning**. The message to love others appears as early as Lev 19:18, "Love your neighbor as yourself." This text was linked to the *Shema* in Deut 6:4 by the "expert in the law" who asked Jesus what was the greatest commandment in the law (Luke 10:27-28). But this **command** is as early as **the beginning.**

How do we understand **beginning**? In the Gospel of John (1:1) the beginning is "the" beginning, prior to creation, in language that echoes the LXX text of Gen 1:1. But here John, as in 1:1, is referring more to the beginning of the gospel's effect in his readers. It is what they had **heard** that brought them to the Christian faith (see 2:24 and 3:11). The reference is similar to the opening lines of the Gospel of Mark. There "the beginning of the gospel" (Mark 1:1) is identified with the public ministry of Jesus' message as proclaimed and received. The **old** is thus about **the beginning** of the gospel in them.

■ **8** John has just said he was "not writing . . . a new command" (v 7). But in the very next breath, he says he is! He has not yet defined the exact nature of the command. Anticipating where he is headed (v 10), John recalls Jesus' words in John 13:34: "A new command I give you: Love one another. As I have loved you, so you must love one another." But first he links the **new command** to the dualistic imagery of **light** and **darkness**. This is reminiscent of the prologue of the Fourth Gospel: "Light shines in the darkness, but the darkness has not understood it" (John 1:5).

The true light is reminiscent of John 1:9: "The true light that gives light to every man was coming into the world." The thought in both Gospel and epistle is eschatological. A new age of light is breaking into the age of darkness. The emphasis here is on the gospel of Christ, "the Word of life" (1:1).

This **light . . . already shining,** however, has not fully eliminated all the **darkness.** The shadows are living on borrowed time and are **passing away.** As in the Gospel, the "true light that gives light" is sweeping back the darkness from all people (John 1:9). We are reminded of Gen 1, which speaks of God separating light and darkness (1:4-5) and of the resultant correcting of chaos (1:1-2).

■ **9** John moves directly to challenge the reader. Any hatred toward another believer is evidence of the **darkness;** it partakes of the spirit of anti-God chaos. Hatred attempts to undo what God, in creation and sovereign rule, is working to accomplish. This is, of course, not possible.

But the question is: Will we interfere with the divine purpose by aligning with the "darkness [which] is passing"? Or will we cooperate with God by embracing the "light [that] is already shining" (v 8)? Paul expresses a similar eschatological expectation when he writes that "the night is nearly over; the day is almost here" (Rom 13:12). The anticipation of this unfolding triumph of **light** over **darkness** places the people of God in "the middle of time" (translation of the original title *Die Mitte der Zeit,* Conzelmann 1954), awaiting a future final victory by "the true light."

If someone **claims to be in the light,** this does not necessarily prove his or her allegiance to God. The dissonance between the sounds one speaks—**claims**—and the clamor that accompanies hatred drowns out mere lip-service (see John's challenges in 1:6, 8, and 10). It is dishonest to claim a state of Christian grace while one **hates his brother** or sister. Hatred apparently describes the false views, superior attitude, and cliquish behavior of the secessionists.

The word **brother** (*adelphos*), a favorite term with John, occurs with great frequency in the remainder of the letter (2:10, 11; 3:10, 12, 14, 15, 17; 4:20, 21; 5:16). The word is used by Jesus in the Gospels (Matt 25:40; 28:10; Mark 3:33, 34, 35; Luke 6:42; 17:3; John 20:17). It appears in Acts (9:17; 22:13) and is commonplace in the writings of Paul. To call one a "brother" is a Christian adaptation of the spiritual "brotherhood" language of Judaism. The designation appears also in a religious sense in Greek secular authors (von Soden 1964, 144-46).

The term **brother** in 1 John does not refer exclusively to male siblings. Greek, like many other languages, uses masculine collective nouns to assume both genders. The term *adelphos* says more about the Greek language than about the limits of divine love (Smith 1991, 58). Recent translations that use "brother or sister" (NRSV) appropriately clarify the *intent* of John's language for modern readers.

Has John narrowed **brother** to mean only Christians who agreed with his christological perspective? Were those who did not agree with Johannine teaching no longer **brothers** (see 2 John 10)? John does not hesitate to label those who had formerly been inside the Johannine community and left "antichrists" (2:18-19).

Does the repeated call in 1 John to love "one another" and to love one's **brother** extend to the secessionists? It seems an open question. It is, however, most likely that John in this context intends **brother** to indicate one still inside the faith community of the Johannine churches. The issue is the behavior of those who were troubling the community, not the world in a neutral (John 3:16) or even negative sense (2:15).

■ **10** In contrast to "hates" and "darkness" (v 9) is **loves** and **light.** Loving one's "brother or sister" (NRSV) means bringing before them nothing that will cause spiritual defeat, **nothing . . . to make him stumble** (*skandalon*). The term *skandalon* pictures a trap or snare laid for an enemy, and, metaphorically, a stumbling block or offence. These words of caution from John arise naturally from his context. The churches were struggling over christological diversity and the resultant issues of leadership and unity.

Jesus calls Peter a *skandalon* when he objects to Jesus pointing toward his destiny on the cross (Matt 16:23). Causing "little ones" to sin is a *skandalon* and receives strong correction from Jesus (Matt 18:6-9). Paul uses *skandalon* while drawing on Isa 28:16 to refer to "a stone that causes [one] to stumble" (Rom 9:33). Strikingly like John, Paul writes of "love [for] one another . . . [as] the fulfillment of the law" (Rom 3:8, 10).

■ **11** Hating one's **brother** demonstrates that one is presently **in the darkness** and **walks around in the darkness.** Such people cannot **know** the way because the **darkness** they have chosen **has blinded** their eyes. Darkness is progressive; it leads to more darkness and eventually to blindness. At stake in loving/hating is spiritual discernment in both Christology and ethics. The issues now simply stated are the understanding of God as revealed in the incarnate Jesus and in the quality of community life that inevitably follows.

This passage speaks of those who moved from light to darkness, and thus increasingly had chosen blindness. Ironically, Paul once hated those who would eventually call him "brother" (Acts 9:17). Here John urges those who call one another **brother** not to hate. While light is being given from God, it is wise to walk in that light—"walk while you have the light, before darkness overtakes you" (John 12:35). In both 1 John and Lev 19:14, not seeing, blindness, or darkness is associated with *skandalon* (Stählin 1971, 339-58).

FROM THE TEXT

Relationships in the Church

As in the first century, so in all ages, people find it easy to forget things already known. This **old command** (v 7) to love God and others needs to be brought before the church from time to time. Truths learned early in one's Christian, even from **the beginning** (v 7), can get lost in the stretch and pull of decision-making in a local body of believers.

The language of family in 1 John is mingled with passages using the words **hate** and **darkness** (vv 9, 11). Significant pastoral challenge arises when, within a congregation, people begin to resent those they should love. The letters of John reflect issues of troubled relationships over theology and leadership, with some people considered "in" and others "out." Unnecessary divisiveness always turns the spiritual journey of a congregation in the direction of **darkness** (vv 9, 11). Darkness always leads away from God and truth. The labeling as evil those with whom we disagree drives us apart.

Eschatology Should Influence Our Ethics

Persons who anticipate a climactic in-breaking of God into history should order their lives accordingly. They should live in view of the nearness of the apocalyptic events depicted in Scripture, aware that these may soon appear. Those who expect a gradual growth of the kingdom of God gaining new ground surely will want to live so as to make its principles and values more and more a reality where they live "on earth" (Matt 6:10).

C. Words for All Ages (2:12-14)

BEHIND THE TEXT

The family language used in these letters draws from at least two contexts. The family was an institution in Judaism. Family themes also derive from OT covenantal images. Jeremiah identifies God as "father" to "Ephraim" (Israel), God's "firstborn son" (Jer 31:9). Ezekiel describes

Jerusalem as a cast-off child whom the Lord adopted and loved (Ezek 16). In Hos 11:1 God calls Israel "my son."

Aspects of first-century Greco-Roman athletic competition appear in vv 13-14. To **overcome** (*nikaō*) was to be a champion who vanquished all foes. Paul makes several references to running a race (1 Cor 9:24-26; Gal 2:2; 5:7; Phil 2:16; see also Heb 12:1). The Greek goddess of victory, *Nikē*, shows the emphasis given to the victor. True conquest, some thought, could only be achieved by the gods (Bauernfeind 1967, 942-45). The language of overcoming in vv 13-14 surely draws on this idea. The letters to the seven churches in Revelation record the Lord's promises to reward all who overcome (Rev 2:7, 11, 17, 26; 3:5, 12, 21).

John continues to emphasize writing (1 John 1:4; 2:1, 7) as he assures his readers in relation to the false teachers. He bases his reminder of the present status of the Johannine Christians in God's purposes in his Son, "Jesus Christ, the Righteous One" (2:1). These sermonic verses provide the foundation for the exhortation to follow in vv 15-17 (Marshall 1978, 134-35; Bultmann 1973, 30).

IN THE TEXT

■ **12-14** An interesting sequence of persons appears twice in these verses—**dear children** (vv 12, 13), **fathers** (vv 13, 14), and then **young men** (vv 13, 14). This reflects John's habit of using family terms to address his readers.

Dear children (*teknia*) in the first set (vv 12-13*b*) may be a way of addressing members of the churches collectively. No value statement about their spiritual development seems to have been intended. The second set (vv 13*c*-14) begins with another collective term **dear children** (*paidia*). This was functionally equivalent to *teknia* in v 12 (see e.g., 2:1, 28).

The references to **fathers** and **young men** could indicate either chronological age or spiritual maturity. In this approach are two overall statements to the entire community (**dear children**) and two categories of believers, the **fathers** and the **young** (Brooke 1912, 43; hesitantly, Akin 2001, 102-3; see Brown 1982, 297-99). Still, the interplay of language throughout this section is difficult to follow.

The **children** (v 13) know whom the **fathers** know, namely **him who is from the beginning**. The parallel with **the Father** in the verse suggests taking **him** as God. Though more likely, as in 1:1 and 2:7, **the beginning** refers to the coming of Jesus in whom the gospel first came to them. Jesus was the one in whom "the eternal life, which was with the Father" (1:2) was revealed. The **young men,** however, have **overcome the evil one.**

The descriptions *shift* in the sections addressed to **dear children.** First, he emphasizes that their **sins have been forgiven** (v 12); next, that they **have known the Father** (v 13). The description directed to **young men** *expands* from **you have overcome the evil one** to add, **you are strong, and the word of God lives in you** (v 14). For **fathers** the descriptions *remain unchanged* in both instances.

These shifts and expansions express nuances of spiritual affirmation poetically, but not necessarily chronologically. The absence of female imagery in the section is curious, given that "the elder" of 2 John addresses churches as "chosen lady" (2 John 1) and "chosen sister (2 John 13).

The passive verb, **have been forgiven,** presents God alone as forgiving sins. The perfect tense indicates that forgiveness brings release from the guilt of the violations of the past and extends into the future (Bultmann 1964, 509-12). The forgiveness of sins is achieved through **his name,** referring back to "Jesus Christ, the Righteous One . . . [who] is the atoning sacrifice for our sins" (2:1-2*a*).

The small word *hoti,* **because** (six times in vv 12-14), suggests that John writes for this reason: his readers are among *the already forgiven*. In this same sense, Brown does not translate *hoti,* treating it functionally as a colon. This is more of a declaration of a present reality: "I am writing to you children: your sins are forgiven" (Brown 1982, 300-301). Smith prefers "because." That is, *as a result of pardon* they are able to refuse the love of the world (Smith 1991, 63).

The perfect tense is used again with **you have overcome.** These **fathers** had previously come to know the One **from the beginning.** That knowing is still true: **you came to know him and you continue to know him.** The victory they had achieved over the evil one was ongoing: **you have conquered and continue to conquer.** The perfect tense conveys both assurance and challenge. The battle, while decisively won by Christ, is to keep playing itself out.

The reference to **children** (v 14) may intend those who are young in the faith. This affectionate term could also indicate that they are under instruction. The English word "pedagogy" is derived from *paidion* and *agō* (lead), thus "led as a child by an instructor." The word **father** (*patēra*, v 14; *pateres*, vv 13, 14) is used three times. When it appears in the singular in 1 John, it always refers to God (thirteen times in the NIV). In the plural, **fathers** addresses leaders in the church (2:13, 14).

Some variation occurs in the phrases translated **I write.** The first three instances employ a simple present tense verb (*graphō*), **I write** or, *I am writing.* The last three verbs are all in the aorist (past tense). They could be translated *I wrote* or *I have written.* But these are probably examples of the epistolary aorist. What was present for John would be past by the time his audience received his letter. Thus, he probably intends a present sense of **I write.** When John later uses *egrapsa* (2:21; 5:13), he apparently intends a present sense. So the shift in tense forms in 2:12-14 may be stylistic only (Smith 1991, 63). Some late manuscripts attempt to harmonize the earlier readings and use the present tense here in v 14.

John speaks also of **young men** (vv 13, 14), who were well-developed spiritually—**you are strong** (v 14). The word can suggest physical strength or spiritual might. The LXX occasionally uses strength to describe a quality of God (2 Sam 22:31). In Revelation the word (translated "mighty" in the NIV) refers to God (18:2), angels (5:2; 10:1; 18:2, 21), and opponents of God (6:15; 19:18). The **young men** were **strong** because **the word of God** was dwelling in them (as in John 15:7: "my words remain in you"). They conquered because the **word of God,** which makes God/Christ known in their lives, gave them overcoming power.

The victory achieved is over **the evil one** (*ton ponēron,* vv 13, 14). The term is used for Satan in 1 John (3:12; 5:18, 19). The language is common in Matthew (5:37; 6:13; 13:19, 38). It appears once in John's Gospel (17:15) and twice in Paul's letters (Eph 6:16; 2 Thess 3:3). This **evil one** stands as the dramatic parallel and adversary to Jesus—"the Righteous One" (2:1). In the Lord's Prayer Jesus taught his disciples to pray for deliverance from "the evil one" (Matt 6:13).

Echoes of the Gospel of John (1:1), as in the opening lines of the letter, appear in vv 12-14 with **from the beginning** and the use of **word.**

FROM THE TEXT

Who Can Forgive Sins?

This controversy is evident in the Gospels (Matt 9:6; Mark 2:7-11; Luke 5:20-24) and extends into the history of Christianity. Is forgiveness of sins a direct transaction between a person and God, through Christ? Or must one confess to a priest or official agent of the church? The discussion draws upon John 20:23: "If you forgive anyone his sins, they are forgiven; if you do not forgive them, they are not forgiven." Protestants tend to understand the pronouncement of forgiveness as recognition of what has *already* been transacted between God and the person. The perfect tense of the verb "forgive" suggests ***they have been forgiven and remain so.***

Roman Catholics appeal to Matt 16:19 and 18:18, claiming a general authority given to the church to dispense forgiveness. First John 2:12, **your**

sins have been forgiven, does not fall conclusively to one side or the other of this debate. Of crucial importance is that forgiveness is experienced only **on account of his name** (v 12). On this all Christians can agree.

Evil in the World

Evil, according to John, manifests itself in **the evil one** (vv 13, 14), but along with thinking of personal evil, Christians are challenged to think of how evil manifests itself institutionally. Systemic evil appears in nations, corporations, and even churches.

The presence of evil in the world is easily demonstrated. Watch any news broadcast for a few minutes. We readily acknowledge evil "out there." But will the church and its leaders recognize and overturn evil "in here"? Are we prepared to address the evil that sometimes rears its ugly head in the way the church functions corporately and in the lives of those who compose it?

Who Is in "the Fight"?

The masculine language in this section (**fathers** and **young men**) may slight the rich diversity of those called to be faithful witnesses. The prophet Joel describes "sons and daughters . . . old . . . [and] young . . . servants, both men and women" suggesting an all-inclusive Christian mission that crosses boundaries of gender, age, and social status (2:28-29). Peter's Pentecost day sermon echoes this refrain (Acts 2:16-18).

D. Love God, Not the World (2:15-17)

BEHIND THE TEXT

A tradition of apocalyptic warnings lies behind the language: **the world and its desires pass away** (v 17). This tradition points informed readers back to OT texts about "the day of the LORD" as a time of destruction (Joel 1:15) and "darkness" (Joel 2:2; Amos 5:18, 20). At that time "the sun will be turned to darkness and the moon to blood" (Joel 2:31). This theme of the world under judgment also appears in several NT passages. In 1 Thess 5:2 "the day of the Lord" is a time of "destruction" and "pains." Second Peter 3:13 warns readers to keep on the path of God's will.

First John has some decidedly apocalyptic features: The world is passing away. Apostasy is a threat because it is "the last hour" (1 John 2:18). "Antichrists" have appeared (2:18, 22; 4:3; 2 John 7). These themes reflect the Roman presence in the first-century Mediterranean world. John's urgency likely relates to the pressure he felt from the increasing social/political tensions between Christians and Rome. The entirety of Revelation can be read as a response to Rome as an anti-God enterprise (Rossing 1999) and as a cry for justice (Fiorenza 1998).

IN THE TEXT

■ **15** John turns to direct admonition as he counsels his readers, **do not love the world** (*mē agapate ton kosmon*). Yet the Gospel of John asserts that "God . . . loved the world" (3:16; *ēgapēsen ho theos ton kosmon*). In the Gospel *kosmos* indicates those for whom Christ died, because loved by God. Here in 1 John *kosmos* speaks of a mind-set hostile to God.

To embrace the world was to stand opposed to the revelation of God in Christ (Marrow 2002, 101). **The world,** due to its alien spirit toward God and all that is holy, creates opportunities for temptations that appeal to normal appetites. So it can lead to misuse of the good gifts of God. Valuing the things of the world disproportionately or illegally is to love things above God. This is idolatry in anticipation of the warning that ends 1 John: "Dear children, keep yourselves from idols" (5:21).

The love of the Father is not in the one who so loves **the world.** Such have closed their hearts against the Father's love directed toward them. They are not allowing God to love them in forgiveness and cleansing (1:7, 9). To love God and to be loved by him belong together: the former is grounded in the latter (4:19; Bultmann 1973, 59; see the commentary on 2:5).

■ **16** The alien-to-God **world** embraces **the cravings of sinful man** (lit. ***the desires of the flesh*** [*sarx*].). In Paul's writings *sarx* often refers to that which manifests itself as hostility toward God rather than to the physical being. It is living "according to the flesh" as opposed to living "according to the Spirit" (Rom 8:5, 4 NRSV). John would agree with Paul that ***flesh*** is the mind-set "on the things of the flesh" rather than on "the things of the Spirit" (Rom 8:5 NRSV). The first is to live for the temporary; the second is to live for the enduring.

The phrase **the lust** or ***desire*** (*epithymia*) **of his eyes** recalls the language of Eden, where Eve "sees" and experiences "delight to the eyes" (Gen 3:6 NRSV). The eyes serve often as the gateway to our affections. John would have his readers guard their eyes.

The boasting of what he has and does (lit. ***the pride of life***) could mean "the pride in riches" (NRSV; Strecker 1996, 59). It calls attention to the problem of an inflated view of self and its attainments. Such arrogance is **not from the Father but from the world** and is marked for destruction along with it (v 17). Wrongful desire and misplaced pride separate us from the holy; but doing "the will of God" leads to life "forever" (v 17).

■ **17** John warns that **the world** is passing **away** (see Behind the Text discussion). This apocalyptic mind-set expresses the tension of the "already" and the "not yet." The "already" speaks of what has been accomplished by the in-breaking of God through Christ's first coming. The "not yet" anticipates what remains to happen at his second advent. Paul voices a similar idea: "this world in its present form is passing away" (1 Cor 7:31). So does 2 Pet 3:12: "That day will bring about the destruction of the heavens by fire, and the elements will melt in the heat."

The idea of a cataclysmic end time derives from the Hebrew prophets. They describe "the day of the LORD" in terms of cosmic signs of judgment (Joel 2:30-31). The end times, however, will be marked by an outpouring of God's Spirit upon all (Joel 2:28-29).

Isaiah thinks of the coming day as a time of "new heavens and a new earth" (Isa 65:17; 66:22). This refrain is picked up by 2 Pet 3:13 and Rev 21:1. The passing of **the world** does not mean the obliteration of the creation (see Rom 8:19-23). For John **the world** that passes **away** is a world order, a system alien to God's purposes. The end will remove permanently any hostile-to-God elements. The end will be much like the beginning. The redemption and renewal of creation will be like a marriage of heaven and earth, when God comes down to dwell among his people. The presence of Jesus causes the creation and all in it to wait on tiptoes with anticipation (Wright 2008, 104-8; Rev 21—22).

FROM THE TEXT

People Will Love Something

Love for **the world** crowds God out (v 15). There is not room in our hearts to love mutually exclusive things. We must choose. The personal dilemma, and the pastoral challenge occur at this point. Some try to live with a divided heart. They mean to love God yet still hold improper affection for lesser things. The remedy, both personally and corporately, surely is to love God and let God's love so permeate us that our lives accurately reflect our true values.

God's Will

To what degree may we know the divine intent for us? That John writes of one who does God's will (v 17) assumes the possibility of understanding what "the will of God" is. How does one know?

First, Scripture can guide toward God's intentions. Second, we need the perspective of godly people now, as well as the collective wisdom of

Christians through the ages ("tradition" in the best sense). They have been equally as desirous to find and do God's will as we are.

Understanding God's purposes grows out of a prayerful and teachable spirit. Praying for God's kingdom to come is to pray for God's will to be done, on earth, in and through us, as it is already purposed in heaven (Matt 6:9-10).

Sensitive spiritual counsel can help us avoid the pitfalls of projecting selfish interests into our decisions and calling them God's will. God's intent always leads to deeper devotion for God and others, for how we serve, and with whom we make the journey.

E. Antichrists (2:18-23)

BEHIND THE TEXT

The **anointing** (*chrisma*, vv 20, 27) draws on a rich complex of images from the OT, though with consistent central meaning. Anointing oil was associated with the priestly functions of the temple (two dozen times in Exodus and Leviticus). Aaron and priests after him were anointed to that role (Exod 29:7). Vessels used in the temple were anointed in a ceremonial dedication (Exod 40:9; Lev 8:10). Kings were anointed when installed into office (1 Sam 15:1; 1 Kgs 1:34; 1 Chr 29:22). Anointing suggests the idea of healing in the shepherd psalm (Ps 23:5), an application continued into the Christian era (Jas 5:14).

The picture is of applying oil to a person or thing; it indicates it was especially designated for the function it was to perform. When Jesus announced his unfolding mission in his hometown synagogue at Nazareth, he framed his ministry with a passage from the prophet Isaiah: "The Spirit of the Sovereign Lord is on me, because the Lord has anointed me to preach good news to the poor" (Isa 61:1; see Luke 4:17-21). This link of anointing with the Spirit of God is a controlling image in all the usages mentioned.

God's Spirit equips and installs persons into places of service. God's anointing dedicates to proper usefulness. The Spirit of the Lord brings healing of every kind. Authority and effectiveness in ministry are due to the Spirit alone. The words "Anointed One" eventually became a messianic title that anticipates a future redeemer (Dan 9:25, 26). The usage of "Christ" as a title for Jesus of Nazareth assumes this messianic expectation language. In Acts 4:26 Jesus is declared the "Anointed One" (Johnson 1962, 563-71; Szikszai 1962, 138-39).

IN THE TEXT

Up to this point in the letter John has said nothing about false teaching. In a new beginning, he takes aim at the false teachers. What perhaps lay under his preceding parenetic (hortatory) material appears now in vv 18-23 as direct confrontation.

■ 18 John's affectionate terms continue—**Dear children.** The family language reflects his relationship to them as their spiritual "father" and perhaps as a man of advanced age. He declares it **the last hour,** a phrase loaded with eschatological implications. Whether John expected Christ to appear in his lifetime is beyond our knowing. His language may be that of a pronouncement of the eschatological *age* of Christ and the church as *inaugurated* by Christ's death, resurrection, and the outpouring of the Holy Spirit (Acts 2:1-4). The full reality of the Kingdom was yet to come (Acts 1:6-7).

Sir Winston Churchill in a speech in 1942 may help us here. In reference to an Allied victory in North Africa during World War II, Churchill cautioned, "Now this is not the end. It is not even the beginning of the end. But it is, perhaps, the end of the beginning." Similar help in understanding John's reference to **the last hour** may be found in the writings of Hans Conzelmann. The German title of his study of the theology of Luke's Gospel was *Die Mitte der Zeit* ("the middle of time"). His work suggests that while many first-century Christians expected a soon return of Christ, its delay caused them to rethink that expectation (Conzelmann 1961, 233-34).

Accordingly, Christ's first coming may be understood as an inauguration of "the end of the beginning." Thus, the church lives in "the middle of time," still expecting the coming of the *eschaton,* **the last hour.** The church is then faced with living out the ethical aspects of God's character over the long term. Faithfulness and faithful confession are not now thought of as belonging only to the end times, but to what the church does in every age. The church lives in patient endurance (Luke 8:15), enabled by the Spirit (Conzelmann 1961, 233-34).

While **last hour** appears only here in the Johannine writings, "hour" appears numerous times in the Gospels. It marks a time of significance, even an appointed or prophesied time. It is an hour when judgment comes, often at the appearing of the Son of Man (Matt 24:36, 42, 44, 50; 25:13; Mark 13:32; Luke 12:39, 40, 46; Rev 3:3, 10). The "hour" in the Gospel of John can refer to Jesus' death as the means to glory, to his resurrection (5:25, 28), and to his ascension—namely his return to the Father (7:30; 8:20; 12:23, 27; 13:1; 17:1). A similar frequent phrase, "last day," speaks of God raising the dead (6:39-40, 44, 54; 11:24; 12:48) in all but one instance.

John writes that **antichrist is coming** with the emphasis that **many antichrists have come.** John is not troubled by a single figure called "The Antichrist" as some cosmic, anti-God personality. Rather, his pastoral concern is with a plurality of **antichrists** that had left the Johannine churches (Painter 2002, 203) and whose influence was already being felt (Kruse 2000, 101). Anyone who took a position about Christ contrary to traditional Christian teaching (the Johannine view) would fall into this "against Christ" category.

Didymus (fourth century) wrote that "it is [precisely] because they were once Christians that they are now called antichrists" (Bray 2000, 186-87). The preposition *anti* can also mean one who takes the place of another, so a usurper, one who presumes to *be* Christ. The Gospels mention "false Christs" (Matt 24:24; Mark 13:22). But here the sense of *anti* is that of one who opposes another.

Antichrist

Although used widely in current Christian circles, the term "antichrist" is rare in the Bible. It appears only in the Johannine letters (2:18, 22; 4:3; and 2 John 7). John uses the term not to focus on a coming singular figure at the end of the age but to describe *even as he wrote* a spirit or teaching about Christ at work among opponents of Johannine Christianity. For John "antichrists" meant *anyone* who took a position denying that Jesus was the Christ (2:22) and specifically that Jesus as Christ had come "in the flesh" (4:2; 2 John 7). This denial of Christ's humanity effectively disallowed the atoning significance of his death (2:2).

A tradition of false Christs appears in Jesus' teachings (Mark 13:5-6, 21-22). But one who claims falsely to be Christ is somewhat different from one who sets himself up as the opponent of Christ. Admittedly, the concept of false Christs sometimes merges with that of antichrists as an eschatological motif.

The phrase "man of lawlessness" (2 Thess 2:3) is often viewed as another way to refer to "antichrist," but the language of Paul and John lacks any clear link. The development of cosmic figures who are the embodiment of evil finds vivid expression in Revelation (see Rev 13:3, 11). While a conflation of images from these texts outside 1 John and 2 John occurs, especially in later understanding, there is little in the Johannine letters with which to pursue a "doctrine" of antichrist(s) (adapted from Rist 1962, 140-43; Watson 1992, 761; Koester 2006, 175-78).

■ **19** John is adamant that these separatists were never truly part of the Johannine Christians. The language of separation (**us** five times in this verse and **they** four times) highlights the sharp differentiation John feels.

Still, it is clear that they had entered into the life of the Johannine community at some point: **they went out from us.** Those who **went out** are likely the "many false prophets [who] have gone out into the world" (4:1) and the "many deceivers [who] . . . have gone out into the world" (2 John 7; Strecker 1996, 63).

The separation was apparently initiated by the opponents. The letter gives no evidence of any type of excommunication. John's claim that **they did not really belong to us** is best understood as his rationale for how the secessionists could conceivably leave the Johannine Christian communities. He could not mean that they had been only *apparent* members (so Marshall 1978, 152). Nor does he imply that those who went out were never truly Christian or were never "saved." The challenge for John and his readers was to understand the unthinkable, that anyone would reject the truth as they understood it.

The word **remained** (*memenēkeisan*) is significant for John (Brooke 1912, 54). The true believer was to remain in God (2:24, 27; see John 15:4-10). By saying that these had not remained, John identifies the separatists as among the "many antichrists" (v 18). Their departure demonstrated they had never, in John's judgment, been *truly* part of the community.

The NIV translation of *hina* as result, rather than purpose, minimizes the impact of the original language. It appears that the going out of the secessionists not only showed who they really were but it also ***was so that*** (*hina*) **they might be made manifest.** The verb *phanerōthōsin* is in the passive voice. This suggests that God revealed them as the traitors they were. The phrase **that none of them belonged to us** is literally ***that they all*** (*pantes*) ***are not of us.***

The issue that led to this break in fellowship was Christology. The dispute over Christ as having come "in the flesh" or not (4:2; 2 John 7) indicates this. The christological controversy appears to be a contention between a fully incarnate Jesus vs. a docetic-type Christology (see Theological Themes in the Introduction).

■ **20-21** With "As for you" (Brown 1982, 341) John states strongly that his readers **have an anointing** (*chrisma*) **from the Holy One,** that is, from God/ Christ (see v 27). Some "antichrists" (v 18) seem to have claimed a special knowledge, perhaps linked to the idea of **anointing.**

John uses **know** frequently in this section (vv 18, 20, twice in 21). He claims that true knowledge resides on the side of the Johannine Christians; they don't need "anyone to teach" them (v 27). He acknowledges no **anointing** (*chrisma*) upon the separatists. He insists that authentic *chrisma* rests only on those who have remained in the Johannine community.

The Greek text employs a wonderful wordplay. To embrace Jesus as Christ (*Christos*, **the anointed one**) who had come in the flesh was to experience **anointing** (*chrisma*). To separate from the Johannine community meant the absence or loss of *chrisma* and also the label of "antichrist" (v 22).

The Holy One may refer to either the Father or the Son. "The Holy One of Israel" is a frequent OT title for God (Pss 71:22; 78:41; Isa 1:4; 5:19; 17:7; 30:12, 15; 37:23; 41:20). Revelation 3:7 speaks of "him who is holy," clearly referring back to the vision of the glorified Christ in Rev 1 (as do all of the seven letters in Rev 2—3). In the Gospels "the Holy One of God" refers to Christ (Mark 1:24; John 6:69).

The Holy One enabled their understanding—**all of you know**. The Greek text lacks the words **the truth** in v 20. Some translations assume a forward reference to v 21, which affirms that John's readers **know the truth** (*tēn alētheian*), otherwise using the same words as here. Some manuscripts have **you know all things** (see John 16:13). Although we could read too much into **all things** (see Brown 1982, 349), both readings strongly affirm the *true* knowledge of the Johannine Christians as over against the *supposed* knowledge of those who had left the fellowship. Truth and falsehood are in contrast: **no lie comes from the truth** (see 3:19; John 18:37). John asserts that no lie has its origin in or belongs to the truth (Brown 1982, 351).

■ **22** The language is sharp. ***The one denying*** Jesus as Messiah is **the liar** and **the antichrist** (see 4:3). Using the definite article—*ho*, **the**—before **liar** and **antichrist** seems to point to one particular person and not many. But the emphasis is on generic character rather than the personal identity of the secessionists. For example, **the liar** is a false teacher. John is saying that *anyone* who denies **that Jesus is the Christ** is *a* **liar** and *an* **antichrist** (see v 18, "many antichrists").

John's focus is not a larger-than-life personality but rather doctrinal error that is hostile to orthodox Christology. He is concerned over the many anti-Christ activists in his time. He demonstrates meager interest in discussing a cosmic Antichrisit figure. John Wesley referred to "the spirit of antichrist" as pointing to "all false teachers, and enemies to the truth" (Wesley 1983, n.p., nn.).

■ **23** The one **who denies the Son** (see John 5:23; 15:23) describes those whose Christology was contrary to Johannine orthodoxy. Embracing a docetic Christology (see Theological Themes in the Introduction), they took tangents that eventually led far from orthodox views. But these opponents, people not entirely devoid of Christian understanding, were probably sincerely trying to understand Jesus' life and teachings.

A close interplay between **Son** and **Father** appears numerous times in the Johannine letters. In v 22 the one who "denies that Jesus is the Christ . . . denies the Father and the Son." Here, no one who **denies the Son has the Father.** The reverse, positive affirmation is also true—**whoever acknowledges the Son has the Father also** (see 1 John 4:15; 5:1; 2 John 9). For John, an appropriate Christology, a fully incarnate Son who reveals the person and work of the Father, is *the* way to an adequate knowledge of God (John 14:6).

FROM THE TEXT

When Is the Last Hour?

The phrase—**this is the last hour** (v 18) challenges the presumption that one will live a long life. One must not presume upon the luxury of many years. Now is the time for a deep embrace of the gospel message and for a close walk with Christ. All serious followers of Jesus seek to live with eternity in view, and so to live day by day with a Christian lifestyle.

Who Is "Antichrist"?

Much energy has been spent on the matter of **the antichrist** (vv 18, 22). Considerable speculation has continued through every age. Prototypes for the Christian idea of antichrist appear in Ezekiel's Gog and Magog. Daniel's beastly images describe oppressors of the Jews. In noncanonical texts like the Testaments of the Twelve Patriarchs a demonic figure seeks to turn Israel aside from the worship of God. For John, however, antichrists were those in the first century with a faulty Christology.

Polycarp (second century) follows 1 John's view of the antichrist as the spirit of heresy, especially denying the actual incarnation (Pol. *Phil.* 7.1). Numerous early Christian writings focused on a mythic creature of evil. Often these extended the images of the two beasts described in Rev 13; 16:12-16; 17; 19:19-21 (for post-NT apocalyptic literature see Charlesworth 1983).

By the Middle Ages some viewed the pope as the antichrist, a link that many Reformers (Wyclif, Huss, Luther, Calvin, Zwingli, Knox, Cranmer) generally supported. A sample of this thinking appears in John Calvin, who allowed that "all the marks by which the Spirit of God has pointed out antichrist appear clearly in the Pope" (1959, 256).

In response, Rome accused some of the Reformers of being antichrists. At various points in church history the label has been assigned recklessly, using inventive readings of Revelation's 666 to identify the antichrist with a wide range of individuals (Rist 1962, 140-43). For a summary of scholarship about the theology of the term "antichrist" see Akin (2001, 267-70).

F. An Anointing and Abiding (2:24-29)

IN THE TEXT

■ **24** John calls his hearers back to **the beginning** (*archēs*, as in 1:1). With renewed emphasis (**See**, the nuance of the pronoun *hymeis*) he urges them to continue embracing the truth of the gospel that has come to them (2:7). A favorite Johannine concept, **remain/remains** (*menō*) appears three times in this verse alone. Forms of the word occur especially in the Johannine literature (forty times in the Gospel, twenty-four times in 1 John, and three times in 2 John).

The word (*menō*) speaks of an abiding relationship his readers were to have with the truth they had heard from the beginning. It assured them of a settled relationship **in the Son and in the Father** (contrast v 22). The mention of both in relation to the Christian's abiding is unique in the Johannine writings. This abiding was a reciprocal reality—when persons "remain" in Christ then Christ remains in them (John 15:4-7). The term carries with it the sense of loyalty to Christ, as well as living in a new realm as a result of God's presence in Jesus Christ (Hübner 1981, 407-8).

■ **25 This is** probably refers to what precedes (v 24) and to the promise that follows. God/Christ (since *hautē* is emphatic, probably Christ) has **promised . . . eternal life. Eternal life** occurs sixteen times in the Gospel of John, most memorably in John 3:16.

The phrase both there and here (1:2; 2:25; 3:15; 5:11, 13, 20) suggests a present quality of life as well as a life that endures into the ages. This **eternal life** is something one *has already:* "God has given us eternal life" (1 John 5:11); and "you may know that you have eternal life" (5:13). This is the **promised** life. The verse repeats related words for both the verb and its object: ***the promise*** (*hē epangelia*) **which he promised** (*epēngeilato*) **us.**

■ **26** John writes with an active pastoral concern about the impact of those who might deceive the Johannine Christians. The secessionists seeking to **lead** them **astray** (lit. ***deceiving*** them). The verb refers to one who wanders (Heb 11:38) and strays from the truth (Jas 5:19) intentionally. Forms of the word occur in 1 John 1:8, "deceive ourselves," and in 2 John 7, "deceivers." John is **writing** to warn them, recalling earlier statements (vv 12-14; 5:13).

■ **27 As for you** introduces a renewed emphasis on the theme of **anointing** (see 2:20). The passage reflects the functions of the Holy Spirit, the Paraclete in the Gospel of John. The idea of **anointing** recalls Jesus' words about the Spirit as One who would teach, call to remembrance, and make Jesus' words clear (John 14:26; 16:13).

Some see the **anointing** (vv 20, 27) as referring to the ritual of baptism or some ritual sealing with oil (Smith 1991, 72). First-century support for this is nonexistent. But **anointing** was linked to baptism by several early Christian authors—Severus of Antioch, fifth century; Oecumenius, sixth century; Andreas, seventh century; Bede, seventh century (Bray 2000, 188). The initial and continuing work of the Holy Spirit in the believer is in view, including especially his teaching role (Smith 1991, 72, 74).

There is irony in John's insistence that the readers do not need **anyone** to teach them as he proceeds to do just that. Probably he meant to caution against listening to any other teachers except those whose message was welcomed in the Johannine churches. John urgently affirms the divine source of the teaching they are to embrace with his emphasis upon **anointing** (twice in Greek here, also v 20).

Sharp dualistic language appears—**real** (*alēthēs*, ***true***) vs. **counterfeit** (*pseudos*, ***false***). The word order highlights the stress John wishes to make. He places *alēthēs* in the emphatic first position—***true it is and not is it false***. Having been taught by the true **anointing,** John commands them to **remain in him** (i.e., Jesus; see v 28).

In the preceding passage, vv 18-23, John set forth the theological error that endangered the Johannine fellowship. The christological heresy was twofold: (1) the denial of the complete humanity of the divine Son, and thus (2) the denial of the full continuity between the Father and the Son in revelatory and redemptive action. This was the *lie* of the false teachers.

Now in vv 24-27 John stresses the two means by which his readers can protect themselves from such error: First, in vv 24-25, it is the apostolic tradition. Second, in vv 26-27, it is the divine anointing. A mind applied to the Scriptures and a heart open to the Holy Spirit are the Christian's spiritual safety net. Such is our graced privilege, the *truth* of the gospel of Christ. This is the way we "abide in him" (NRSV).

■ **28-29** John makes a transition with these verses from the importance of a correct Christology to the necessity of an appropriate ethic. How Christians are to live as "children of God" (3:1) occupies the apostle through 3:24. In 2:28—3:3 John brings the motif of the future return of Christ to bear on his ethical imperatives.

■ **28** After strong warnings and accompanying appeal, John again employs warm, personable language—**dear children.** As believers **continue in him,** they will **be confident** (*parrēsia,* "**courage, confidence, boldness, fearlessness,**" BDAG 2000, 781) when Christ **appears** (lit. ***is made manifest***). John uses *parrēsia* to speak of being confident before God in an eschatological sense (here and 4:17). But the term also speaks of boldness to approach God in prayer now (3:21; 5:14). Thus the Christian *already* can enjoy judgment day confidence in the presence of God.

The verb *phaneroō* indicates making something plain (see v 19). John affirms Jesus as the One who reveals God's saving love through the incarnation (3:5, 8). In 1:2 "the life appeared" and God's revelation continues in the church's living tradition of Jesus (Müller 1993, 413-14). The passive voice of the verb suggests that the appearance of Christ was a presentation by the Father.

Remaining in Christ prevents one from **being made ashamed.** The passive indicates that God can make rebels ashamed. The word *parousia* (**coming,** only here in the Johannine writings) meant generally the arrival or presence of someone (see 1 Cor 16:17; 2 Cor 10:10; Phil 1:26; 2:12). However, in the NT *parousia* developed a special nuance as referring to the future appearing or presence of Jesus to rule, raise the dead, and fully establish the kingdom of God (Matt 24:3, 27, 37, 39; 1 Cor 15:23; 1 Thess 2:19; 3:13; 4:15; 5:23; 2 Thess 2:1, 8; 1 Tim 6:14; 2 Tim 1:10; 4:1, 8; Titus 2:13; Jas 5:7; 2 Pet 1:16; 3:4).

The word *parousia* was used for the visit of a king or emperor (Brooke 1912, 66; Diessmann 1995 [1927], 268-70). The NT usage is an example of a Christian employing words and titles from the public arena as subversive protests against the blasphemous practice of emperor worship (Brooke 1912, 67). The true Lord of all, not the Caesar but Jesus, will appear as the one before whom "every knee should bow" (Phil 2:10).

The *parousia* involved going out to welcome a royal or powerful figure who was arriving in a city. It did not have the idea of going somewhere with that royal figure (Wright 2008, 128-36). In some early church writings the return of the Lord is called *hē deutera parousia,* **the second appearing** (Justin, *Apology,* 1:52). An auditory wordplay may be present in the verse. The text promises that **children** who **continue in him . . . may be confident** (*parrēsia*) **. . . at his coming** (*parousia*).

■ **29** John's shift of emphasis to ethics now becomes direct. God (or Christ; with 2:6; 3:3; 4:17; so Brown 1982, 382) is **righteous,** and **everyone who does what is right** gives evidence of having **been born of him.** The antecedent of **him** is unclear. If related to v 28 then it is Christ, but most often in Johannine usage it refers to God (see 3:9; 4:7; 5:1, 4, 18; John 1:13; von Wahlde 2002, 319-22; Brown 1982, 384). The emphasis on doing **right** sounds like James, who insists that a right relationship to Christ should manifest itself in a life of righteousness (Jas 2:18). John says we do **what is right** (lit. *what is just;* see Mic 6:8) as a result of the new birth.

The righteousness of God, revealed in the incarnate life of Jesus (1 John 2:6), is lived out as a present and continuous activity. Righteous living is evidence that one has undergone a spiritual rebirth. The perfect passive verb (*gegennētai*) suggests **has been born of God and continues as God's child.**

Righteousness is more than how one is *viewed* by God. The righteous person is one who allows the life of God into which one **has been born** to be lived out.

This figure of spiritual birth—**born of** God—appears as a new idea in the epistle (Marshall 1978, 167). However, the concept of spiritual birth ws already implied in the frequent use of **children** in 1 John (five times in ch 2). The intentional use of spiritual birth imagery is clear from here on (3:9; 4:7; 5:1, 4, 18). The language echoes the Gospel of John (John 1:13; 3:6, 8). John maintains a distinctive status for Jesus, who alone is "son" (*huios*) of God, whereas Christians in 1 John are always "children" (*teknia* or *paidia*). But Jesus (Matt 5:9) and Paul (Rom 8:14; Gal 3:26; 4:4-7) both speak of believers collectively as "sons" (*huioi*) of God (Marshall 1978, 168).

FROM THE TEXT

2:24-29

Constancy in One's Relationship with God

The word *menō* (**remain**, v 27; **continue**, v 28) suggests that Christian faith is not confined to special moments of religious experience. Since the Christian faith is mostly lived in the routine of ordinary days, our spiritual development requires a routine to stabilize us.

Sporadic flights into emotional high moments, without comparable depth developed by Bible study, prayer, and worship, offer little that builds spiritual backbone. John urges the value of continuing trust—**remain in the Son and in the Father** (v 24) and **continue in him** (v 28). The text also confirms the benefit found in solid teaching—**See that what you have heard from the beginning remains in you** (v 24; John 15:7).

God's Voice in Scripture and Persons

It pays to remember. Being reminded often keeps us doing what is right. So much of life consists of relearning what we already know. Peter wrote, "So I will always remind you of these things, even though you know them" (2 Pet 1:12). Maintaining a teachable spirit is a lifelong journey. Reading and meditating on Scripture nurtures our Christian development.

We learn also by being open to what the Spirit of God may be saying to us through others. The will of God is often better understood as we listen to the voices of those who compose the covenant people.

While there is great strength in belonging to a committed faith community, we dare not attempt to live the Christian life in mere human strength alone. The text speaks importantly of an **anointing** (v 27). This grace gift of the Spirit stabilizes individuals and churches spiritually, keeping both on track. Spiritual drift, unchecked, can lead us much further away from God than we may be able to imagine. But being attentive to the promptings of the Spirit keeps our Christian experience current.

The Lord's Coming and Our Service in the Meantime

Far too often godly people so anticipate the second coming that they invest all their energy on being ready for an early exit from the world. But we are here to live out kingdom values throughout our entire life.

The goal of the Christian life is *not to depart* from this world. Rather it is to invest ourselves in the present *kingdom in this world* so that we can receive him **confident and unashamed** (v 28). We will welcome him as the king who has appeared among us, bringing a wonderful, final answer to the prayer so many of us pray—may "your kingdom come . . . on earth" (Matt 6:10).

III. CHRISTLIKE LOVE NOW AND WHEN CHRIST APPEARS: 1 JOHN 3:1-24

A. When He Appears: A Call to Cleansing (3:1-6)

IN THE TEXT

■ **1-6** John continues with his ethical concerns as impacted by the appearing of Christ. Verses 1-3 have his future appearance in mind; but vv 4-6 return to his first coming as John reintroduces the sin terminology from 1:7—2:2, 12.

■ **1** John commands the reader to *see* or *remember* (*Idete*, an imperative) **how great is the love the Father has lavished on us.** The verb *eidon* is used as a revelatory declaration with prophetic insight in the Gospel of John—"Look [*Ide*], the Lamb of God" (Thomas 2004, 147; John 1:29, 36, 47; 19:14, 26-27). Another form, *idou*, appears in Revelation related to the coming of Christ (Rev 16:15; 22:7, 12). The NIV leaves *idete* untranslated, subduing the strong exhortation. Other versions render *Idete* as "See" (NASB, NRSV, ESV) or "behold" (KJV). The reader is likely being enjoined both to *recall* and to *understand* (see *eidōmen* in 1 Cor 2:12).

This verse recalls the visual language of 1:1-4 where one sees God's love by looking upon Jesus. This **love** . . . **lavished** by **the Father** has been wonderfully given—**how great** (*"wonderful"* [BDAG 2000, 85] or massive). Mark 13:1 uses the same adjective to describe the immense stones and magnificent buildings of the Jerusalem temple complex. In Matt 8:27 the word denotes the disciples' surprise at Jesus' great power (Brooke 1912, 80). The perfect tense of **lavished** (*dedōken*) indicates that this love, given in the past, continues to have effect.

Such lavish divine love is the foundation for inclusion in God's family. By this means one enters into relationship with God and receives the power to remain in spiritual community. John employs family metaphors to depict spiritual relationships and ethical obligations (van der Watt 1999, 491). These images reflect the power of family identity in the ancient Near East. People lived so as not to bring dishonor to their family. Loyalty toward one's family excluded all other loyalties (van der Watt 1999, 497, 510).

The **Father gave** (*dedōken*) this love; it was not earned. God's lavish love comes as a gift to us. It is not based on merit, for God takes the initiative. We have opportunity to become true spiritual offspring of God only because divine love has been first offered to us. This initiative by God is often called prevenient grace. The word "prevenient" is formed from two Latin words meaning "to come before." Prevenient grace makes our coming to God possible, because God has first come to us (see John 6:44).

John makes a bold declaration. What his readers are *declared* to be—**children of God**—they actually *are* (***and we are!***). The passive voice of **called** suggests God as the one who makes the declaration. This is no merely, in-name-only, positional relationship to God. The *character* of God becomes a part of who we are. Just as the Creator planned for the original pair to reflect the divine image, so here the readers *are* what God has declared them to be (Bruce 1970, 85-86).

Participation in the family of God makes the believer a mystery to **the world**. The non-Christian **does not know** the Christian because it **did not know him**. This nonrecognition of Jesus appears also in John 1:10. There the Greek words, although in a different order, are identical (Thomas 2004, 149). Ignorance of mind and heart toward Jesus' true identity prevents **the world** from recognizing Jesus' followers as **children of God**. They are unable to understand why Christians act and live as they do. As God's **children** by birth we are to live as those who cannot be understood apart from Jesus. To truly know us, they must learn to know him. And we hope that as they learn to know us, they will learn to know him.

■ **2** John continues affirming family status—**Dear friends** (lit. *beloved ones*; see also 2:7; 3:21; 4:1, 7, 11). Being **children of God** is not something delayed for the future at the end of the age—**when he appears.** It is *already* true—**we are** (*esmen*) truly God's family **now** (*nyn*). Still, John says the present family likeness pales in comparison to what is to come. The experience of being God's child is **now,** but the full reality of that transformation is not yet. Futuristic ("not yet") eschatology and realized ("already") eschatology stand in tension in Johannine writings. Due to this mixed nature Johannine eschatology can be described as a "progressively realizing eschatology" (van der Watt 2007, 74-76).

Such future hope **has not yet been made known.** The passive voice suggests that the disclosure comes at God's discretion. The text is reserved in speculating about eschatological details, a modesty that contemporary Christians should consider (Smith 1991, 80). This yet-to-be-experienced, future relationship with God comes only as it is revealed by God. The fullness of that revelation awaits a future day. The **not yet** (*oupō*) language is at home in apocalyptic settings (Brown 1982, 392-93). The same word is used by Jesus in the eschatological discourses when he speaks of "wars and rumors of wars." But he says that the end is "not yet" (Mark 13:7 NASB; "still to come" [Matt 24:6]).

The statement **when he appears** (*ean phanerōthēi*), or **when he has been made manifest,** fulfills the expectation of the **not yet been made known** (*oupō ephanerōthē*). And this is the certain truth of becoming like Christ. About the future state **we know . . . we shall be like him.** Present sight will be improved majestically, enabling followers of Christ to **see him as he is** in resurrection splendor. Postresurrection knowledge will perfect the seeing/knowing of Jesus by the disciples (Smith 1991, 78). The final vision of Christ will mean a full and unhindered knowledge of him. The veil diminishing the radiance of his holiness will be removed. The seeing is **just as he is.** Seeing Christ **as he is** will be to see him with new eyes of understanding, as for the very first time.

The standard for holiness is quite clear. Holiness is supremely to **be like him.** Being God's offspring calls for us to reflect his character. Choices, values, attitudes, lifestyle—all these are increasingly to conform to the image of Christ. Seeing Jesus will have the effect of looking in a mirror, but with one substantial difference. Rather than seeing ourselves as we now are, we will be enabled to see ourselves in the possession of the shared glory of Christ (Marshall 1978, 172-73). With Paul's expectation, "all of us, with unveiled faces, seeing the glory of the Lord as though reflected in a mirror, are being transformed into the same image from one degree of glory to another; for this comes from the Lord, the Spirit" (2 Cor 3:18 NRSV).

■ **3** John makes ethical application of v 2 with a simple, declarative statement: **Everyone who has . . . purifies.** It is precisely the one who *is purifying himself* who possesses the **hope** of likeness to Christ. A changed present life proves the authenticity of the future hope. Such a resplendent **hope** (*elpida*, only here in the Johannine literature) calls the readers to holiness in the present. Salvation climaxes in Christ's coming and the **hope** of our resurrection. This eschatological yearning points toward a sharing in Christ's glory; it is already begun by our now being children of God (Mayer 1990, 438).

All will appear in God's presence at the end of the age. Such **hope** compels us to a full surrender to him now. A **hope** with Christ as its focus inevitably has a purifying effect on those who trust in Christ (Bruce 1970, 88). Eschatology drives ethics, and ethics makes our eschatology credible. We have a future appointment with God. But we are already citizens of God's kingdom and are to live daily by kingdom values.

Believers strive for a life of purity because Christ **is pure** (*hagnizei . . . hagnos*). The pronoun **he** translates the demonstrative pronoun *ekeinos* (lit. *that one*), a term often used in 1 John to refer to Jesus (Smith 1991, 78; 2:6; 3:3, 5, 7, 16; 4:17). The pronoun makes a specific designation—*that one*. The incarnate, earthly Jesus (2:6) defines the purity in view.

The word **pure** (*hagnos*) means holy, belonging to God (BDAG 2000, 13). The purity of Christ calls for his disciple to embrace that same purity. Yet, interestingly, *hagnos* is never used in the Gospels to identify Jesus (Brown 1982, 397). The verb form (*hagnizō*) appears only here and in John 11:55 in the entire Johannine corpus. More frequent in the Johannine literature is *katharos*, "clean" (John 13:10, 11; 15:3; Rev 15:6; 19:14; 21:18), *katharizō*, "to make clean" (1 John 1:7, 9), and *katharismos*, "cleansing, purification" (John 2:6; 3:25).

The measure of true holiness is Christlikeness. Holiness is not first and foremost adherence to rules or standards. Rather it is the divine life being lived out through us. The phrase **just as** (*kathōs*, used of comparison) **he is pure** involves the possession of the same kind of character Christ displayed. We will see Christ "as he is" (v 2) and that unhindered seeing leads to a purity of life *that is like his*.

But what does John mean by **purifies himself?** The basic idea is of the preparation required to enter the divine presence (Brown 1982, 397-98). The cultic background of the terminology is that of ritual purity (Strecker 1996, 91). In John 11:55 those preparing themselves for Passover went to

Jerusalem "for their ceremonial cleansing" (*hagnisōsin*, see Exod 19:10-11). But here the term should be understood ethically as in the rest of the NT (Jas 4:8; 1 Pet 1:22). The concerns of "lawlessness" and "sins" follow immediately (1 John 3:4-6).

Related language appears in John 17:19 when Jesus said, "I sanctify myself" (*hagiazō emauton*). This is Jesus' preparation just prior to his return to the immediate presence of the Father. Jesus' self-sanctification (making himself holy!) is his dedication to the cross to fulfill the will of the Father ("that they too may be truly sanctified"). It is the ethic of the redemptive mission of the Christ, the supremely revealed way of life.

Yet one cannot humanly accomplish the cleansing, hallowing work required to conquer sin. Only the holy God can fully purge and hallow. To purify self is to be understood in the context of the pardon and cleansing from sin (1:7, 9; 2:1-2, 12; 3:4-6) that is available only through Christ's atoning death (2:2; Brown 1982, 398). But after accepting Christ's sacrifice for sin we present our lives "as living sacrifices, holy and pleasing to God" (Rom 12:1). It is in this placing of our redeemed lives fully at God's disposal that the call to purify self should be understood.

This full consecration to God is evidenced by ongoing choices toward the holy. The present tense of *hagnizei* suggests an ongoing, dynamic translation—***be continually purifying.*** This kind of living faith honors God and adheres to Scripture. A surrendered life gives God unhindered space in which to work. To the degree that we invite God's purifying presence into our lives, to that degree we are engaged in purifying ourselves.

The fullness of "what we will be" (v 2) is not yet known. Yet, in the present we are preparing to stand in the presence of the Holy One by an ongoing, obedient response to this word from God. Purity is not presented as *future reward* for the Christian. Rather it is a *qualification* for seeing God someday ("Blessed are the pure in heart, for they will see God" [Matt 5:8]).

■ **4** John's return to the topic of sins (see 2:12) highlights an ongoing tension in the letter. The reality is that sin may occur (2:1). The goal to which we are called is that sin be dethroned. John sets forth a definition of sin (*hamartia*) as **lawlessness** (*anomia*), a combination of *nomos* (law) and an alpha prefix that negates the word. In some instances the word means a person who does not know the law. Gentiles can sin apart from, or independently of, the Mosaic Law (1 Cor 9:20-21).

Anomia

The words *hamartia* and *anomia* are used as equivalent expressions in the LXX of Ps 32:1. Employing synonymous parallelism, the text reads "Blessed is he whose transgressions [*anomiai*] are forgiven, whose sins [*hamartiai*] are covered."

The idea of *anomia* as lawlessness suggests apocalyptic tones. In the Olivet Discourse, Jesus says that "wickedness" (*anomian*) will be multiplied (Matt 24:12). Earlier, Jesus spoke of false prophets who would work *anomia* (Matt 7:22-23). Second Thessalonians uses *anomia* in an eschatological setting to describe "the man of lawlessness" (2:3) and "the secret power of lawlessness" (2:7).

In the second-century writing the *Didache* (16:3-4), the last days, false prophets, and *anomia* are closely associated (Brown 1982, 400; Richardson 1943, 178). A "son of lawlessness" who is a false Christ appears in the post-NT writing *Apocalypse of Elijah* 3:1-10 (Limbeck 1990, 1:106; Charlesworth 1983, 729-30).

So *anomia* was understood as a final outbreak of evil, as rebellion against God. Such would place one in the company of God's enemy the devil (vv 8-10) and with the earlier mentioned "antichrists" of 1 John 2:18 (Marshall 1978, 176-77). This lawlessness of spirit is part of an eschatological opposition to God and cannot be reconciled with a confident waiting for his return. One cannot be eager for the return of the Lord and at the same time in rebellion against him (Thomas 2004, 155).

Two senses may be present in 1 John 3:4. *First*, sin is a breaking of the law. People create a *performance* record of violations; they break the law in an ongoing way.

Second, people may have *a spirit hostile* to the laws of God—**sin is a lawless spirit.** Sin may be understood especially as a *lawless attitude* toward God (Bruce 1970, 89). Thus, sin is a *condition* from which believers must be set free (Smith 1991, 82). Paul writes similarly of sin as an inner compulsion that combats his better, spiritual judgment (see Rom 7:23).

Foundationally, John appears to believe that people sin because they are first sinners. They have an anti-God attitude that manifests itself in opposition to the purposes of God. Thus, the most fundamental need for everyone is to find correction for the core character problem, an answer that will turn the heart's affections strongly godward. Such a solution would make it as natural to do the right, the holy, as formerly it was "natural" to do the wrong, the sinful.

■ **5** Such a radical correction of the sin problem finds strong expression here. With similar terminology to that he had just used for Christ's future coming (3:2), John writes now of Christ's first appearance: **You know that he appeared** (*ephanerōthē*) **to take away our sins.** The incarnation, and by extension, all of Christ's life and work, were for the purpose of taking away (*arei*) sins. Other manuscripts, preserving perhaps the better reading, have simply "take away sins" (NRSV, NASB), without specifying whose. A minority of manuscripts read "the sins of the world," perhaps an attempt to harmonize with 2:2.

The verb *airō* is used in the Fourth Gospel with the sense of a change of location (John 2:16; 11:39, 41; 19:31, 38; 20:1, 13). Sins are taken away by the atoning work of "the Lamb of God" (John 1:29) whose death was a representative bearing away of sin (Radl 1990, 41; Marshall 1978, 177; see 1 Pet 2:24; 1 John 2:2; 4:10).

But the term may imply more than simply to **take away.** It can also suggest removal in the sense of destruction. John 11:48 uses the word to refer to the possibility that the Romans "will . . . take away" (*arousin*) the temple and the Jewish way of life. The Jews in John 19:15 call for the death, by execution, of Jesus, "Take him away [*aron*]! Crucify him!" (see Luke 23:18). Paul receives the same kind of death threats from the crowds in Jerusalem—"Rid the earth of him! He's not fit to live!" (Acts 22:22; see 21:36). These usages suggest not just a new residence for sin, but its eventual removal by defeat/destruction (Radl 1990, 1:41).

John is not presenting Christ as having come simply to counterbalance sin in the human heart, that is, to hold down evil so as to give holiness a *chance* at succeeding in the believer. Christ came to complete a decisive victory over sin. Oecumenius (sixth century) asserted that since Christ, who had no sin, came to take away sins, there was no excuse for the practice of ongoing sinning (Bray 2000, 197). For John purity meant freedom from sin (Marshall 1978, 174).

■ **6** The text now declares that for **the one continually abiding in** (*menōn*, a present participle) God/Christ, the habit of sin is broken. The verb that follows is also present tense and may be rendered—**does not continue to practice sin.** John contends for a Christian faith that moves one to a higher level of living. God defeats and ultimately destroys sin. God cannot coexist with it.

Two perfect tense verbs appear. The first, **has not seen him,** strongly affirms that the person continuing to live habitually in sin has never truly seen Christ initially and certainly does not have Christ in view now. The second, **has not known him,** stresses that such a one has never authentically **known** Christ and obviously does not know Christ now. True vision and knowledge have abiding results (Brooke 1912, 86). These verbs provide a direct contrast to the opening lines of the letter.

Abiding in Jesus means sin is excluded. Conversely, ongoing sinning means that Christ is not known. John's views here are consistent with the dualism expressed throughout (Smith 1991, 83). This verse does not declare *occasions* of sin to be impossible. Rather it asserts that *a sinful life* does not characterize the child of God (Bruce 1970, 90). As one is constantly abiding, one is simultaneously kept from the practice of sin. The image of sinlessness is a lofty call to holy and consistent living in obedience before God.

FROM THE TEXT

Becoming Part of the Family

Calling Christians **children of God** (v 2) affords preaching themes around the images of birth (John 3:16; 1 Pet 1:23) and adoption (Rom 8:15, 23; Gal 4:6). These and other NT analogies draw from OT language referring to Israel as God's "son" (Hos 11:1; Jer 31:9).

Some people misunderstand the idea of being a child of God, insisting that all people are God's children. This is true in a sense. All are created with immeasurable value and a residual image of God the Creator. But faith in Christ and obedience to him demonstrates our spiritual birth. Jesus said that some are, by their choices against God, offspring of the devil (3:10; John 8:44).

Supporting Life in the Church

The church has a responsibility to nurture new believers—the **children**. We would not leave a newborn child to survive on its own. In the same way we give special attention to those new to the Christian faith. Also, if the church is healthy, offspring will be a natural outcome. Lack of new **children** should signal us to find out what is undermining the health of the body. How we tend to the spiritually wounded among us also indicates our commitment to spiritual life.

Being Well-Prepared for Meeting Christ

Health of spirit is needed to stand in Christ's presence someday. The powerful phrase **what we will be** (v 2) speaks of an eternal life beyond our present comprehension. Christ's presence on that future day will mean the full correction of infirmities and weaknesses. Theologians sometimes refer to this end-of-the-way work of grace as glorification.

John is clear that the correction for *sinning* includes forgiveness as an essential aspect. The correction of *sinfulness* requires cleansing as a mandatory element. Both can, and should, occur here, and now. But the full restoration of all that was marred by sin, those *residual effects*, will be corrected **when he appears** (v 2). Then, our unobstructed view of him will transform us so that we will be like him. Christ's coming to **take away our sins** meant "to destroy them all, root and branch, and leave none remaining" (Wesley 1983, n.p.). Adam Clarke also emphatically urged God's remedy for sin in this life: "He came into the world to destroy the power, pardon the guilt, and cleanse from the pollution of sin . . . can it be supposed that he either *cannot* or *will not* accomplish the object of his own coming?" (Clarke n.d., 6:914).

B. Destroying the Devil's Work (3:7-10)

IN THE TEXT

■ **7** With **Dear children,** a favorite term (3:2, 7, 21; 4:1, 7, 11), the author continues to use family language to express his ethical concern in vv 7-10. Belonging to God by birth (v 9) as children (vv 7, 10) is to be part of a spiritual family, yet one still subject to being led **astray.**

This family likeness of heart, described as **right** (*dikaios*), is lived out through right acts—**He who does what is right** (*tēn dikaiosynēn*, **righteousness**). God's people reflect God's character. The standard for righteousness in persons is the righteousness of Christ—**just as he is righteous** (*dikaios*). The expression is similar to the earlier "just as he is pure" (v 3). This is the fourth time that Christ has been called **righteous** or "just" (1:9; 2:1, 29). The adjective describes the nature of Christ's life as always righteous in character and just in all his dealings (Brown 1982, 404).

In classical Greek usage the *dikaios* person was one whose behavior fulfilled obligations to both "the gods" and his fellow humans (Brown 1978, 353). The OT idea of righteousness (*dikaiosynē*) moves toward the idea of behavior consistent with the relationship between God and persons. The *dikaios* person is devout and demonstrates God's righteousness in godlike dealings with others (Brown 1978, 355).

■ **8** The consequences of one's life are evidence of one's allegiance. Committing sin demonstrates allegiance to **the devil** whose **sinning** was **from the beginning.** John 8:44 is similar; the devil is described as "a murderer from the beginning . . . a liar and the father of lies" (van der Watt 2007, 38). The absence of sinning displays allegiance to God, who is holy.

John continues to clarify the theme in various ways. **The reason** Christ came was for the purpose (*eis touto,* **unto this**) of conquering sin. The verb *lysēi* means in some cases to release, but it can also mean **to destroy,** to do away with completely (see Eph 2:14; John 2:19. Here John insists that God aims to achieve a decisive and unmistakable defeat of sin.

Poetic parallelism in vv 5 and 8 suggests that taking away sin and destroying the devil's works are the same (Thomas 2004, 164).

- "He appeared [to] . . . take away our sins" (v 5).
- "[He] appeared to destroy the devil's work" (v 8).

Verses 7 and 8 contain a similar poetic parallelism:
- "He who does what is right is righteous" (v 7).
- "He who does what is sinful is of the devil" (v 8).

These lines highlight two mutually exclusive spheres of existence. One can belong to only one realm and will bear the imprint of that realm and allegiance (Brown 1978, 362).

In v 8, reference to Christ's appearance speaks of his past coming to the world, his first advent, to break the back of sin. But in 3:2 John writes of his still future coming to the world, a second advent, fully and finally to establish a cleansed, sin-free environment of righteousness.

Calvin rightly understood "that the flesh and its lusts do not prevail, but are tamed and as it were yoked, so that they are checked" (1959, 272). His language suggests more a suppression of sin than its conquest. Yet, Calvin did not contend for a Christianity that allowed sin to flourish. Rather, he believed the Spirit of God brought superiority to the believer. Earlier Didymus (fourth century) taught that sin is not intrinsic to human nature. It is accidental, a result of intrusion into God's plan for humankind (Bray 2000, 198). A full overturning of the curse of sin is the final answer from God.

■9 This verse is artfully structured as a chiasm (Thomas 2004, 165), a repetition of lines in mirror fashion:

    a–**No one who is born of God**
        b–**will continue to sin,**
            c–**because God's seed remains in him;**
        b'–**he cannot go on sinning,**
    a'–**because he has been born of God.**

John returns to the metaphor of new birth (2:29). As indicated by the chiasm, **God's seed** is the central idea. Clearly sin and Christ cannot finally coexist. The **seed** (*sperma autou*) of God, by its very nature, expels sinning. The word *sperma* conveys the imagery of having offspring rather than planting and harvest. **God's seed** means the very life of God deposited into the believer. A likely association of *sperma* is to the Spirit (Brooke 1912, 89; John 3:6, 9; see Brown 1982, 408-11).

The gnostics thought of preexistent divine seed as begetting divine children (Brown 1982, 411). John may employ this language with a similar nuance. That is, to belong to God means the divine life resides in such a person.

The "anointing" described earlier by John (2:20, 27) involved being taught by the Spirit. The same idea may be at work here. In 1 Thess 1:5-6 the Spirit and the word of God serve together to achieve new birth. By extension, the Spirit and God's word insure the growth of the new life, and the divine life within necessarily expels sin.

John insists that an ongoing practice of sin means that the life of God is being choked off or was never present. God's life within one achieves radical transformation. Sin, formerly natural, or better, typical of humanity, now becomes unnatural (Bruce 1970, 92). When **God's seed** is nurtured it **remains in** a person and life happens and grows.

John cannot be saying that to sin is impossible in the life of the Christian. Else 1:8, 10; and 2:1 are emptied of meaning. It is not that it is impossible to sin, but that it is possible not to sin. Sin can happen, but it is an intrusion. Sin, when accommodated, puts one's spiritual life—**God's seed**—in jeopardy. When the life of God is given the opportunity to do as it will, it expels sin just as lighting a candle dispels darkness. The more that light expands, the more the darkness flees. There may be gradations of the light's success. Shadowy corners may still exist. But everywhere the light is given access it conquers darkness.

John has already strenuously challenged the secessionists' claims to sinlessness (1:8, 10). Nevertheless, this passage insists that true followers of Christ will experience freedom from sin as God's holy character resides within. The text argues for a spirituality that eliminates willful acts of sinning as long as one fully abides in Christ. Sinning is never the norm in the lives of believers (van der Watt 2007, 63). One cannot simultaneously actively obey God and willfully disobey him. "He whose life is governed by the law of love—love for God and for his fellowman—cannot sin because he cannot, at one and the same time, both love another and intentionally sin against him" (Blaney 1967, 380).

John Wesley addressed the matter like this: "But 'whosoever is born of God,' while he abideth in faith and love, and in the spirit of prayer and thanksgiving, not only doth not, but cannot, thus commit sin" (1978, 5:227).

The Christian's status as a child of God is a present reality, and freedom from sin is associated with it. Indeed, the more that this divine **seed** transforms the Christian, the more unlikely it is for the Christian to sin (Brown 1982, 431).

■ **10** Christ "appeared" (*ephanerōthē*) to "take away our sins" (v 5) and so "destroy the devil's work" (v 8). What Christ came to do will ***appear*** (*phanera*) in a life that does **what is right**. John insists that righteousness is relational. It is relational first toward God—**children of God**. This brings a positive relationship toward others. One rightly related to God will **love his** "brothers and sisters" (NRSV).

Anyone who does not do what is right is clearly among **the children of the devil** (*diabolou*; see John 8:31-59). Sins of omission, right actions one fails to do, can be as great an evidence of a failed spiritual condition as the sins one commits. John clearly assumes the presence of an evil one in the world whose influence is always contrary to the right. Similar to Jas 2:18, v 10 determinedly holds faith and works together. God's love for his children lives in the routines of life. His love flows in gathered worship but also, and authentically, in loving service that finds the people of God scattered into the world.

Verse 10 summarizes and concludes John's concern for "right" living that has governed 2:29—3:9. With the use of family metaphors John applies the twofold coming of Christ to the Christian ethic. This subtle polemic against the false teachers climaxes in the return of the theme that now takes over—**love** for the **brother** and sister (see 2:9-11). Thus, v 10 functions as a transition to what follows in 3:11-18, and to a large degree in 3:11—4:21.

FROM THE TEXT

Free from Sin

The statement **cannot go on sinning** (v 9) creates challenges for the Christian minister. How is one to preach/teach on this difficult text? Some would simply avoid it altogether, but that is irresponsible. It runs the risk of creating a "canon within the canon," adopting a selective approach to what texts are authoritative for faith and practice. John both acknowledges sin (1:8, 10; 2:1) and calls his readers to live free from sin (see discussion at 1:8).

If we accommodate sin in our lives, we too readily dismiss the call to holy living in this writing. Our approach must embrace the entire text. Sin does occur, but it can never be the standard for Christian living.

First John 2:1 reassures that God has in Christ made provision for sin when it intrudes into the life of a believer.

The task of the preacher is to offer hope for the restoration of those who have failed and fallen. At the same time we must call all to live in consistent obedience to God's *known* standards, which means a freedom from *willful* sin.

The Devil and Evil

Some find it fashionable to dismiss the idea of a personal **devil**. But four times this text speaks of such a one (vv 8 and 10). The word **devil** appears some three dozen times in the NT. A personal anti-God being is clearly viewed as real and formidable by the NT writers.

The seriousness with which many Christians view the devil comes in the wording of the baptismal creed still used in many churches. The officiant asks, "Do you renounce the devil and all his works?" (for its history see Gilmore 1949, 9:488-89).

Two extremes exist in modern Christendom. In one, believers seem obsessed with the devil. Lack of personal discipline or outright sin (e.g., gluttony or greed) are attributed to demonic activity. Financial pressures due to imprudent spending habits are excused as Satan's doing. Physical illness that derives from undisciplined eating, or a sedentary lifestyle, is blamed on the devil. Such spiritual sloth and theological error is offensive to thoughtful, conscientious Christians.

On the other hand, some Christians do not take seriously enough the enormity of evil in the world. They don't embrace the doctrine of the fall, preferring a view of humankind as evolving upward. Such minimizing or ignoring the problem of systemic and individual sin leaves no truly adequate answer for the problem of evil.

C. Love and Hate, Life and Death (3:11-15)

IN THE TEXT

■ 11 John states why he emphasizes the theme of love in v 10. The command to **love one another** was in **the message** (lit. news or announcement) that is not new (1:5). It was part of the faith **from the beginning**, which John's audience had **heard** from the time of their earliest experience as Christians. The **message** recalls 1:5. The term first appears in the move from the revelation of life in Jesus Christ (1:1-4) to its redemptive and ethical application in 1:6—2:11 (Strecker 1996, 107-8).

The call to love is a present reality experienced in community—**you** (plural), **we**, and **one another**. The living out of mutual **love** among the Johannine Christians did not depend on feelings, since it could be commanded (John 13:34; 15:12, 17; 1 John 3:23). It was an obligation that one could and **should** do. To love was to act in the same loving ways Christ modeled.

■ 12-13 Early biblical narrative relates a sad tale (Gen 4:1-16) that John develops as a negative illustration. John reminds his readers that because **Cain** "was from the evil one" (NRSV) love had so disappeared from his heart that he could murder his own blood brother. Casting his lot with **the evil one** took **Cain** much further into depravity than he could have imagined. **Cain** first **belonged to the evil one** and subsequently committed murder.

John's only explanation for Cain's action was "because his own deeds were evil and his brother's righteous" (*dikaia*, NRSV).

The verb *sphazō* (**murdered**) always includes a sense of violence (Brooke 1912, 92). It described the especially heinous crime of killing one's family member (Michel 1971, 7:932, 934). In the LXX it often has sacrificial connotations (Gen 22:10; Exod 29:11; Lev 1:5; Num 11:22). Forms of the word are found in the NT only here and in Revelation (5:6, 9, 12; 6:4, 9; 13:3, 8; 18:24). The term most often refers to the crucifixion of Christ or the killing of Christ's followers. John depicts Cain's violence as arising from a heart already compromised toward evil. Because his allegiance was wrong, wrong acts followed.

The verse reminds us that we should not be **surprised** (*thaumazete*, "*wonder, marvel, be astonished*" [BDAG 2000, 444]) if **the world hates** us (see Acts 7:31; Rev 13:3).

The **world** has already been depicted in 1 John as hostile to God (1 John 2:15-17; 3:1; see also John 15:18-20). John will describe it later as the domain of false prophets and antichrists (1 John 4:1-5), a place given to "the evil one" (5:19), and thus a sphere to be overcome (5:4-5).

■ **14** With vv 14-15 John introduces a new dualism—life vs. death. This adds to his previous dualisms: light-darkness, righteousness-sin, love-hatred. He continues to see in either-or terms as he applies his gospel to the situation in his churches.

John speaks from within the community. The pronoun **we** (*hēmeis*) at the beginning of the sentence emphasizes the pronoun already implied in the verb *oidamen*—**We know**. The sense is *we ourselves know this!* What is being so emphatically affirmed? It is a dramatic spiritual transformation—**from death to life**. The perfect tense verb **we have passed** (*metabebēkamen*) conveys the idea of a settled relocation, of having "crossed over [*metabebēken*] from death to life" (John 5:24).

The Gospel uses the same verb to write of Jesus' approaching death—"the time had come for him to leave [*metabē*] this world" (John 13:1). So here John describes a spiritual transformation. They had not just "turned over a new leaf"; they had received a new life. Their previous condition was spiritual **death** (*thanatou*). Now, by their faith in Christ, God had brought resurrection **life** (*zōēn*) to them. Acting toward others in loving ways is the supreme evidence of spiritual life—**because we love our brothers**. A lack of loving deeds demonstrates that professing Christians remain in spiritual **death**.

Just who are **our brothers** ("one another," NRSV) in the mind of the elder? Those who "went out" from the Johannine fellowship (2:19) surely were not thought of as family. Indeed, those who left are labeled "false prophets" (4:1), "deceivers" (2 John 7), and "antichrists" (2:18; 2 John 7). The **brothers** whom the readers are called to love were those believers clearly still in harmony with the teachings and practices of the Johannine churches. John may emphasize the command as a condemnation of the attitude and behavior of the secessionists.

In 2 John there is a strong prohibition against even granting hospitality (food and lodging) to itinerant preachers whose Christology was in error. The Johannine discomfort over who is to be welcomed/loved and who is not to be welcomed may be the reason for some of the textual variants of this verse. Most likely the original reading of the latter part of the verse was as rendered in the NIV—**Anyone who does not love.** It would be a generic statement that some scribes apparently wanted to make more specific. Consequently, some manuscripts were emended to read ***love the brother,*** and others more specific yet as ***love his brother.***

■ **15** The text goes radically further. The one who **hates his brother** not only still resides in death but spreads a death-dealing spirit toward others. Love leads to life, lack of love leads to death; both are contagious. Like Jesus, who linked "angry with his brother" (Matt 5:22) to murder and consequent judgment, John warns of the danger of lost love.

When love leaks out it is often replaced by hatred. When hatred seeps in, a person opens the door to the possibility of becoming a **murderer** (*anthrōpoktonos:* ***a man killer***). The word appears only one other time in the NT where it refers to "the devil" as "a murderer" (John 8:44). The text of 1 John 3:15 speaks of the spiritual condition—**eternal life**—that could be forfeited by hatred toward our Christian **brother** and sister.

FROM THE TEXT

Living in Love Toward Others

Why is love so important? Because a lack of love invites in **the evil one** (v 12), and that can lead to murder. The motives that lead to hate, envy, lust, and murder begin in withheld love. People who want to justify low-level living ask, "How much do I *have* to do?" Christlike love asks, "What is the lavish thing to do? How much *may* I do?"

All sin is a distortion of God's purposes. Misshapen love toward others can become a desire to control rather than to honor them. Normal God-given sexual desires can become lustful thoughts and actions outside of God's will. Appropriate self-esteem can, if unchecked, move to a life turned in on self. Necessary financial concern for one's family can mutate into greed and miserliness.

Losing the Way

Spiritual apostasy can manifest itself as hatred for "a brother or sister" (v 15 NRSV). The passage speaks of having **passed from death to life** (v 14). Implicit in these words of warning is that one once among the people of God may yet become captured by hate and experience the loss of **eternal life** (v 15). Clearly 1 John warns against moving outside the faith community. Those who do reject the truth of God's love and forfeit eternal life. Salvation is relational; when the relationships with God and God's people are broken, the life one enjoys in those relationships is also lost.

From Hate to Murder

How could a brother murder a brother? The story of Cain and Abel highlights the profound danger of fratricide that lurks in every heart. Unchecked, anger and jealousy grow. Eventually hatred follows. Sadly, wrong attitudes can lead a person, or a nation, to believe that murder of another is the best option.

D. Love in Action (3:16-24)

BEHIND THE TEXT

Genuine Christian faith expresses itself in tangible ways. The OT is replete with calls to be generous to "the fatherless" and to the "widow" (Deut 10:18; 24:17-21; 26:12-13; Isa 1:17, 23; Jer 7:6; 22:3; Ezek 22:7; Zech 7:10). Such admonitions to care for the poor and disadvantaged continue into the NT. Jesus had compassion on hungry multitudes and fed them (Matt 14:14-21; Mark 6:30-44; Luke 9:10-17; John 6:1-13). The early church distributed food to the widows as part of their ministry (Acts 6:1). James had sharp words of warning to the rich who did not treat others with justice (Jas 5:1-6).

The ethic of love that John stressed in 1 John 3:11-15 he now describes in two ways in vv 16-24: first, what love looks like in practice (vv 16-18); and second, how such love relates to Christian assurance (vv 19-24).

IN THE TEXT

■ **16** This section stands in sharp contrast to the tragic example of Cain. Instead of killing his brother, Jesus surrendered **his life** (*tēn psychēn autou*, **his soul**) for others (Brown 1982, 473). John argues that humankind would not be capable of knowing the full extent of what love looks like without seeing it in Christ's self-sacrifice on the cross. It is **by this** that **we know what love is.**

The death of Christ was not a colossal accident; it had a purpose. His was a life given, not taken from him. The NIV inserts the name **Jesus Christ** for the word *ekeinos* (**that one**). In 1 John *eikeinos* consistently refers to the incarnate life of Christ (2:6; 3:3, 5, 7; 4:17). He **laid down his life** (see John 10:11, 17-18). No earthly ruler had the power to take his life, not even the Roman governor Pilate (John 19:11).

His surrendered life had others in mind. It was **for** (*hyper*: **in behalf of**) **us.** John contends that the only adequate response to this love is to live a life of selfless sacrifice, that is, to live like Christ. Such living is *not to earn merit with* God, but *to express gratitude toward* God. This sacrifice and emptying of self extends as far as giving **our lives** (see Phil 2:5-11 for a vivid portrayal of Christ's other-centered living).

Christ's example calls his followers to live **in behalf of** (*hyper*) **our brothers.** The repetition of *hyper* implies that our sacrificial living is of the same sort as that of Jesus, who was willing to die for another. The brief section beginning with v 10 presents the spiritual family language of "brother" numerous times (vv 10, 12-17). The appeal to give ourselves for our **brothers** and sisters stands in sharp contrast to Cain's fratricide.

■ **17** Passing love on to another is not merely to express warm thoughts. Shared love has substance. Love consists of giving goods, **material possessions** (lit. **the life** [*bios*] **of the world**). The word *bios* appears rarely in the NT and always suggests life in its external aspects; it expresses concern over the affairs of material existence (Ritz 1990, 219; Brooke 1912, 97). In 2:16 the NIV translates it as what one "has and does." Probably it is intended here as the "things of life" the necessities of life in the world. When the prodigal younger son asked his father, "Give me my share of the estate," the father "divided his property" (*bion*, Luke 15:12).

When others have material lack we can open our hearts and respond to their need. Or, instead, we can have **no pity.** The Greek text is vivid, saying one may be tempted **to lock** (*kleisēi*) **away one's inner being from him.** To refuse to help another when God has placed the means in our hands is to lock those resources inside ourselves away from the needy other. The verb *kleiō* suggests a key or locked door, holding someone outside (Matt 23:13; Luke 11:7). To have **no pity** is to close off compassion to another.

John employs the word *splanchna* (lit. **intestines**) metaphorically to refer to one's **inner being.** At that time *splanchna* conveyed the idea of the innermost center of a person, where deep feelings reside. For modern readers in most cultures, a translation stressing feelings of compassion captures the sense.

John raises the rhetorical question: How can we fail to meet the tangible needs of another without blocking God's love toward us and the other? We cannot maintain our material security at the expense of others and at the same time and in the same measure experience the love of God. We put our own spiritual security in jeopardy whenever it is not **in him**. Jesus taught that the way to save one's life is to give it away (Mark 8:35).

■ **18** With warm words—**Dear children**—John urges moving from lip service to lived-out love. True love works; it expresses itself in **actions** (see Mark 13:34). One can feel love and not act on it—loving **only with words or tongue**. But such love is of doubtful value. A "love" that is only **words** is not really love at all (v 17; Matt 7:16-20; Jas 1:22; 2:16). The faith of which John speaks sees needs and acts to meet them. One with material means to help and in whose heart God's life is active will instinctively show God's love by sharing with others (Bruce 1970, 97).

■ **19** In vv 19-24 John brings together the themes of appropriate Christology and the corresponding ethic. Out of pastoral concern he deals with the obligation to love (vv 16-18) as it relates to Christian assurance (see 2:1).

This then or "And by this" (NRSV) signals John's application of love's demand to the believer's conscience. John presents the grounds of Christian assurance first in theological/christological terms (vv 19-20) and then as ethical in character (vv 21-22). The reference of both is to love in action.

Only a faith that works can **set our hearts at rest**. The plural **hearts** translates the singular *kardia*. So the text speaks of *one* **heart.** Biblical writers occasionally used the concept of corporate personality in which one person represented the whole community. Here, the many is placed with a *singular* noun, **heart.** The net effect is to stress the unity of the body of believers. Although we are many, we have one heart. And when this one-in-heart group acts in love, our common heart can be **at rest** (*peisomen*, lit. **we will persuade;** see Heb 13:18) in the **presence** of God (*emprosthen autou:* **before him**). The expression "reassure . . . before him" (NRSV) suggests the judgment seat of God or Christ (Matt 25:32; Luke 21:36; 2 Cor 5:10; 1 Thess 2:19; 3:13).

The verb **we know** (*gnōsometha*) is a middle voice suggesting knowledge that validates the claim of the person—*for* **ourselves.** A few manuscripts read simply *ginōskomen* (**we are knowing**). This knowledge assures us **that we belong to the truth** (see the sidebar "Truth" at 1:6).

■ **20** Yet the heart may not be a reliable indicator. The issue is our exercise of love as we perceive it. That is, have we failed to love as we ought (see 1:7, "fellowship with one another," 1:3; 2:6; 3:18)? At this point we *are* in need of assurance! We may live under self-condemnation, although our actual spiritual condition, known better by God than by us, is secure. A troubled heart may reflect an unnecessarily anxious condition, lacking in trust. But God is **greater than our hearts;** his mercy is the deciding word. He is more merciful to us than is our own conscience. John wants his readers to find their assurance from God, who in spite of knowing **everything** about us yet loves us immensely.

But what is the **everything** God knows, that we are better or worse than we think? Have we failed to love, or have we loved better than we think? That is, God "knows we are basically lovers of the brethren (v 14) and as such, are 'of the truth' (v 19)" (Bultmann 1973, 57). Is our assurance fundamentally grounded in our performance or in God's love and mercy?

Since the issue here is **whenever our hearts condemn us,** we take it as the latter—the christological ground of assurance (2:1). God's forgiving love in the "blood of Jesus" (1:7; 5:6, 8; see 1:9; 2:1-2; 4:9, 19) **is greater than our hearts** (see Nauck 1957, 78-82). The condition is our troubled hearts, the consequence is that God in Christ is greater than our hearts. And the explanation is that God knows us better than we know ourselves. We can trust his love!

■ **21** Now the condition is **if our hearts do not condemn us.** We *are* loving others to the best of time and ability with the consequence that **we have confidence before God.** Our conscience is clear. Why? Because we are obeying "his commands" (v 22; see vv 23-24). The ground of the Christian's assurance is now that of one's ethical response to God: we are genuinely loving. But fascinatingly, if not profoundly, living in obedience to God involves for John both believing and loving (v 23). Our response is beyond what legalism or moralism could ever require.

Thus, the love of the all-knowing God enables the people of God to have **confidence before God.** In Greek, *parrēsian* conveys the meanings ***"courage, confidence, boldness, fearlessness"*** (BDAG 2000, 781; see also 2:28; 4:17; 5:14). Strengthened by the Judge before whom all will someday stand, we can come, not fearfully, but with assurance. God calls us to be holy and enables us to become what he requires. Thus the confidence we enjoy is both now (specifically related to prayer) and preparation for the future (see the commentary on 2:28).

Two textual variants in the verse are worthy of note. The manuscript evidence is evenly divided between two readings relating to *kardia*. As in v 19, the singular noun *kardia* in Greek is translated as "hearts" because it is followed by the plural possessive pronoun **our** (*hēmōn*) in some manuscripts. John stresses the corporate personality of the church. Although many, they are of one heart. Other manuscripts omit the pronoun and read simply **the heart.** This avoids the apparent grammatical problem of a singular noun with a plural pronoun.

The second variant reading comes at the phrase **do not condemn us.** The majority of manuscripts read simply that the heart ***does not condemn.*** But several add **our** and a few read ***your*** (singular). The simpler, less specific reading is likely the more original—***if the heart does not condemn.*** The addition of pronouns was probably due to scribal attempts to clarify whether the message is directed to **us** or **you** (plural). The difference is slight. Both are possible. John could be *identifying with* his readers or *speaking to* them.

■ **22-24** The Christian's right to be assured is now made fully clear with these verses. The condemned conscience due to our failure of love is met by the greatness of God's forgiveness in Christ (vv 19-20). Christians who practice love have clear consciences, due to the sanctifying and assuring presence of the Spirit, as they live before God and for others (vv 22-24).

John explains that Christian assurance is confirmed by living in obedience to God's **commands**. Obedience is doing **what pleases him** (v 22, **what is acceptable before him;** see John 8:29). The obedient or pleasing life enables us more readily to believe God for answered prayer (see 1 John 5:14-15). We **will receive from him** (3:22, a present tense—***we are receiving;*** see Mark 11:24).

And what are some of the answers to prayer that contribute to the Christian's "confidence before God" (1 John 3:21; see on 5:16-17)? In 3:24 at least three appear. One is to be in God's presence—to **live in him.** Another is to have the life of God **in us.** This is the first mention of God dwelling in the believer. Several divine qualities have already been said to live/remain in the Christian. These include "truth" (1:8), God's "word" (1:10), the "anointing" (2:27), "God's seed" (3:9), and in 3:15 "eternal life" (Thomas 2004, 194).

The third answer to prayer is the inner witness of **the Spirit he gave us.** This is John's first explicit reference to the Spirit. But the Spirit is surely present as the agent of "anointing" earlier at 2:20, 27 (Bruce 1970, 100, 102; see 4:1, 13; 5:6, 8). Although the Spirit is an underemphasized presence in 1 John, this is still a strong affirmation. The Christian knows that God/Christ lives within, by virtue of the Spirit's testimony to the gift of God's presence.

Another answer surely is to become increasingly conformed to the likeness of Christ by God's indwelling presence. Further, to be like Christ leads to generous gestures toward others. What better answers to prayer might one **receive from him** (v 22) than to be at peace with God, others, and self?

The assurance inspired by the Spirit is experienced most profoundly in the ability to **believe in the name of** God's **Son, Jesus Christ** and to **love one another** (v 23). The presence of the Spirit enables the Christian to receive God's love and to respond to this love with love to others. This emphasis parallels the exchange between Jesus and "an expert in the law." There eternal life is said to rest in supreme love for God and selfless love for neighbors (Luke 10:25-28). John insists that faith toward God will be evident in tangible love toward others. Believing in the Son and loving **one another** constitute one **command**. A single purpose clause connects them as one. Faith that works flows from faith in Christ.

No authentic faith can circumvent Christ, for this faith is **in the name of his Son**. The emphasis on one's **name** appears often in Scripture. The name of persons could refer to their authority and character. All that a person represented was assumed within his/her **name** (Haas, DeJonge, and Swellengrebel 1972, 97; see 5:13 and 3 John 7).

Six times in Revelation **name** refers to God/Christ (2:13; 3:12; 11:18; 14:1; 16:9; 19:13). The most extensive usage of **name** is in Acts (29 verses, with 27 referring to God and Jesus). The absolute use in Acts 5:41, "suffering disgrace for *the* Name" (emphasis added), reflects a use of the phrase as a title for Jesus (as in 3 John 7).

The assurance of living in God/Christ comes in several ways. First, there is the confidence that comes from *living consistently* before God (1 John 3:22). Second, there is the assurance of this text, the witness of *Scripture* (v 24). Third, there is the witness of *the Spirit* (v 24). The Holy Spirit is a gift to us that confirms what Scripture promises and what our life has embraced. Confidence before God is more than hopeful optimism. It is an assurance that **we know** (*ginōskomen*). Forms of the word occur thirty-five times in John's letters, giving strong assurance to the readers.

Much in 1 John 3 has been encountered earlier, but these are not the repetitions of a meandering mind. Rather, they are deeply felt themes returned to in a calculated way. Loving one another not only can nurture the relationship among persons but also insures ongoing intimacy between the believer and God.

The crowning evidence of this mutuality of life is that God gives the Spirit. Obeying God's **commands** and doing **what pleases him** (v 22) demonstrates faith in God's **Son, Jesus Christ** (v 23). God demands that we **love one another** (v 23). Our obedience to this and, indeed, all God's commands means we **live in him** (v 24). The **Spirit he gave us** (v 24) bears witness to the intimacy of this relationship. It is this Spirit of faith and love who enables us to believe and to love, thus enabling us to know that God lives in us. So God (Father), Jesus Christ (**Son**), and the Holy **Spirit** all are affirmed together in this portion.

There is another "trinity" of sorts present. God's love for one believer flows to other believers. All three—God, believer, and believer—share reciprocal expressions of love in action. John will write more explicitly of this as he returns to the assurance theme in 4:7-21.

FROM THE TEXT

The Most Magnificent Expression of Love Is the Cross

When Isaac Watts surveyed the cross, he found that nothing of earth would satisfy like knowing the one who died for all. The cross brings vividly before us the servant of the Lord who "bore the sin of many" (Isa 53:12). The cross recalls Jesus, the good shepherd, who lays down his life for his sheep (John 10:11, 15).

The dying Christ, willingly giving himself up for others, serves as a challenging model for ministry. God defines **love; love** is self-sacrificing, even unto death (1 John 3:16-17). Love is active, not reactive. To love God is to commit to love the family of God (van der Watt 1999, 508-10). To minister in Christ's name is to serve with a spirit marked by less of self and more of him. When we serve faithfully where God has planted us, we daily lay down our lives for others. In ministry we give a portion of our lives for others every day.

Asking for Anything

John's claim that believing prayer assures us that we may **receive from him anything we ask** (v 22) poses theological challenges. What is the nature of prayer and stewardship? In a section that speaks of receiving **anything,** the text also confronts us with a clear obligation to give **material possessions** to our **brother in need** (v 17). The word **anything** could be wrongly construed to mean more material resources, justified by having more to share with the needy after all!

But it is only *after* we have demonstrated generosity through **actions and . . . truth** (v 18) that we can experience a heart assured by God. Only after we have given to others are we positioned to **ask** for *self*. Even then the one who prays has **confidence before God** (v 21) only because of a habit of doing what pleases God. If we are close to the heart of God, we will find ourselves asking largely for others and little for self.

Standing Before God

We find assurance and peace in being thoroughly known by God (see Heb 4:12-13). Yet it is ironic that for many, the thought of standing before God brings anxious thoughts, even dread. But God's examining presence in our lives now flows from his grace. God is for us, not against us, and at work to build holiness within us, preparing us daily for that future day. When we embrace this truth dread disappears.

IV. TESTING THE SPIRITS AND TRUSTING GOD'S LOVE: 1 JOHN 4:1-21

A. Test the Spirits (4:1-6)

BEHIND THE TEXT

While dualistic language is characteristic of 1 John, this section is especially marked by dualisms. The opposing pairs in these brief verses include: **Spirit of God** (v 2) and **spirit of the antichrist** (v 3); **truth** (v 6) vs. **false** and **falsehood** (vv 1, 6); **from God** (vv 2, 3, 4, 6) and from **the world** (vv 1, 3, 4, 5); **the one who is in you** (v 4) and **the one who is in the world** (v 4). These sharp contrasts depict a pronounced *ethical* dualism within Johannine Christianity.

The contrasting categories demonstrate points of connection with the Gospel of John—life and death, God and the devil, free from sin and enslaved to sin, truth and lies, light and darkness (see van der Watt 2007, 32-33, for a detailed list). This highly dualistic imagery reflects a Jewish mind-set comparable to the Dead Sea Scrolls from Qumran. The Qumran community and the Johannine Christians shared certain vocabulary—light/darkness, truth/falsehood, and spirit language (see Behind the Text for 1 John 1:5-10). These similarities suggest a common thought world. But we cannot prove conclusively any direct influence between the Johannine Christians and the Jewish sect at Qumran (van der Watt 2007, 142-43).

Within this dualistic mindset John employs sharp adversarial language. He labels opponents **false prophets** (v 1) and **antichrist** (v 3). The terms are part of the rhetorical vocabulary of 1 John and draw on both OT prophetic tradition and Jesus' teachings. The major writing prophets (Isaiah, Jeremiah, Ezekiel) warned of "false" prophets who preached without being truly sent with God's word (Isa 44:25; Jer 14:14; Lam 2:14; Ezek 22:28).

Jesus mentions pseudo-prophets in the Sermon on the Mount: "Watch out for false prophets" (Matt 7:15). In the Olivet Discourse he warns that "false Christs and false prophets will appear and perform signs and miracles to deceive the elect—if that were possible" (Mark 13:22; see Matt 24:11, 24, and Luke 6:26). Both OT and NT writers readily affirm that sometimes those who claim to be prophets are, in fact, proclaiming lies.

The reference in Mark 13:22 to "false Christs" carries a different nuance than the term "antichrists" in the Johannine letters. It is quite a different matter for one to claim falsely to *be* the "Christ" than for one to be *hostile* to Jesus as the Christ. While a degree of overlap could obtain, and likely does in many minds, the terms are not to be equated.

Popular end-times writings about "The Antichrist" in the modern era might lead one to expect a wide array of "antichrist" texts in the Bible. But the term appears only in the Johannine letters (five times in four verses). John may have anticipated an end-times personification of evil (1 John 2:18), although whether in the near or distant future is hard to say. He was more agitated about false teachers who had departed from the Johannine faith in his time (4:3; see 2:19; 2 John 7). These secessionist opponents he deemed *anti*-Christs (*against* Christ), who denied both the Father and the Son by dismissing the real humanity of Christ (1 John 2:22-23).

IN THE TEXT

■ **I** John addresses his readers again as **Dear friends** (*beloved ones*, as in 2:7; 3:2, 21; 4:7, 11). This term of affection, however, is immediately followed by stark words of warning. This section of the letter is a call for discernment. An undiscriminating embrace of the message of false prophets, alleging to speak under divine inspiration, would surely be disastrous. Wrong **spirits** (*pneumata*) would surely bring John's hearers to spiritual harm. The connection of this passage with 2:16-23 is clear as it again deals with christological error.

This is the only instance in the Johannine writings where readers are admonished to **not believe** (*mē . . . pisteuete*). However, it clearly echoes Jesus' warnings in the Synoptics. He warned his disciples "do not believe" when false reports of Christ's appearing come to them (Matt 24:23, 26; Mark 13:21). John had just commanded his readers: "believe in the name of his Son" (1 John 3:23; also 5:13). Of stylistic interest is the possibly deliberate alliteration of the Greek words in the opening line of v 1: *panti pneumati pisteuete* (Brown 1982, 485). This may have been intended as a memory device, and surely would have captured the ears of the hearers.

The spirits out and about in **the world** were to be carefully examined (*dokimazete*). In the LXX *dokimazō* sometimes referred to a test to determine that an accurate count of money was made (Gen 23:16; 1 Chr 28:18; 29:4). It can refer to the testing of precious metal by fire to assure its purity (Prov 17:3; 27:21; Wis 3:6; Sir 2:5).

In the NT the word relates to character (Rom 5:4) and to genuineness of faith (1 Pet 1:7). Paul admonished the Thessalonians, "Test everything" (*panta de dokimazete*, 1 Thess 5:21). A Christian writing not long after 1 John agrees that testing prophets is necessary (*Did.* 11:12) and makes their behavior a criterion of genuineness (Brown 1982, 506). The readers of 1 John are *commanded to examine* the spirits (imperative mood). The testing was an ongoing obligation (***keep on testing***).

Proper testing would discern those genuinely **from God** in contrast to those who were **false prophets** (*pseudoprophētai*). These pseudo-prophets represented a serious and immediate challenge to the Christian faith as practiced by John and his readers. Those who had separated from the Johannine churches had become enemies of the faith in his eyes.

Further, they had apparently taken a significant number of people with them. The text reports they were **many** (*polloi*). This echoes an earlier reference to "many antichrists" (2:18) and seems to foreshadow the "many deceivers" of 2 John 7. The repetition of **many** in each case and the quite similar characteristics attributed to them argue for these as being the same group. In 2 John the elder warns against the "deceivers" and equates them with "antichrist" (Strecker 1996, 133).

John describes the arena of these opponents' activity as outside his communities—they **have gone out** (*exelēlythasin*). The prepositional prefix *ex-* attached to the verb emphasizes a place. In 2:19 *ex* appears five times as John describes those who had left the Johannine community. The secessionists were no longer in the churches identified with John but were competing with them. These false prophets, formerly called "antichrists" (2:18), had transferred their citizenship **into the world** by having **gone out** from the Johannine churches (2:19). Symbolically, **the world** is the domain of anti-God activity (see Theological Themes in the Introduction).

The verb **have gone out** (*exelēlythasin*, perfect tense) suggests that these pseudo-prophets had previously departed from the Johannine churches and had remained separated from them. There may be no significant distinction in the alteration between the simple past and the perfect tense (Brown 1982, 490). But the perfect tense seems to highlight a past departure of some from the Johannine community that had continued as an established separation. The simple past tense, the aorist, would have served well enough if John was only reporting a past event.

■**2** An ongoing refrain throughout the letter stresses that the litmus test of orthodoxy is Christology, specifically the issue of the incarnation. The criteria as to **how you can recognize the Spirit of God** turns fully on Christology. The secessionists seem to have embraced a Christology that so emphasized the deity of Christ that his full humanity was denied. John, in contrast, affirmed a docetic-rejecting, fully "Emmanuel" Christology. For John Jesus and the Christ were one and the same. The eternal Son had entered completely into the human experience—**has come in the flesh** (*en sarki elēlythota*). The preexistent Christ was manifested as God's glory in human form (Brooke 1912, 109) in that he *became* flesh (*sarx*, John 1:14).

The verb **has come** (*elēlythota*, in the perfect tense) points not only to the fact of the incarnation but also to its enduring significance (Yarbrough 2008, 221; Rensberger 1997, 112). Is John saying there was a permanency about the incarnation? The perfect tense certainly supports such an understanding. As such, even the glorified Christ remains fully human. His incarnational presence is a continuing reality (Marshall 1978, 205). Christ, who came in the flesh, *continues* to be the incarnate Son (Thomas 2004, 203).

When Jesus appeared in postresurrection glory to disciples in Jerusalem he reassured them they were not seeing a "ghost" (*pneuma*, **spirit**): he had "flesh [*sarx*] and bones" (Luke 24:39). The promise of 1 John 3:2

"when he appears, we shall be like him" suggests that our resurrection bodies will be like Christ's incarnate and glorified body. The age to come is not an abandonment of creation but an affirmation of it (Wright 2008, 147-63).

The embrace of a fully human Christ was something to be acknowledged (*"claim, profess, praise,"* BDAG 2000, 708 s.v. *homologeō*). John the Baptist used the term to insist he was not the Christ—"He . . . confessed" (*hōmologēsen*, John 1:20). Paul before Felix employed it to affirm his clear allegiance to the Christian way—"I admit" (*homologō*, Acts 24:14). In Matt 10:32 the acknowledgement called for is crucially christological, with destiny tied to the confession—"Whoever acknowledges [*homologēsei*] me before men, I will also acknowledge [*homologēsō*] him before my Father in heaven."

■ 3 Verses 2b and 3 stand in antithetical parallelism. The positive, confirming confession leads to a discrediting denial (Jones 2009, 164):

"Every spirit that acknowledges that Jesus Christ has come in the flesh is from God" (v 2).	"But every spirit that does not acknowledge Jesus is not from God" (v 3).

These are confessions that imply community. To fail in the confessions was to refuse to participate in the community (Jones 2009, 168). Both elements of the confession—"Christ" and "in the flesh"—are essential (Culpepper 1998, 268). Of the five uses of **antichrist** in these letters (2:18, 22; 4:3; 2 John 7) all focus on the denial of the man Jesus as the Christ. Two of the three passages (4:3; 2 John 7) make explicit that the denials included his coming "in the flesh" (Burge 1996, 175).

The battle for allegiance was more than intellectual. John understood the struggle as a spiritual battle. Spirit language abounds (3:24; 4:1, 2, 3, 6, 13). The same word (*pneuma*) is used both positively (God's Spirit any spirit that rightly confesses Jesus) and also negatively (the spirit of **antichrist** and wrong confessors). The readers are warned not to trust **every spirit** but to "test the spirits" (v 1). The validation of "the Spirit of God" (v 2) comes when a "spirit . . . acknowledges that Jesus Christ has come in the flesh" (v 2). But **every spirit that** failed to **acknowledge Jesus** as **from God** was identifying itself as **not from God**. The distinction was the genuineness of a prophet's claim to divine inspiration.

Instead of **not acknowledge** (*mē homologei*) **Jesus,** some manuscripts read with a much more stern sense—**nullifies** or **destroys** (*lyei; "destroy, bring to an end, abolish,"* BDAG, 607 s.v. *lyō*; see 3:8 where the same verb is used). Although **destroys** is supported by only a minority of manuscripts, some interpreters prefer it as the more difficult reading (Lieu 1991,

46). Brown argues in favor of *lyei* in part by recalling the sense of 3:8 (1982, 496). Still, the majority reading is probably to be preferred (Haas, DeJonge, and Swellengrebel 1972, 103). The harsher reading, **destroys,** may be an expression of the second-century christological debates (Rensberger 1997, 113).

Instead of the **Jesus** in the first clause, some later scribes seem to have added the title "Christ" to emphasize the earthly aspect of the confession.

A number of manuscripts add **in flesh having come** (in harmony with v 2 and 2 John 7) in order to interpret the point as failure to confess Jesus' coming in the flesh (Smith 1991, 98-99). Different manuscripts link coming in flesh as variously related to Jesus, the Lord Jesus, or Jesus Christ. The numerous variant readings demonstrate how central this verse was to the christological controversies reflected in these letters.

An unsatisfactory confession of Jesus was taken as opposition to Christ. The drama was a spiritual contest between "the Spirit of God" (v 2) and **the spirit of the antichrist.** The Greek text does not have **spirit,** simply *kai touto estin to tou antichristou* (**and this is the ... of the antichrist**). The word *pneuma* is ellipsed and taken for granted as the most recent noun that agrees with the Greek neuter article *to*. The construction here permits reading the verse as either **the antichrist** or "the antichrist spirit" ... **is coming.**

The false prophets of v 1 among the secessionists had so aligned with an errant theology that they were labeled by John as having a spirit of **antichrist.** Such a spirit could be present in "many" individuals (2:18). John seems not much interested in a distant future eschatological figure—*the* Antichrist. Rather, anyone in his time proposing an incarnation-denying Christology demonstrated their allegiance to an anti-Christ *group* that was **already in the world.** His concern was the **now** (*nyn*) of the Johannine churches.

Whether John anticipated a single, cosmic figure as an end-times personality is difficult to ascertain. He did understand his era as part of the eschaton—the end times (**now** and **already**). But his eschatological concerns were focused on *a number of individuals* whose teaching was undermining the faith of the churches within his sphere of influence. He seems little interested in future events and characters. The teachings of these first-century opponents, already characterized as "many antichrists" in 2:18, were potent and dangerous. John's pastoral instincts were on high alert (see the sidebar "Antichrist" at 2:18 and the From the Text section of 2:18-23).

The focus of this verse, indeed of John's writing, is christological. A comparison of 2:18-22 and 4:1-3 reveals how each passage returns the attention back to Jesus. In the first instance, right relation to the Father leads to a correct view of the Son. In the second case, right relation to the Spirit leads, again, to a correct view of the Son. John depicts the Son as central (Burge 1996, 176). Yet John's Christology has inherent soteriological implications. For him, Christology determines the faith and life of Christians as he demonstrates throughout the letter. The bond between theology and ethics is essential.

■ **4** The status of the Johannine Christians as **dear children** is tied to their being **from God**. Their character was to be marked by righteousness and refusal to sin, expressed as love toward God and their fellow believers (Lieu 1991, 39). Although called **children**, they had gained spiritual victory and continued to be victorious (as implied by the perfect tense of *nenikēkate*: **have gained and keep the victory**).

John resumes his earlier mention of age-group categories in 2:12-14 ("dear children," "fathers," and "young men"). In 2:13-14 he wrote that "young men . . . have overcome the evil one." Here **children** have **overcome** those who were of "the spirit of the antichrist" (v 3) and **the one who is in the world.**

John does not say when and how this victory was gained. Does he refer to what Christ accomplished at the cross, viewed in Johannine circles as an ironic victory? The Gospel refers to Jesus' appointment with the cross as his hour of "glory" (see John 7:39; 12:16; 17:5).

Children overcome as their personal faith embraces the Christ of the cross (see 5:4-5). They had accepted the Johannine declaration of the gospel and experienced its continuing effect lived out through them. Forms of the Greek word for victory—*nikē*—appear in every "letter" to the seven churches in Rev 2—3. The risen Christ promises reward to everyone "who overcomes" (Rev 2:7, 11, 17, 26; 3:5, 12, 21). This makes victory something *yet to be fully accomplished.*

In this section of 1 John, the victory was already *somewhat* achieved. Because of **the one** (either God [vv 4, 6] or Christ) living in them, they were indwelt by divine power. That power had already trumped (*meizōn*: **greater**) **the one who is in the world.** The overcoming of these Christians was not their achievement, but in God's strength, already real in their lives because God resided in them.

■ **5** John negatively highlighted "the one who is in the world" (v 4), referring back to "the spirit of the antichrist . . . in the world" (v 3). There are also *a number of opponents* (note the plural **they** and **them**) who are **from the world** (*ek tou kosmou*). The **world** represents the devil and all opposed to God (Lieu 1991, 83).

John also draws a sharp line of contrast between those of the world and his churches. Note the parallel construction:

They are from the world (v 5).	"We are from God" (v 6).
autoi ek tou kosmou eisin	*hēmeis ek tou theou esmen*

This recalls a passage from the Gospel: "If you belonged to the world, it would love you as its own. As it is, you do not belong to the world, but I have chosen you out of the world. That is why the world hates you" (John 15:19; see 17:6-24). One's allegiance, John contends in 1 John 5, affects both how one hears and how one speaks. Those allied with the world and the leader "who is in the world" (v 4) have learned to speak the same language. The Greek text literally says *of/from the world they speak* (*ek tou kosmou lalousin*), though **viewpoint** does catch the sense. The use of *from* is not intended in the sense of separation and distance, but rather refers to origin and nature (Smith 1991, 100).

The speaking occurs in the present tense. The action takes place in John's time. When we **listen** in the biblical sense, we will necessarily order our lives by what we hear. The classic example in the *Shema* ("Hear, O Israel, and be careful to obey" [Deut 6:3]) appears in the NT as well. Listening to Jesus means conforming to his teaching (Matt 17:5), responding appropriately, and being reconciled (Matt 18:15).

■ **6** John contended that true believers would tune out messages from "the world" (v 5). They would refuse to give heed to the "false prophets" (v 1) who had left the Johannine churches ("gone out into the world," v 1). John calls his readers to reject the docetic Christology of the secessionists. They should instead listen to him and those allied with him. He insists that when people do **not listen to us** and choose to listen to a contrary gospel, they show themselves to be **not from God.**

A positive statement of this principle appears in John 8:47: "He who belongs to God hears what God says." Developing orthodox Christianity is seen in the contested questions between John and his opponents. For John, teaching alien to his views clearly placed a person in the arena of **falsehood** or ***deceit***. Listening to him was to listen to **truth**. A person will inevitably heed one spirit or another.

FROM THE TEXT

Christology

Christological consensus took centuries to achieve in the formal creeds of the churches. In 325 the Council of Nicea declared Christ to be "begotten, not made" and "of one substance with the Father." The Council of Chalcedon in 451 affirmed Jesus Christ to be at once fully God and fully human (Smith 1991, 101-2). Some Christians still minimize the humanity of Jesus in favor of a strong assertion of his divinity. Others so emphasize his humanity as to obscure or reject his divine nature. John insists that both are essential for human salvation.

Choosing Friends

Our friends and the social contexts we embrace incline us toward certain habits. Our associates affect how we entertain ourselves and how we spend our time and money. Admittedly, we cannot always choose our environment. But we are always to choose for the holy, rather than contrary to it. Susanna Wesley advised her son John,

> Whatever weakens your reason, impairs the tenderness of your conscience, obscures your sense of God, or takes off your relish of spiritual things; in short, whatever increases the strength and authority of your body over your mind, that thing is sin to you, however innocent it may be in itself. (Wallace 1997, 109)

Choices of habits and associates derive from our sense of the character of God and God's expectations for how life is to be lived. Christians must continually ask, What is Jesus like? What sort of gospel should we proclaim? And, How should we then live? Choices shape habits. Habits influence direction, and direction determines destiny.

Discerning the spiritually nurturing influences of life from the damaging ones is seldom easy. How do we reject aberrant teachings and at the same time remain open to the new thing God may be doing? We must live anchored by Scripture and committed to the Christian community. The collective wisdom of God's people, current and past, can help us find the way. But the task is not something done just once. It is a continuing assignment, a daily response of discipleship.

B. God's Son an Atoning Sacrifice (4:7-15)

BEHIND THE TEXT

For a discussion of "atoning sacrifice" see the sidebar "*Hilasmos*" at 1 John 2:2.

IN THE TEXT

■ **7** John returns to his concern for mutual love (see 3:11-24) as he appeals to his **Dear friends** (*beloved*) to live in love—**let us love** (in the subjunctive mood). Love should manifest itself in relationships with **one another**.

Love originates in God and flows *out* from God. God's love comes to all, both by creation and from grace (Marshall 1978, 212); anyone can choose to receive and express this divine love.

John is clear that one who expresses God's love toward others manifests the very character of God (Akin 2001, 177; Brooke 1912, 117). Acting in love presents evidence that one is **born of God and knows God.** John brings together in **born** and **knows** the language of physical generation and intimate relation to enforce his point. This acknowledges God for who and what he is—a God of love (Strecker 1996, 144).

When John writes **Everyone who loves,** he is not saying that acts of love provide conclusive evidence that one is a Christian. The word *agapōn* (a present active participle), suggests continuous action and is best understood as *everyone who keeps loving others.* John stresses that an obvious *lifestyle* of love demonstrates that the life of God is truly present in us. On such a basis one **knows** (*ginoskei*: **he is presently knowing**) God.

■ **8** This present knowledge of God and the true nature of love is not a secret disclosed only to a select few. It flows out of a relationship available to all. Loving is to be a lifestyle. Thus, John states that to live in a habitual condition of **not loving** is to live as strangers to God. Those who live in this way do **not know God** because **God is love.** By manifesting love, we demonstrate that we know God. Our character becomes increasingly what we were created and redemptively re-created to be. When we are born of God, we begin truly to **know God.**

To develop in relationship with God and God's people is to deepen this knowing. As a child spends time with parents and others in the immediate circle of family and friends, that child begins to know a number of things by intimate experience. This knowledge is based on, and enriched by, relationships children have with those they know well. Just so, the absence of love reflects ignorance of **God,** who **is love** (see 4:18).

John's inspired assertion that **God is love** indicates the basis of the preceding command to love. None of the Johannine equations: "God is spirit" (John 4:24), "God is light" (1 John 1:5), or **God is love** here is an ontological definition of God's being. None exhausts all that might be said about God. These assertions function rather as descriptions of the characteristic ways in which God works in revelation and redemption.

■ **9 God showed** (*ephanerōthē*) **his love** in the person of the incarnate Christ in his first advent (John 1:14; 3:16). In 1 John 2:28 *ephanerōthē* refers to Christ's *future* coming "when he appears." God's love motivates both the first and second comings of Christ.

John makes two emphases. God's love is experienced corporately, in worshipping communities—**among us.** But God's love is also experienced quite personally—***within us.*** Divine love transforms individuals and churches. The authentic experience of God is always personal, but never solitary.

God ***has*** sent [*apestalken*, perfect tense] **his one and only Son.** Christ's mission to the world continues to have impact. The **sent** one enlisted others and sent them (John 20:21; John 17:18; see Rom 10:15). The verb *apostellō* means to send on a mission as an official representative ("apostle"). The arena of the missionary activity of God in 1 John—**the world**—is nearly always a reference to an anti-God locale or mind-set (2:15-17; 3:1, 13; 4:1, 3, 4, 5; 5:4, 5, 19; also 2 John 7). However, it is also of necessity where God does his saving work (2:2; see John 3:16).

The phrase **his one and only Son** (lit. ***his son the only begotten***) echoes John 3:16. It also reminds the reader of John 1:14, where the glory seen in Christ was "the glory as of the only begotten from the Father" (NASB). In the Gospel of John *monogenēs* combines the ideas of "only begotten" and "well-loved" (Bruce 1970, 108). The word conveys not so much an "only child" idea as it does a child especially beloved.

In Heb 11:17 Isaac is the *monogenēs* of Abraham, who also fathered Ishmael. Isaac is the unique son, a "one of a kind" son in that through him the promise continued (Jones 2009, 183). Likewise Jesus is the unique Son of God in the sense that he is fully divine (Earle 1984, 107). Through him all God's promises are fulfilled. By sending his *monogenēs* Son, God demonstrates the unlimited reach of his love toward us. As the ***only begotten*** Son of God Jesus alone can mediate salvation (see John 1:18). Further, because Jesus is *monogenēs* one must place faith in him alone; there is no other. To fail to believe in Jesus is to come under judgment (Büchsel 1967, 737-41).

The sending of the ***only begotten*** Son makes God's life in us *possible*—**that we might live.** But it does not *guarantee* it. Nor is the life irrevocable. The verb is in the subjunctive mood, suggesting that the life is conditional. One may have life by accepting Christ, but one may forfeit life by rejecting Christ. The offer made, and the ability to respond, are all of grace. God **sent** Jesus. And only because of his initiative toward fallen, broken, sinful humanity can we hope to return to life.

To **live** does not refer to physical life (*bios*). The word for life here is a cognate of *zoē*, emphasizing the quality of life. "Eternal life" in the NT always uses *zoē* (three times in Matthew and Luke, twice in Mark, sixteen times in John, and nine times in Paul's letters). One might live and breathe physically and yet be utterly devoid of the abiding life of God. The life God offers is to know, and be known, by him. It is to live in intimate relationship with the Creator.

Genesis warns that eating of "the tree of the knowledge of good and evil" (Gen 2:17) means "you will die" (3:3). The result was not immediate physical death, but relational separation from God symbolized by eviction from Eden. Spiritual death begins with disobedience. The life offered by God is only **through him** (lit. ***by means of him***) whom the Father sent. No other source for life exists; God alone, as revealed in Christ, is the only source of true life. To disobey is to distance oneself from God and increasingly embrace death. To obey is to embrace God and to experience his life, flowing from the Son.

■ **10** The initiative for spiritual transformation comes from God. Love for God is in us because **he loved us.** God has taken the initiative, since as fallen creatures, we often exhibit selfishness rather than the selfless love of God (Smith 1991, 107). Love is grounded in God's perfection, not in human imperfection (Yarbrough 2008, 239). This broken relationship with God can only be restored by Christ (Burge 1996, 188). A person may authentically know love because of the efficacy of Jesus' saving death (Yarbrough 2008, 240). God sent **his Son** to demonstrate his love definitively (Brooke 1912, 119).

In v 9 the perfect tense describes the sending of Christ, stressing the *continuing effects* of the incarnation. Here the aorist tense emphasizes *the event* of God's act (Marshall 1978, 214). The mission of Christ was for a precise and profound purpose. The **Son** came to do for us that we could not do for ourselves. Pardon for our sins was achieved by God assuming the consequences of our rebellion (Marshall 1978, 215). The purpose of the sending of the **Son,** beyond his incarnation, was to bring us back to God (Akin 2001, 180). Christ's saving death calls attention to the enormity of divine love (Culpepper 1998, 270). The sending had reconciliation in view—the **Son as an atoning sacrifice for our sins.**

The word translated **atoning sacrifice** (*hilasmos;* NIV, NRSV) is "propitiation" in some translations (ASV, ESV, KJV, NASB, NKJV) and "expiation" in others (RSV, see NJB). Propitiation turns the thought toward the Son as appeasing God the Father, the offended party. Expiation emphasizes the cleansing and resulting restoration of sinners. This is achieved by a sacrifice that removes sin (Brown 1982, 519).

The translation **atoning sacrifice** leaves the precise emphasis of the word to the reader (see the sidebar *"Hilasmos"* at 2:2). In the LXX *hilastērion* identified the "mercy seat" (see Heb 9:5) as the place of reconciliation. The term had a technical cultic or sacrificial meaning in relation to the Day of Atonement (Lev 25:9) as well as a general reference to God's forgiveness (in Ps 130:4; Lieu 1991, 63).

Both propitiation and expiation make important theological points. God, who is wronged by human sinning, is reconciled by Christ's death in propitiation. The change is from the divine side. Sin is serious and requires sacrifice to be atoned for. The Johannine theology of the cross in the Fourth Gospel emphasizes Jesus' death as exaltation. But passages with sacrificial imagery do appear (Jones 2009, 184) in John 1:29 and 36. Jesus is handed over to death at the time of the slaughter of the Passover lambs (John 19:14-16). Sacrifice is also implicit in the sacrifice of the shepherd for his sheep (John 10:11).

But the coming of the Son addresses the need for sins to be removed or cleansed in expiation. This regards the change from the human side of the atoning event. Sin in human life must be removed by a thorough purification.

By insisting on suffering due to sin and by suffering in behalf of sinful humanity, God demonstrates that (1) sin is serious and must be radically dealt with, and (2) God is gracious and makes the reconciliation possible (2 Cor 5:18-19). God reconciles by sending the Son. But God is also the one who is reconciled by what the Son accomplished on the cross **for our sins.** The objects of God's initiative are reconciled to God through a remission of, and cleansing from, **sins** (*tōn hamartiōn*). Just as John includes the many in **our** violations that required the cross, so also the many are included in God's provision.

■ **11** The love of God is described in the same way as the familiar John 3:16—**God so** (*houtōs*) **loved.** This love that sent the Son, John insists, **ought to compel us to love one another.** The word **ought** (*opheilomen*) suggests a moral debt owed (see Matt 18:28; Rom 13:8). The emphatic pronoun *hēmeis*, **we,** intensifies the statement, since it is already implicit in the verb ending. Right spiritual relationship in the *vertical* plane—God to humankind—will rightly manifest itself in a relationship of love on the *horizontal*—person-to-person.

■ **12** That God is unseen is a consistent biblical emphasis. An identical statement appears in John 1:18: **No one has ever seen God.** Exodus 33:20 is representative of OT teaching. There the Lord told Moses, "You cannot see my face, for no one may see me and live." The NT describes God as "invisible" (1 Tim 1:17; Heb 11:27).

The perfect tense of **has . . . seen** stresses that God was not seen in the past and continues to be unseen in the present. Although no one can directly see God, **God** is knowable to some extent since he **lives in us** as we live out his love for others. Love from God, incarnate in *followers* of Jesus, powerfully demonstrates God's purpose in the world (Bruce 1970, 109).

Even if God cannot be seen directly as gnostic heretics thought, God can be seen when his people act in love. John insists that divine love infused into us can be perfected. That is, it fulfills its purpose or achieves its end (*telos*), among us as we live in love. Love **is made complete** (*teteleiōmenē*, see 2:5 and 4:17-18). This passive participle probably presumes God as the unexpressed Actor, who perfects believers—brings us to the goal he has in mind for us. Christian perfection is not a human achievement based on merit or struggle. It is God graciously at work, achieving his intentions for us as **we love one another.**

■ **13** John writes throughout in sharp disagreement with the secessionists' claim they had a special, esoteric knowledge. But he insisted that he and all true believers in his community, possessed a definite knowledge of their own: **We know** (*ginōskomen*)! The verb is a Johannine favorite, appearing nearly forty times, but only a handful of times in the Synoptics.

And what do Johannine Christians claim to know? That **we live in him** and that God lives **in us.** This profound mutuality of relationship continues the theme and language of v 12*b*. The NIV here translates the verb *menei* as "lives in." Elsewhere it prefers "remains" (sixteen times in the Gospel of John, and in 1 John 2:24, 27). The KJV typically renders *menō* "abides" to describe this close relationship between God/Christ and believers (see especially John 15:4-10).

The evidence confirming that God abides in human hearts is he has **given . . . of his Spirit** (see 3:24). ***By this*** (*en toutōi:* untranslated in the NIV) relates v 12 to the character of the **Spirit** received. The presence of the Spirit of God is the Spirit of love (vv 7-12) and of faith (vv 14-16; see vv 9-10). The presence of the **Spirit** in believers and within the worshipping community was not a human achievement.

Throughout, the text keeps grace clearly in view. God initiates, God abides/lives in, and God brings believers to completion. Christians are not, however, swept along irresistibly by his grace. We respond by welcoming his Gift. But even our ability to respond is thanks to his grace (Eph 2:8-9).

The **Spirit** had been **given** (a perfect tense verb) as an abiding reality. Further, the **Spirit** is received, not through a solitary pursuit of God, but by a believing community—**us.** The pursuing God gives the Spirit, having engendered in us a desire for God.

■ **14** The claim, **we have seen,** points back to v 12. We "see" God in a sense, despite the fact that "no one has ever seen God" (v 12). John claims, **we have seen . . . that the Father has sent his Son to be the Savior of the**

world (see v 10). Linked to the Spirit's presence in the community of love is a faith-seeing of God's activity in salvation: "The seeing of faith evinces its certainty in the fact that it carries its testimony with it" (Bultmann 1973, 70-71). The ability to love and the ability to believe assures us of the Spirit's presence (see 5:10).

John's shifts in verb tenses here seems self-conscious. He says **we have seen** in the perfect tense, indicating a past vision with a continuing impact. The present tense that follows, **we . . . testify,** suggests an ongoing practice of telling the story of **the Father** God who **sent** the **Son to be the Savior.**

Savior, from *sōtēr,* appears only here and in John 4:42 in the Johannine writings. This title "has parallels in Hellenistic worship of heroes and in the Roman cult of the emperor, as well as in the worship of healing gods in the Hellenistic period" (Strecker 1996, 158). In the LXX God is *sōtēr,* especially in the Psalms and Isaiah.

In the NT the term "savior" is used of God occasionally, but most often refers to Jesus (Luke 2:11; John 4:42; Acts 5:31; 13:23; Phil 3:20; 2 Tim 1:10; Titus 1:3-4; 3:6; 2 Pet 1:1, 11; 2:20; 3:18). The salvation God intends is **of the world,** an unlimited offer of transformation for all who were once hostile to God.

■ **15** John holds the door of opportunity wide open for all—**anyone (***whoever***)**. No one is excluded from God's invitation. Any may come by confessing Jesus as God's Son. The translation **acknowledges** might seem to suggest consent alone. But the verb conveys a more public and active sense of confessing (*homologēsē*) or making a public and life-shaping claim (Matt 10:32). In the Gospel of John, confessions of faith in Jesus could get one expelled from the synagogue (John 9:22; 12:42). In Rom 10:9-10 confessing Jesus as Lord is inextricably linked to God's saving work (Hofius 1991, 514-17).

Throughout the letter, John stresses relational Christianity, a faith not bound to a legal code. Rather it requires involvement in a love relationship with God through Christ: **God . . . in him and he in God.** From this, obedience and doctrinal consistency flow. This privilege, the result of the Savior's work (v 14), is effected through the confession that **Jesus is the Son of God** (see 1:9).

FROM THE TEXT

Godlike Qualities in Not-Yet-Christian People

Countless acts of love in service and compassion are done by people with no religious motivation. Are they also manifesting the character of

God? Surely so, even if they don't acknowledge it, and even if they do not allow that God exists!

Compassionate work by individuals or groups of people is evidence of *grace from God working through them. God is graciously working to bring them to faith.* The smallest capacity for love is due to grace (Akin 2001, 177). This grace that precedes self-conscious Christian faith is sometimes called prevenient grace, a grace that "comes before." Because God is at work in redeeming ways in all lives and systems, God's character can be demonstrated even among those who are not yet overtly aligned with God.

Godlike Qualities in Christians

God calls Christians to exemplify the qualities of God, most notably his **love.** Just as God became manifest in **the world** by sending **his one and only Son** (v 9), so followers of Christ are called to make the love of God apparent in **the world** (vv 9, 14). Faithful following of Christ enables the unseen God to be seen in acts of love toward one another.

God in Three Persons

The full expression of the Godhead appears in this section. In vv 7-15 **God** appears thirteen times, **Son** four times, and **Spirit** once. The activity of the Father is a love-motivated sending of the **Son** (vv 9-10, 14). The **Son,** by his death for sins, enables life (v 10). The **Spirit** confirms the relationship between God and believers, and among fellow Christians (v 13).

C. Perfect Love Drives Out Fear (4:16-21)

IN THE TEXT

■ **16** John affirms the present experience of churches. They have knowledge **(we know)** and faith **(rely on,** lit. *we have faith in, pepisteukamen*). John describes past experiences that continue to impact the present. The force of these perfect tense verbs can be conveyed as *we came to know and continue to know* and *we believed and continue to believe.*

God and love are synonymous—**God is love** (repeating 4:8). God defines true love. This strong and clear equation is expanded by the idea of living (*menōn,* **remaining**—a present participle) **in love,** which is to live **in God.** The imagery is of settling down in God's love, taking up secure residence in the heart of God. Christian faith is not occasional but constant. Faith is not just for big events but lived out in all the moments of life's routine.

John expresses love as absolute—**in love;** and thus unlimited. "He is thinking not only of God's love for human beings or that of humans' love for God but also of the love of human beings for one another" (Strecker 1996, 161). None of the three aspects can be isolated from the others.

■ 17 This living in love, which is to live in God and to have God live in us, causes God's love to be **made complete**. It is love brought to wholeness (*te teleiōtai*, from *telos*: **end, goal, purpose;** see on 2:5 and 4:12). It accomplishes the purpose for which it was created (Boice 1979, 119). This perfecting work (in v 18 forms of *telos* are translated "perfect") is not a human achievement. The passive voice of the verb describes the divine action that brings wholeness. God perfects believers. Some overstress the human activity of "following Christ" as the means of perfect love (so Smith 1991, 114).

Still, God's accomplishment is not achieved apart from the human response. The perfecting work of God occurs in people who are part of a believing community—**among us** (*meth' hēmōn*, suggesting **in company with us** or **in cooperation with us**; Brown 1982, 527). Then it comes to expression in our love for others. God's love finds completion or perfection—its true end (*telos*)—to the extent that it is shared among others (Burge 1996, 189). Holiness develops not so much in solitude as in relationship.

Quiet and withdrawn-from-the-routine times may be part of spiritual formation. But the true test of holiness occurs when God's love is manifested in the community's contacts with others. John emphasized that God's love is not for private enjoyment but is meant to be shared. First-person plural language (**us, we**) appears three times in this verse. God desires so to transform Christian communities that we **will have confidence** (see 2:28) in his presence as we face the future (2:28; 4:17) and as we pray here and now (3:21; 5:14).

This work of God that brings spiritual wholeness is not to be postponed for some far-off day. Indeed, the holy God who desires to perfect holiness in us begins to do so **in this world,** the very place where antichrists (2:18, 22; 4:3), false prophets (4:1), and deceivers (2 John 7) operate.

God's universal love can be so *lived out through us* that others may see in some measure what God is like. We participate in God's nature *now:* **in this world we are like him** (lit. *just as that one is also we indeed are in this world;* see 2:6; 3:7).

John expects believers to be conformed to the likeness of Jesus in love in the *present* (Lieu 1991, 90). Holiness is not reserved only for after death. Calvin said: "What God is in heaven, He bids us to be in this world, that we may be reckoned his children" (1959, 295). This astounding promise, to be **like him,** can hardly be overestimated. Sharing in the nature of God is a present possibility (2 Pet 1:4). It is a reality not withheld until after death. It is the only adequate preparation for death, when we stand before God **on the day of judgment.** This firm foundation is forever linked to God's love at work among people. Confidence before God and Christian love go together (Bruce 1970, 113).

Day of Judgment

The concept of a future judgment day appears early and frequently in Scripture. "Day" does not refer merely to a twenty-four-hour time. In Hebrew practice it refers to decisive historical events. Isaiah spoke of "the day of the LORD" (13:6, 9) and "the day of vengeance of our God" (61:2). Jeremiah mentions the "day of the LORD's anger" (Lam 2:22), as does Ezekiel ("the day of the LORD's wrath" (7:19). In the LXX, all these become the Greek phrase "the day of the Lord" (see Joel 1:15; 2:1, 11, 32; 3:14; Amos 5:18; Zeph 1:14-16).

The phrase "day of God" appears seldom in the NT (2 Pet 3:12; Rev 16:14). In the NT "the day of the Lord" has an apocalyptic association with Jesus as *kyrios* (see 1 Cor 1:8; 5:5; 2 Cor 1:14; Phil 1:6, 10; 2:16). Intertestamantal Jewish literature includes similar expressions (*1 En.* 10:6; 16:1; *Jub.* 5:10; 24:30; *4 Ezra* 7:113; *Pss. Sol.* 15:13).

These various Jewish and Christian texts envision a time of accountability when individuals and nations will stand before God. In the presence of God's glory, where holiness is the standard for judgment, all that is wrong will be made right. Evil will be justly punished. Righteousness will be rewarded. This divine and human drama brings God's just judgment upon all, living and dead. The judgment of the dead seems to presuppose their resurrection, an idea most clearly found first in Dan 12:1-3. It can be argued, however, that it was anticipated in Ezekiel's vision of the "resurrection" of the nation of Israel from the "dry bones" of Babylonian exile (Ezek 37:1-14), and a return to the land of Israel.

Throughout Scripture, judgment is expected at an appointed time in God's calendar. Eschatological judgment is not one of many events in which God judges individuals and nations throughout history. Rather it is the one grand and fearsome event of judgment, marking the transition from the present age to the age of the fullness of the kingdom of God. (See Jesus' parable of the Son of Man separating "sheep" and "goats" to "eternal punishment" or "eternal life" in Matt 25:31-46; and the "great white throne" judgment scene of Rev 20:11-15; Hiers 1992, 79-82; and Jenni 1962, 784-85.)

The hallowing, perfecting work of God in this life offers us reassurance for the future day of judgment. As a collective body of Christ, we will stand holy before the holy God "perfectly restored . . . changed from glory into glory . . . lost in wonder, love, and praise" (Charles Wesley, "Love Divine, All Loves Excelling"; Kimbrough 1987, 82).

■ **18** The expression **perfect love** refers to being loved perfectly by God. But this is only part of the story. Certainly the origin of all love is God, and we know how to love only "because he first loved us" (4:19). But God's love is not only something *we receive*. It also *transforms* us and *enables our response* of love to God and for others (Haas, DeJonge, and Swellengrebel 1972, 113). Abiding in God's love, living in the flow of **perfect love,** we are enabled to love one another authentically (Painter 2002, 283).

In a relationship of mutual love there is **no** necessity for **fear** in God's presence (Marshall 1978, 224). Love is personified as the agent expelling all fear. The power of love triumphs over fear (Strecker 1996, 167). This **perfect love,** which originates from God, achieves its purpose in persons, toward one another, and returns to God. This process **drives out fear** (Rensberger 1997, 122). Love on that day cannot be condemned by Love! Fear is ***cast out*** (*exo ballei*), a phrase recalling the judgment of evil persons expelled into the darkness (Matt 8:12; 22:13; 25:30) and the exorcisms of evil spirits by Jesus (Mark 1:34—*exebalen;* Mark 1:39—*ekballōn*).

The statement **there is no fear** has occasionally been forced to say more than it does. The deliverance effected by divine love removes the fear of **punishment** (*kolasin*). In the NT the word only occurs here and in Matt 25:46, where it denotes "eternal punishment" (*kolasin aiōnion*). So the fear from which one is delivered is the fear of standing before God at the final day ("the day of judgment," v 17). **The one who fears** is continually (a present continuous participle) anxious about his or her eschatological appointment with the divine Judge. God's love at work in believers takes that fear away.

But one may still fear other things. Indeed, people should learn to fear some things in the interest of personal safety and to be good stewards of the life given them. But perfected love can so harmonize our lives with the character of God that coming into the presence of the Holy One holds no dread for us. The holy character of God can express itself in blazing judgment on sinners. Or, that holiness can effect a thorough cleansing of sinners, totally transforming them. This holiness in believers grants peace, because it meets the divine requirement. God prepares us by his **perfect love,** which flows to us and through us to others. This enables us to come into the divine presence with confidence (v 17).

■ **19** We are able to love since God **first loved us** and thereby enables our human response of loving. This is a statement of fact—**we** do **love,** rather than an exhortation—"Let us love." Love is not self-originated, but it is of divine origin (Brooke 1912, 125). Love, like holiness, finds its source and definition in God. We cannot become truly holy or genuinely loving by our own striving. Only when we have received the holy love or loving holiness of the Creator God can we claim these qualities. So it is all of grace.

Some scribes felt the need to expand the text by clarifying the object of the human love. Some manuscripts read **we love God;** others **we love him;** and still others **we love one another.** But the best manuscripts support the shorter reading: simply **we love**—a love without designation and without limit.

■ **20** The proof of love is seen in action. In a succinct way John contends that love for one's **brother** and sister, who are **seen,** gives credible witness to one's love for God, who is **not seen.** John minces no words. Whoever **hates** (see 2:9, 11; 3:15) a **brother,** while claiming to love God, **is a liar.** The Greek word order particularly emphasizes this—**liar he is** (*pseustēs estin*).

Even though unloving people may be publicly identified with the church, failing the love test relegates them to a category reserved for serious offenders. The designation **liar** applies to those who disobey God's commands (2:4) and who deny that Jesus is the Christ (2:22). Liars are antichrists (2:22), who deny God and Christ.

Many manuscripts simply declare at the end of v 20 that liars **cannot love** (*ou dynatai agapan*). Others pose a rhetorical question: **How is he able to love** (*pōs dynatai agapan*)? The semantic force of the two readings is identical. The question clearly expects a negative answer (Haas, DeJonge, and Swellengrebel 1972, 114).

■ **21** Love for **God** is evidenced by the attitudes and relationships one has toward a **brother** and sister (*adelphon*). The term **brother** indicates a member of the Johannine community (fifteen times in 1 John, three times in 3 John). This loving is neither automatic nor dependent on feelings. If **love** can be commanded, John presumes obedience is a choice. Obedience is an act of volition, not an involuntary emotional response. The **command** is to do the right thing, regardless of how we feel about another. If we can obey the **command** to **love,** then surely we can disobey it. Otherwise the command is not truly such, and we are not responsible for what we do.

FROM THE TEXT

God's Love Comes Through Many People

Any truly loving expression has its origin in the **God** who is **love.** Love flows from God through people (v 16), whether or not that person acknowledges God. Even atheists and agnostics are part of God's work in **this world** (v 14) when they act in love. When we express God's love to others, we simultaneously draw closer to God's heart.

Perfect Love Takes Time, but Can Be Real in Us Now

Perfected or **complete** love (v 17) encompasses a span of time. The perfecting of God's love in persons began with God's declaration in Gen 1 that all creation was "good" (Gen 1:18, 21, 25), even "very good" (Gen 1:31). The restoration of what sin forfeited takes place through the cross, and enters our experience as we respond in faith to God's offer in Christ.

Further, the perfecting of love is a living, present reality. It is done in us by God **in this world** so that **we are like him** (v 17). John intends to counter the secessionists who denied that Christ came in the flesh (4:2; 2 John 7). Finally, the completing of God's love in us **in this world** (v 17) prepares us for the future **day of judgment** (v 17), when we will need the **confidence** God promises.

Lived-Out Love

The profession of Christian faith obligates believers to express that faith in loving acts expressed toward others (v 20), both in the church and beyond. Pastoral practice that helps people reconcile to one another is essential to the church's mission. Loving **brother** and sister in the church frees us to love God fully (v 20) and demonstrates that God's love is truly resident in us.

V. LIFE IN THE SON, DEATH IN DEPARTING: 1 JOHN 5:1-21

A. Overcoming Faith (5:1-5)

BEHIND THE TEXT

The statement **Jesus is the Christ** (v 1) combines an exalted, honorific title and a personal name. **Christ,** from the Greek word *christos,* means "anointed." In the LXX it translates the Hebrew word for "Messiah." In the OT, Messiah refers to the king of Israel or Judah (twenty-nine times; see, e.g., Saul in 1 Sam 24:6; David in 2 Sam 19:21; and Solomon in 2 Chr 6:42).

In the NT the Aramaic form *messias* appears only in John 1:41 and 4:25. In both instances Messiah is immediately followed by its Greek equivalent. All other occasions in the NT (over two hundred) use the Greek *christos* alone.

Expectation of an anointed one as something *more* than an earthly king, however, became part of Israel's future hope. This expectation is present in both the OT and intertestamental literature. In some minds, the anticipated one became an eschatological heavenly redeemer (see Isa 9:1-7; 11:1-9; Mic 5:2-5; and Zech 9:9-10).

Messianic expectation included for some the idea of a forerunner, or advance agent, who would prepare the way for the coming Messiah (Mal 4:5-6). The Gospels describe John the Baptist as "a messenger . . . who will . . . prepare the way for the Lord" (Mark 1:2-3; see Mal 3:1; Matt 3:1-3; Luke 3:1-18; John 1:6-8, 19-23). Mark explicitly claims that John the Baptist fulfills the Malachi passage.

In the time of Jesus, there were competing views about the Messiah. Some held a "low" Christology (earthly in origin), viewing the Messiah as a Davidic king, who would arise to rid Israel of its century-long Roman occupation. Others espoused a "high" Christology, envisioning the Messiah as a heavenly redeemer figure. This view was partly informed by the description of the enthronement in heaven of a Son of Man figure in Dan 7:13-14. Writings associated with the name Enoch also use Son of Man language to depict a heavenly champion of the righteous (*1 En.* 62:7-9; 69:30-36; 71:14).

Christian messianic expectation in the NT includes both conceptions. Jesus was regarded as a Davidic king and the heavenly Son of Man. The Gospels identify him in the Davidic sense seventeen times but use "Son of Man" more than eighty times (all in sayings of Jesus apparently about himself). Messianic expectation in the NT also clearly understands Jesus in terms of the Suffering Servant of Isaiah (esp. ch 53). The Gospels depict Jesus as a persecuted righteous man, who suffers in behalf of others.

The Qumran community imagined a future in which one or two Messiahs would be active. Some texts of the Dead Sea Scrolls (DSS) envision a royal, Davidic figure—a *kingly* Messiah called "the Branch of David," the "Messiah of Israel," and the "Prince of [all] the Congregation." They also anticipated a *priestly* Messiah, called the "Messiah of Aaron," "the Priest," and the "Interpreter of the Law" (Vermes 2004, 86).

Both the Johannine and Qumran communities expected an eschatological victory. Qumran *expected* the victory to occur soon. For the readers of 1 John the end-times victory had *already been achieved* by Christ and was *a continuing conquest* in the congregations (Schnackenburg 1992, 230 n. 103; Bultmann 1973, 78 n. 17).

When John challenges his readers to believe **that Jesus is the Christ** (v 1), the definite article (*ho,* the) highlights the title. Jesus is *the* Messiah. In most instances in these letters, the more typical and fuller usage "Jesus Christ" appears (1:3; 2:1; 3:16, 23; 4:2; 5:6, 20; 2 John 3, 7). "Jesus" without "Christ" accompanying it occurs five times (1:7; 2:6; 4:3, 15; 5:5), although the designation "Christ" is seldom far removed. Other important identifiers also appear, including "Son" and "Son of God." "Jesus" appears alone only in 2:6; "Christ" stands alone only in 2 John 9.

IN THE TEXT

■ **1** John's concerns for correct Christology (2:18-27; 4:1-6) and the ethic of love appropriate to it (2:7-11; 2:28—3:18; 4:7-21) now come together (see also 3:1-24).

The letter conveys a welcoming ecumenical tone. The use of **everyone** appears to invite all who will believe into the Christian community. The present participle seems to emphasize *continuous* believing—***everyone who keeps on believing***—not a once-for-all moment of spiritual rebirth. Ongoing belief and obedience (v 2) provide evidence that one **is born of God**. The phrase *ek tou theou* (***out from God***) suggests that believers have their origin in God (see 2:29; 3:9-10; 4:7; 5:18).

The errant beliefs about Jesus held by the secessionists excluded them from the category of "brother." Thus, they were not among those John's audience were to love (Brown 1982, 566). The different Christologies of the Johannine and of those who "went out from us, but . . . did not really belong to us" (2:19) should be kept in mind.

The assertion here that **Jesus is the Christ** stands in stark antithetical parallelism to the secessionists' denial cited in 2:22 that ***Jesus is not the Christ*** (Brooke 1912, 128). John is urgently working against inroads by those with a dangerously variant Christology. The unifying center for John was a correct embrace of Jesus, who had "come in the flesh" (4:2), as God's anointed, **the Christ.**

Both faith and spiritual birth figure importantly in this section of 1 John. It stresses faith seven times in five verses (vv 1, 4, 5, 10, 13). Spiritual birth is mentioned in vv 1 (three times; see on **father** and **child** below), 5, and 18 (twice). The perfect tense **is born** underscores the spiritual birth as a past event with consequences in the present.

Having experienced spiritual birth, the natural response is to love **the father** (many translations supply the word **child** for a more readable translation). The Greek text, however, reads that ***whoever loves the one begetting loves also the one begotten from him.*** Thus, the person who loves God will surely also love God's offspring (see 4:19).

■ **2** Love is by nature reciprocal. It originates in God, because "God is love" (4:8, 16). It circles back to the Creator, as believers worship him and love others (4:19-21). The evidence that one truly loves God is demonstrated in **carrying out** (lit. ***doing***) **his commands.** Some manuscripts read *keeping/obeying* rather than *doing*, consistent with v 3. **This is how we know that we love the children of God** because we embrace and are living out God's **commands** (4:20-21).

God's love works in redeeming ways. Love, flowing from God and multiplied by the lives it invades, draws us into relationships with others. This verse reflects the spirit of "the greatest commandment in the Law" (Matt 22:36; see vv 37-40; Lev 19:18; Deut 6:4). Worship, an obedient response to God, originates with God and expresses itself in relationships between people. To love God supremely and to love neighbor as oneself summarizes the law (Mark 12:28-31; Luke 10:27).

■ **3** Obedience to God is *expected:* **This is love . . . to obey.** Disobedience to God can never be construed as normal Christian practice. It undermines community. **Love for God** means unwavering devotion to God's **commands.** Similar sentiments appear in the Fourth Gospel. Love for God means obeying or keeping (forms of *tēreō*) Jesus' "command" (John 14:15) or his "teaching" (John 14:23; 14:24).

This is not a standard humans can meet unaided. God's directives **are not burdensome** (*bareiai*), but we are not able to obey without divine assistance. Jesus calls down woe upon the "teachers of the law and Pharisees" who lay "heavy loads [*barea*]" of traditional regulations on others (Matt 23:2, 4). He criticizes them, using another form of the *bar-* word family, for their neglect of the "more important [*barytera*]" matters of God's demand (Matt 23:23). Acts 15:28 underscores the desire not to place unnecessary burdens (*baros*) on Gentiles coming to faith in Jesus.

John does not consider the commands of God a burden to be endured. Rather, when Christians obediently embrace them, we give *evidence* of our new, divinely given life. That new life is lived in victory because *God empowers us so we can obey* (Haas, DeJonge, and Swellengrebel 1972, 116).

■ **4** John emphasizes victory again: **everyone born** (*gegennēmenon*) **of God overcomes the world.** The Greek perfect participle implies that those born of God continue in their new way of life. Those who do are *already* victorious. The words **overcome/overcomes** in vv 4-5 (from *nikaō*) and **victory** (*nikē*) in v 4 derive from the same Greek root.

The risen and reigning Jesus is already victorious. The aorist participle (*nikēsasa*, v 4b), replacing the previous *nikai* (v 4a), means "has overcome" (NASB). Christians participate in the "once-for-all" victory of Jesus over the world (John 16:23) by their faith (Marshall 1978, 229; Bultmann 1973, 77).

What do believers overcome? Earlier John mentioned overcoming "false prophets" (4:1) and "the spirit of antichrist" (4:3). Here it is **the**

world. This is not a new opponent. All three expressions describe those who left the Johannine community (2:19).

The promise of **victory** is thematically similar to phrases at the end of each of the seven letters in Rev 2—3. There the one "who overcomes" is promised appropriate rewards: "I will give" (Rev 2:7, 11, 17, 26; 3:5, 12, 21). In 1 John, overcoming is tied to **faith,** that is, to ongoing trust in God. This faith is not individualistic, but corporate/communal (Jones 2009, 209). We are not left to survive alone. It is **our** shared faith, held in common with the entire community, that enables us to participate in the victory already won by Christ (Haas, DeJonge, and Swellengrebel 1972, 117).

Curiously, the participial phrase translated **everyone** (*pan*) **born** is in the neuter gender. Perhaps this is because the Greek word for child (*teknon*) is neuter (Marshall 1978, 228). If so, the phrase may have had John's audience in mind—*every child of God born.* But the word *pan* might be translated *everything* and suggests a wider application to v 4. Jones calls the neuter here and in 2:16 "all inclusive" (2009, 209).

Redeemed persons, certainly, and perhaps all of creation will experience new life from God in the new age and share in the victory of **faith.** Cosmic redemption, perhaps only hinted at here, appears clearly in Paul's thought: "The creation itself will be liberated from its bondage to decay and brought into the glorious freedom of the children of God" (Rom 8:21). A vivid picture of universal worship appears in Rev 5:13: "I heard every creature in heaven and on earth and under the earth and on the sea, and all that is in them, singing" to God and the Lamb.

First John 5:4 uses the same root word in both the subject and the accompanying participle. Thus, the latter part of this verse may be translated: ***This is the conquest that conquers the world.*** Such Hebraic repetition strongly emphasizes the victory. Other examples of this rhetorical device appear with other words. In v 9, "the testimony [*martyria*] of God, which he has given" (*memartyrēken*); v 10, "the testimony [*martyrian*] God has given" (*memartyrēken*). In v 15, "what we asked" (*ta aitēmata ha etēkamen*) is literally **the requests we have requested.** In v 16 "commit a sin" (*hamartanonta hamartian*) is literally **sinning a sin.**

■ **5** John employs language used earlier—"that Jesus is the Christ" (v 1). Verse 5 shifts the language slightly. The faith **that overcomes the world** now belongs to those who believe **Jesus is the Son of God** (see 2:22-23). The phrase **Son of God** (or "Son" alone, referring to him), appears more than twenty times in 1 John. Nearly half appear in ch 5 (vv 5, 9, 10, 11, 12, 13, 20). Early Christians referred to Jesus as both "Christ" (v 1) and **Son of**

God. The parallel structure of vv 1 and 5 reflects a synonymous parallelism typical of Hebrew poetry:

"Everyone who believes that Jesus is the Christ" (v 1)	He who believes that Jesus is the Son of God (v 5)
pas ho pisteuōn hoti Iēsous estin ho Christos	*ho pisteuōn hoti Iēsous estin ho huios tou theou*

For Johannine Christology, the incarnate Jesus *is* the Christ *as* the Son of God (1:3; 4:10, 14).

FROM THE TEXT

Living in Love

What if everyone who claimed to be **born of God** (v 1) would manifest it by consistently loving others? God reaches out in love to establish a relationship with us. When God's love takes root in us, it spreads into the lives of others. Love acts. It is not always easy to know what to do, but part of loving is to live in accordance with what one *already does* understand.

Living in Joy

The language of **not burdensome** (v 3) speaks of a faith anchored by joy. Jesus warned of those who laid heavy religious demands on others and advised, "Do not do what they do" (Matt 23:3). He described his demands on those who come to him by comparison: "My yoke is easy and my burden is light" (Matt 11:30). What might happen if a revival of glad, obedient response to the word of God swept the churches and homes of our world?

B. Witnesses to the Truth (5:6-12)

BEHIND THE TEXT

The validity of personal testimony in the OT was linked to a specific number of credible witnesses. According to Deuteronomy "two or three witnesses" were necessary to establish guilt or innocence on criminal charges (19:15). Only on this basis could a person be sentenced to death (17:6).

This requirement is mentioned several times in the NT. Hebrews warns its readers against rejecting Christ. Arguing from the lesser to the greater, its author reasons: "Anyone who rejected the law of Moses died without mercy on the testimony of two or three witnesses." It goes on to point out the greater "testimony" of "the Son of God" and "the Spirit of grace" (10:28-29).

Jesus applied the principle of "two or three witnesses" to his instructions for resolving disputes in his church (Matt 18:15-16). Paul used the standard to determine whether an accusation could be sustained against an elder (1 Tim 5:19). He seems to have understood his repeated testimony alone, whether in person or by letter, as satisfying the requirement (2 Cor 13:1-3; Carver 2009, 360). This OT standard as to what constitutes credible witnesses is central to this section of 1 John.

IN THE TEXT

■ **6** Does v 6 echo the Gospel of John? On the cross Jesus' side was pierced and "blood and water" (*haima kai hydōr*, John 19:34) came forth. This resulted in the "one seeing it" affirming his testimony (*martyria*) as "true" (*alēthē*, 19:35).

The convergence of **water** (*hydatos*), **blood** (*haimatos*), **witness** (*martyroun*), and **truth** (*alētheia*) in the present passage is striking. The language surely reflects a familiarity with the Fourth Gospel, and possibly direct dependence upon it. It may also echo John 3 (see **water** [*hydatos*] and **Spirit** [*pneumatos*] in v 5).

Brown surveys the various theories as to the possible meaning of **water and blood** in 1 John 5:6. He narrows them into four groups. Those referring to: (1) the sacraments of baptism and the Eucharist; (2) the incarnation; (3) the baptism and death of Jesus; and (4) the meaning of the death of Jesus. He identifies the latter as solving more problems than any other theory, since it emphasizes the saving effect of the death of Jesus (Brown 1982, 575-78).

However, many interpreters embrace the third category (Culpepper 1998, 272; Smith 1991, 123; Marshall 1978, 231; Bruce 1970, 118). Bruce notes that the sequence (water, then blood) corresponds to the historical order of Christ's baptism and passion. The double affirmation—**by water and blood**—may have been intended to counter Gnosticizing views. Some taught that "the Christ" (a spiritual being or "Christ-Spirit") descended upon Jesus at his baptism and left him prior to the cross (Smith 1991, 124; Bultmann 1973, 80; Bruce 1970, 118).

John's opponents could accept that Jesus came **by water,** if this was understood as a reference to his baptism. But they could not affirm the genuineness of the incarnation, if coming **by water** indicated his natural, human birth. Neither could they embrace Christ's death on the cross, if this was the reference **by blood.** John, however, affirmed both the incarnation and the crucifixion as significant salvation moments, in opposition to secessionist views (Marshall 1978, 232).

Brooke correctly observed that baptism marked the beginning of Christ's work and the cross its consummation in the Synoptic Gospels (1912, 133). But the Fourth Gospel never explicitly mentions Jesus' baptism by John. Only an awareness of the Synoptic parallels even hints at it.

From the Johannine perspective, incarnation embraced the full bodily existence of Jesus, from birth to death on the cross (Jones 2009, 211; Burge 1996, 202). The reference to **blood** almost certainly refers back to 1:7 ("The blood of Jesus . . . purifies us from all sin"), which clearly refers to the redemptive significance of Christ's death (Jones 2009, 211).

The role of **the Spirit** as the one **who testifies** seems to correlate well with John 15:26-27, where he is "the Spirit of truth," the "Counselor." The Gospel passage also reports the Spirit's testimony "from the Father" "about" Jesus. The disciples were also obliged to be witnesses. Their testimony was to be enabled by the Spirit sent to them by the "absent," though present, Jesus (John 16:7; see the sidebar "Truth" at 1:6).

John places enormous significance upon faithful witness as he nears the conclusion of his letter. This theme recalls the opening statement, "The life appeared; we have seen it and testify to it" (1:2). In ch 5 John employs forms of "witness" and "testimony" ten times in five verses (vv 6, 7, four times in v 9, three times in v 10, and v 11).

The **water and blood** may have sacramental overtones (baptism and Eucharist). If so, they witness to Jesus' saving work in a repetitive way (Smith 1991, 124). But the Fourth Gospel never explicitly mentions the institution of Communion.

A cluster of variant readings occur in v 6. Some manuscripts read **water and blood.** Others have **water and *spirit*.** Still others give **water and blood *and spirit*** (all three) in various combinations. These all appear to be later scribal attempts to harmonize the epistle's wording with the Gospel parallels already cited.

■ **7-8** These verses hint at Trinitarian language: **there are three that testify.** These three continuously witness (*martyrountes*, a present participle). In the previous verse "the Spirit" was the witness (*to martyroun*) "who testifies." Now the witnesses are **three.** Later scribes could not resist extending the thought into overt language about the Trinity.

Some late manuscripts of the Vulgate (a Latin translation of the Bible created by Jerome in the late fourth and early fifth century) expand the reference to mention three witnesses that "testify in heaven: the Father, the Word, and the Holy Spirit, and these three are one." This obvious theological expansion of the text does not appear in any known Greek manuscripts before the sixteenth century. Nor is it quoted by any early church writers. It surely would have been, if it had been a part of the original text (Marshall 1978, 236; see the careful excursus in Akin 2001, 198-200).

The language of **three** may hint at a Trinitarian tendency in John's thinking. But, more likely, it was a Johannine expression of the Hebraic standard of "two or three witnesses" (Deut 19:15). John reports that **three witnesses of the gospel story—the Spirit, the water and the blood—are in agreement.** He stresses the agreement of their common testimony because they have come from the witness of "the Spirit [who] is the truth" (v 6).

■ **9** John argues here from the lesser to the greater (technically, *a minori ad maius*). If people receive human **testimony,** then they will be even more inclined to receive **the testimony** (*martyria*) **of God.** God's character defines integrity; so divine testimony is immensely superior to that of humans. God's testimony is focused on the person of Christ—**about his Son**). The threefold testimony (v 8) is the superior **testimony of God** (Strecker 1996, 192-93). The Gospel of John insists that God provides reliable testimony about Jesus (5:37; 8:18; see the sidebar "Faithful Witness and Martyrdom" at 1 John 1:2).

God **has given** his testimony about his **Son** in the past. Yet the testimony still resounds in the present (the verb *memartyrēken* is in the perfect tense). John invites his readers/hearers to enter into the story and embrace the testimony about God's Son.

■ **10** Embracing God's word gives an inner witness **in his heart** (lit. *in himself*). Other manuscripts read simply **has the testimony in him,** but *in himself* has the best manuscript support. The word **heart** is a paraphrasing addition to the text. The confirmation of faith is all-encompassing, involving outer behavior and inward conviction, mind and emotions, head and heart. The cognitive truth of God's witness grasps us at the center of our beings—what the Bible often calls the **heart.** The witness of God is not to be intellectualized, but interiorized. That is, the witness has to become the possession of faith (Schnackenburg 1992, 240). This simply means that "the event of faith is the witness" (Bultmann 1973, 82). Our very ability to believe constitutes God's witness to our hearts (see Rom 5:5).

Other textual evidence in v 10 varies. There is strong support for the reading **does not believe** (or, ***trust in***) **God.** Other manuscripts, however, have **does not believe *in the Son*,** while still others have **does not believe *in the Son of God.***

John sharply insists that the one resisting **the testimony God has given about his Son** makes God **out to be a liar.** The secessionists prefer their own version of the truth. The word order is emphatic: ***liar he has made him.*** The traitors to the Johannine community have not merely made a one-time inference that God is liar. Their stubborn insistence on their alternative Christology is a standing affront to God. They persist in their false views (*pepoiēken*, **he has made,** is in the perfect tense).

■ **11** John's statement, **this is the testimony,** echoes the beginning of the letter (1:5; so Culpepper 1998, 272). The witness of **God** to his **Son** comes with a life-changing offer. God **has given eternal life** (see on 1:2; 2:25; 3:15). The Greek order is emphatic: *eternal life God has given to us* (Haas, DeJonge, and Swellengrebel 1974, 122). Many expect to have **eternal life** without surrendering to the lordship of Christ. But eternal life comes only by faith in Jesus Christ: **this life is in his Son.**

■ **12** John concludes: **He who has the Son has life.** To reject God's testimony about his incarnate **Son** is to reject the **eternal life** offered only through that Son (v 11). Rejecting the Son brings God's wrath (John 3:36) and death. Verse 12 is a tightly packaged example of poetic form of antithetical parallelism:

- He who has the Son has life.
    ho echōn ton huion echei tēn zōēn
- He who does not have the Son of God does not have life.
    ho mē echōn ton huion tou theou tēn zōēn ouk echei

Verses 11-12 encapsulate the essential thrust of the entire letter. *Salvation life is found only in the Son of God.*

FROM THE TEXT

Faithful Witnesses

The plan of Christ was to call and train some ("the twelve"), who would tell others. They, in turn, would tell others. All who have heard the gospel are part of this chain of faithful witnesses. The chain reaches from the first testimony of the discovery of the empty tomb and encounters with the risen Christ into the present. Like relay runners, we receive the baton of fiduciary faith and are responsible to pass it on. Faithful witnesses have *a personal responsibility*. But do not stand alone. Our testimony joins the chorus of "a great cloud of witnesses" (Heb 12:1) who share the same mission (Acts 1:8).

Personal Integrity

How can **we accept man's testimony** (v 9) if those who witness lack integrity? Social stability, familial balance and health, and spiritual relationships all require persons whose words are true. People in every age have, sadly, demonstrated the human ability to conceal and distort the truth. We must live truthfully and consistently that others may find it easy to believe us. Nonetheless, despite our best efforts, **God's testimony is greater.**

Spiritual Assurance

Having an inner confidence of a right relationship with God can hold us steady in the most difficult of circumstances. When John Wesley experienced his "heart-warming" encounter with God on May 24, 1738, he wrote in his Journal: "An assurance was given me, that he had taken away *my* sins, even *mine*, and saved *me* from the law of sin and death" (1978, 1:103). Only God's Spirit can give such assurance.

Wesley's second sermon on "The Witness of the Spirit" describes Christian assurance as

> an inward impression on the soul, whereby the Spirit of God immediately and directly witnesses to my spirit, that I am a child of God; that Jesus Christ hath loved me, and given himself for me; that all my sins are blotted out, and I, even I, am reconciled to God. (Wesley 1978, 5:124-25)

C. Assurance of Eternal Life (5:13-17)

BEHIND THE TEXT

The phrase **eternal life** is frequent in the Johannine writings. It occurs six times in 1 John (1:2; 2:25; 3:15; 5:11, 13, 20), and sixteen times in the Gospel. In the Synoptic Gospels it appears only eight times. It is a distinctively NT concept. A similar idea in the OT appears only in Dan 12:2, which refers to "everlasting life," with a clearly future reference. The Johannine literature especially emphasizes the present experience of **eternal life.**

IN THE TEXT

■ **13** John refers to what he had already written (aorist tense, see the commentary on 2:14). The NIV translates this as a present—**I write,** understanding the verb as referring to the finished letter from the perspective of his readers. John did not refer to an earlier letter. This is an "epistolary aorist." The writing of the letter occurred in the past from the reader's perspective, although John naturally was writing in his present time. This accounts for the difference between the literal and dynamic equivalence translations (Earle 1984, 109).

Smith suggests that 1 John may have originally ended with 5:13. He refers to similar "ending problems" with the Gospels of John and Mark and

Romans (1991, 121-22). But Jones convincingly demonstrates that 5:13-21 resembles a classical epilogue (2009, 223).

Thirty-six times in 1 John and once each in 2 John and 3 John, the author claims to write so his hearers might **know.** The statement **so that you may know,** in the subjunctive mood, indicates that John recognized that their knowing was conditional. Their confidence of having life depended on their response to the source of life. The word *hina* introduces a "purpose" clause. John wrote *in order that* they might know. He intended that his communities might be totally confident that they had **eternal life** as a reality, personal and corporate (**you** is plural). But this was contingent on realities beyond his control.

The phrase **to you who believe** translates a present participle. This stresses the necessity of ongoing faith: *to you who continue believing.* Believing **in the name of the Son of God** is more than an event. It may begin in a moment of trust, but it demands ongoing assent. When surrender to God happens, life and obedience must follow (Brooke 1912, 143).

There is a sequence of believing statements in ch 5 (vv 1, 5, 10, 13). With each the language shifts to stress new points. These four verses highlight the poetic parallelism and the development of faith. The Christian

believes that (*hoti*) **Jesus is the Christ** (v 1)
believes that (*hoti*) **Jesus is the Son of God** (v 5)
believes in (*eis*) **the Son of God** (v 10)
believe in (*eis*) **the name of the Son of God** (v 13)

Faith has an intellectual *content*. Christians accept as true *about* Jesus that he is the Christ/Son of God. Faith also has a relational dimension. It is *trust placed in a person*. The shift in vv 10, 13 emphasizes this nuance of personal trust (Jones 2009, 226; see Matt 18:6; Mark 9:42; John 14:1; Acts 24:24; 26:18).

John expands the statement that one believes in **the Son,** to believe also **in the name of the Son of God.** This may point to the use of "the name" in the technical sense found in Acts 5:41 (see the commentary on 1 John 3:23 and 3 John 7). To **believe in the name** is a typically Johannine construction (John 1:12; 2:23; 3:18; 1 John 3:23; 5:13). It implies complete personal surrender to the divine revelation in Christ (Hartman 1981, 520).

■ **14-15** John connects the Christians' assurance of eternal life with confidence in prayer. Our **confidence** (see the commentary on 2:28; 3:21; 4:17) that our prayers will be answered must not assume that God *must* do as we request. As we **ask** (lit. *request,* translated twice in v 16 as "pray"), our asking will first change us. John may employ the middle voice to mean to ask *for oneself* (Brown 1982, 609; Westcott 1952, 190). The text assumes that those asking will become more and more aligned with God's intentions (Haas, DeJonge, and Swellengrebel 1972, 125).

The point of praying is not just getting things from God, but getting "on the same page" with God. Prayer is not a technique by which we may gain just **anything** (lit. ***whatever we might ask***). Rather, it is a means of gaining intimacy with God. As we learn to **ask . . . according to his will,** we know God **hears us.** Surely the greatest benefit of praying is moving nearer to the heart of God. As we increasingly learn what God wants, we enter more fully into the joy of the answers **we have . . . asked of him** (Marshall 1978, 245). The instances of **we** (six times) and **us** (twice) reminds us that praying is done best in agreement with like-minded Christians.

Several verses in the Fourth Gospel strongly resemble vv 14-15. John 14:13 reports Jesus' promise, "I will do whatever you ask in my name." In 15:16 he assures that "the Father will give you whatever you ask in my name"; in 16:23, that "my Father will give you whatever you ask in my name." All these statements must be read with the key words of Jesus' last discourse. John 15:7 is foundational: "If you remain in me and my words remain in you, ask whatever you wish, and it will be given you." Christian prayer is always shaped by the words of the Lord and a healthy relationship with him.

John writes to the believing community: **If we know that he hears us . . . we know that we have what we asked of him.** Believers may have confidence that God hears them, because they together ask in harmony with God's will. What John promises is that those who sincerely seek the will of God in their lives will find it.

Many sincere believers misunderstand prayer in "Jesus' name." They imagine that a tag line at the end of their prayers somehow obligates God to deliver on their requests. In fact, praying in "Jesus' name" means asking consistent with the purposes of God working through Jesus, by the Spirit.

Praying **in the name** (v 13) is to ask **according to his will** (v 14), never contrary to it. Would any true child of God want anything other than God's will? Petitioning God **in the name** means that we accurately represent the *character* of Christ in all ways—his life, death, resurrection, and coming rule. Praying **in the name** affirms the *continuing presence* of Christ in the world by the Spirit, who helps us pray (Carver 1996, 81-89).

Misguided, magic-oriented asking achieves little more than frustration and spiritual anemia. Asking outside of God's will achieves nothing positive. When we pray in the name of Jesus we seek God's will. Only in this way may we move forward with clear assurance. God, who put it in our hearts to pray in this way, is at work enabling the answer. That is, **we have the request we have requested from him.**

■ **16** In this difficult verse, the question appears to continue to be with assurance related to our prayers. How does confidence in praying (v 14) affect our assurance of eternal life (v 13)? Is John saying that some objects of intercessory prayer will aid our confidence and others will not? Does he emphasize that prayer has its limits? What are the distinctions he wants us to recognize?

Is praying for a "brother committing a sin not leading to death" (NASB) a prayer we can voice with confidence (vv 14-15)? Is praying for one whose sin **leads to death** not a prayer we can pray with confidence? How can we know the future consequences of a particular sin? Do particularly heinous sins need more than intercession? How do we know we need not pray under such circumstances? Does John mean to suggest that we can never pray for such sinners or about such sins? Does John, on the other hand, suggest that our praying alone can secure divine forgiveness for the lesser sins of others without their praying?

John earlier stated his purpose for writing as that his readers might never sin (2:1). Here, however, he acknowledges the possibility that believers may sin. A **brother** or "sister" (NRSV) may **commit a sin** (*hamartanonta hamartian*, lit. **sinning a sin,** an LXX way of speaking; Brown 1982, 611) and need correction. The present participle **sinning** may suggest falling into a sinful pattern, not just committing an isolated sin (Bruce 1970, 124; Blaney 1967, 402; Brooke 1912, 146-47).

John affirms that Christians are obliged to pray for each other—**he should pray.** Asking God in behalf of another is especially warranted when a fellow Christian struggles or makes overtly sinful choices. God's children are family, entrusted with the gospel, and responsible for each other. The family language (**brother**) probably refers to the believers of the Johannine churches, as distinguished from the secessionists (2:19). This obligation to pray for fellow believers is contrasted with other sinners for whom we are apparently not obligated to pray. The tone is similar to that of Jesus in John 17:9, "I am not praying for the world."

The difference turns on what John means by **a sin that does not lead to death** (*hamartian mē pros thanaton*) in contrast to **a sin that leads to death** (*hamartia pros thanaton*). A few OT passages link sin to physical death (Num 18:22; Deut 22:26; see also *Jub.* 21:22; 26:34; 33:13, 18). The second phrase seems to suggest a situation in which the sinner is beyond the reach of divine grace. This explains why John does not require his readers to pray for such people. But can that truly be the meaning? Is anyone beyond God's grace?

Is it possible that John has a specific sin in view? Some have appealed to the traditional Roman Catholic distinction between "mortal" and "venial" sins. Are there specific sins that, when committed, release other Christians from praying for such persons?

John's meaning is problematic. The context suggests the arena of prayer that is in God's will (vv 14-15). Christians are urged to understand that it is not God's will that any should perish (2 Pet 3:9). Thus to pray for someone to come to repentance would seem to be to pray within God's will.

Bruce has suggested that, since the letter battles the dangers of incarnation-denying docetic Christianity, the secessionist opponents are in view here. The **sin that leads to death** is then understood as false christological beliefs, a *heretical position in which one chooses to persist*. Leaving the fellowship of the Johannine Christians was viewed as abandonment of the group within which eternal life was found (Bruce 1970, 125).

Those who had left the Johannine community (identified as "antichrists" in 2:18 and 2 John 7) deliberately chose a path of separation. This apostasy from the true faith seems supported by the appeal to "keep yourselves from idols" (1 John 5:21). This may be understood as being on guard against false teaching (Bultmann 1973, 87, 90)—ideological idolatry. Stubbornly remaining in their false beliefs opposed to John's teachings meant they would die in their sins. Thus, the secessionists were committing **the sin that leads to death** (Jones 2009, 230; see John 8:24; van der Watt 2007, 63). This coheres with other passages in 1 John that make spiritual death a result of *persisting* in sin, demonstrated by a failure to love (3:14), and a resultant denial of Christ (5:12).

Thus there was the prospect of help for the Johannine Christian (the **brother**) but not for those who continued outside the Johannine circle (Brown 1982, 611). John's churches were discouraged from even praying for the secessionists, to leave their fate to God.

The **sin that leads to death** for John referred to sins that were incompatible with being children of God (Marshall 1978, 247). These sins would include denying that Jesus is the Christ, the Son of God (2:22-23); refusing to obey God's commands (2:4); loving the world (2:15-17); and hating fellow believers (2:9, 11; 3:15; 4:20).

Calvin understood the sin unto death as referring not to "a partial fall, or the transgression of a single commandment, but apostasy, men alienating themselves completely from God" (1959, 311; see Matt 7:6; Rom 1:28).

Although John assumed his first-century readers would know his meaning, firm conclusions elude us in the twenty-first century. Scholarly discussion offers a variety of views as to the reference of **the sin unto death.** Jones lists eight (2009, 231).

The phrase may have been intended to demarcate clearly between the remaining Johannine Christians and those who had broken away from them, as noted above. In any case, no legitimate permission to cease praying for another in the modern era can be derived from this text.

That John uses the Greek word *pros* (**to**) here seems to suggest a "death" that has not yet occurred, since *pros* can carry the sense of "tending toward" (Jones 2009, 231; Liddell 1996, 1497). Thus, John's intention cannot have been to prohibit his original audience from praying for those already physically dead.

■ **17** This verse equates **unrighteousness** (**wrongdoing**) and **sin.** Extending the analogy, if all unrighteousness is sin, then righteousness would manifest itself as an absence of sin. Although only briefly mentioned here, John's assumption is clear. We can, if we submit to the will of God, stop the practice of sinning. Thus, praying for that to happen in the lives of others is right and expected—**he should pray** for the **brother** (v 16). Sin may still intrude, but it need not control the Christian. Even if sin and the child of God occasionally meet, they cannot live together in harmony (Akin 2001, 212).

A few manuscripts omit the negative Greek particle (*ou*), thus changing v 17 to **there is a sin unto death,** bringing it into agreement with v 16*b*. But the textual variant here only highlights the problematic wording. Early scribes, like later interpreters, were hard pressed to make complete sense of the passage.

FROM THE TEXT

Praying Urgently for Others

The **assurance** of praying in God's **will** is preceded by the spiritual certainty of knowing **that you have eternal life** (v 13). One who has believed **in the name of the Son of God** (v 13) is well-positioned to pray. The **assurance** also stands on the foundation of God's purposes—**his will** (v 14). Prayer for those who struggle spiritually is a high calling and within God's will. Our prayers cannot override the contrary choices of others, but intercessory prayer may soften their hearts.

Sin and Death and Life

That there is a **sin that leads to death** (v 16), one that is beyond being prayed for, is a frightening thought. Although the complete sense of what the text means escapes us, the warning is clear. Sin is lethal; and some sins kill more quickly than others. No matter what the speed, the road of rebellion against God always has death as its final destination. But letting the nudges of the Spirit, aided by the prayers of God's people, draw us godward increasingly leads to life.

The distinction between the sins for which the reader is urged to pray versus those for which prayer is not required has some interesting historical developments. Concerning the "sin unto death" Augustine especially focused on ending one's life in "perversity." Oecumenius similarly understood that only sins not repented of lead to death (Bray 2000, 226-27). In the medieval period there developed a distinction between mortal sins (confession to another was needed) and venial sins (private requests for forgiveness were deemed adequate, Lieu 1991, 113).

D. Things We Know (5:18-21)

BEHIND THE TEXT

Nearly half of the eleven NT occurrences of the phrase **the evil one** (v 18) appear in 1 John (2:13, 14; 3:12; 5:18, 19; see Matt 5:37; 6:13; 13:19, 38; John 17:15; Eph 6:16; 2 Thess 3:3). In the Gospel passages the phrase appears in discourses by Jesus. Two instances in Paul likely reflect that use. The frequency of the phrase in 1 John suggests that the Johannine community closely identified with this memory of Jesus.

The warning against **idols** (v 21) demonstrates a long-standing tradition in the Hebrew Bible. The prophets warned strenuously against idolatry, although their calls often met with mixed results. Warnings against idols appear as early as the Ten Commandments (Exod 20:4), and numerous times thereafter in the OT ("idol" thirty-seven times, "idols" one hundred fifty-seven times, and "idolatry" four times).

Although explicit NT references to idolatry are more limited. There are twenty-seven instances for all three terms combined. But the teaching remains clear and consistent: God's people must never substitute lesser things for God. John may echo the language of idols found in the sharp warnings of Rev 2—3. Those chapters resemble Paul's urgent appeals to the Corinthians, especially on the subject of "food offered to idols" (1 Cor 8:1, 4, 7, 10; 12:2; Rev 2:14, 20; 9:20).

IN THE TEXT

■ **18** **We know** is a favorite Johannine phrase, appearing in seventeen verses (2:3, 5, 18; 3:1, 2, 10, 14, 16, 19, 24; 4:13, 16; 5:2, 15, 18, 19, 20). The three closely spaced instances here (vv 18, 19, 20) give these verses a rhythmic cadence (Burge 1996, 216).

John's ethical concern is restated in summary fashion as he concludes with a bold proclamation of deliverance from the oppressive power of sin: **anyone born of God does not continue to sin** (3:6, 9). The practice of sin is broken by the abiding results of the new birth (*gegennēmenos*, a perfect participle) not by some later experience (Brooke 1912, 148). John allows for no "sinning religion" here.

The three verses are all in the present tense (*ouch hamartanei*: **he is not continuing to sin**; *tērei*: **he is keeping**; and *ouch haptetai*: **he is not touching**). They suggest that freedom from sin is an ongoing and relational matter (Smith 1991, 136). Christians do not habitually sin. They do not live in sin (Burge 1996, 216). But living without ongoing sin is not automatic. It requires meaningful moral decisions (Smith 1991, 136). Not sinning is a divine and human joint enterprise.

The sense in the middle of the verse is unclear. **The one who was born of God** seems also to be the same one who **keeps him safe**. We might expect the text to say, "The one who was born of God, God keeps that one safe" (Schnackenburg 1992, 253). Several interpreters understand **the one who was born** (*gennētheis*) **of God** to refer to Jesus (Strecker 1996, 208; Marshall 1978, 252; Bultmann 1973, 88-90).

The grammar, however, seems rather to indicate that the one **born of God**—that is, the Christian—is also the one who keeps safe. But what does that mean?

Some manuscripts attempt to solve this enigma by reading **himself** rather than **him**. This would call for the translation **keeps himself safe**. Neither variant reading is fully satisfying.

Regardless, John's meaning seems clear enough: Christians are protected, whether by God/Christ or by themselves. The issue is much the same. We can protect ourselves only because we have been born of God (Brown 1982, 622).

The power of God is greater than **the evil one**. This is a given. Jesus said, "The prince of this world . . . has no hold on me" (John 14:30). Yet many Christians live as if Satan has the upper hand in their redeemed lives. Evil is real. But it is severely limited by the sovereign permission of

God. Evil cannot go further than God allows. Indeed, Jesus prayed for this very protection for his followers and their future converts (John 17:15).

John makes a bold statement: **the evil one does not touch him.** The promise is confusing at first glance. All of us have felt at some time or other the "touch" of evil upon our lives. But **touch** (*haptetai*) here has more to do with contact that clings—that holds on and won't let go. This same verb appears in the admonition of the risen Jesus to Mary Magdalene not to hold on to him as before, since he was ascending to God (John 20:17). The verb can refer to binding relationships like marriage (1 Cor 7:1). Thus, John seems to say that the one born of God cannot be held fast, bound in the clutches of evil. The Christian and **the evil one** have no sustained relationship. Being children of God excludes lesser allegiances.

■ **19** John again declares **we know.** We have an experiential certainty, given by God. It is not "insider" secret knowledge, not esoteric super-spiritual insight only a few can fathom (as gnostics thought). Those who are truly from God are kept safe. They have the assurance of sufficient knowledge.

John's readers **know** they **are children of God.** At the same time John makes the staggering claim that **the whole world is under the control of the evil one.** This is hyperbolic language. When John says **the whole world** he recalls the dualistic worldview in which the spirit of antichrist stands in hostile opposition to Johannine Christians (see 2:15-16). John does not, of course, mean that every last portion of the globe and all of those on it are being manipulated by satanic forces. His point is clearly that the true **children of God** are **safe** (v 18), despite those who oppose them. Even now they are being kept from **the evil one.**

■ **20** How may one know the truth? Only as it is revealed to us from God: **the Son of God has come and has given us understanding.** John's confidence in the ethical security of his communities (v 19) has a christological basis, which is carefully and clearly constructed.

Truth exists, and it is knowable. Truth resides in, and is communicated through, a person—**him who is true.** A clear mind, **understanding** (*dianoian*), comes from the Father through **the Son of God.** The perfect tense of the Greek verb translated **has given** suggests that God *continues to open* our minds to more truth in Christ.

The truth can be lived in by ordering our lives by revealed truths *about* God. But John claims more. The faith to which he points involves also *living in right relationship with the author of the truth.* That is, **we are in him who is true,** namely **we are in . . . Jesus Christ.** When we enter into relationship with God's **Son,** we enter into the truth. Truth is uniquely incarnate in Christ. But truth also becomes incarnate in those believers who trust in Christ. Receiving this incarnated truth restores us to the knowledge of the one **true God,** whom to know is **eternal life** (John 17:3).

The phrase **He is the true God** is ambiguous. Is John referring to the Father or Jesus as **the true God?** He translates *houtos* (***this one***). Its immediate antecedent is clearly **Jesus Christ.** Both phrases **him who is true** and **his Son** are in the dative case, confirming this identification.

After careful analysis, Jones agrees that a strong case exists for linking **the true God** and **eternal life** with the **Son** (Jones 2009, 235). Thus, this text makes one of the NT's most lofty affirmations of the divine nature of Jesus. Jesus is **the true God,** who is **eternal life.** This bold closing assertion in 1 John recalls a similar statement in John 20:28—Thomas's declaration of the risen Jesus, "My Lord and my God."

John was striving mightily to insure that his readers grasped how secure they were in knowing God through Christ. Such knowledge linked them intimately with God and all who belong to God. In such a relationship, their present condition and future destiny was **eternal life.**

John was persuaded that the Christian's assurance is the presence of the heavenly Christ living out the character of the earthly Jesus in the daily life of those who are **in his Son Jesus Christ.** Assurance is a continuing theme throughout the letter. This is not presumption since it bears witness to him who **is the true God and eternal life.**

■ **21** The epistle closes by repeating some of the themes with which it began. John employs family language—**Dear children**—in his personal benediction. Accompanying this warm conclusion, however, is a clear reminder that compromise is deadly. John's pastoral concern drives him to speak words of assurance, but also of caution. He commands the readers: **keep yourselves** (an imperative verb form).

One's response to God is necessarily personal; no one can obey *for* another. Yet our response to God happens *among* others. John is, like all true ministers, both pastor and prophet. He nurtures, affirms, and loves. But he loves his audience too much to gloss over the dangers they face.

Without warning, his final sentence mentions the threat of **idols.** He offers no explanation or elaboration as to the specific dangers his readers face. His words may warn against sin generally or perhaps even against literal idolatrous images.

But in their present context the meaning of **idols** probably summarizes his explicit warnings throughout the letter against the secessionists and their false Christology (Smith 1991, 137; Marshall 1978, 255-56; Bultmann 1973, 90; Bruce 1970, 128). Thus, John's admonition sets before his hearers the clear choice between the incarnate, crucified, risen, and reigning Christ, who gives **eternal life** (v 20), and any counterfeit (Hills 1989, 285-310).

With this final focus on Jesus as the Christ who is the unique revelation of God, the writing ends. A minority of manuscripts conclude the epistle in a liturgically appropriate way, with a clear, final ***amen.***

FROM THE TEXT

Redeemed So the Practice of Sin Is Broken

Habitual sinning ceases for those truly born of God. Genuine Christian faith is manifested in a life of *obedience to the known will of God*. Christian life cannot coexist with habitual disobedience to God's law.

One's definition of sin is important here. Some define "sin" as any lack of perfect conformity to the law of God, known or unknown. Even unintended mistakes and subpar actions, because one doesn't know any better, would fall within this definition.

Wesleyans believe there is a great difference between missing the mark due to ignorance and missing the mark due to disobedience. Reformed theologians define both as sin. John Wesley, however, defined "sin, properly so called" as "a voluntary transgression of a known law" of God (1978, 11:396). The resurrected Christ empowers believers to obey. Through the indwelling presence of the Holy Spirit, believers may be victorious over sin. That is, sin defined as deliberate rebellion or self-conscious disobedience. Neither Wesley nor Wesleyans profess "sinless perfection." But Scripture holds out the promise of "perfect love" (1 John 4:18). On this basis, Wesleyans refuse to minimize the possibilities of grace, including God's power to enable believers not to sin (see 1 John 2:1-2; 3:3-6, 9).

Redeeming the World

The **whole world . . . under the control of the evil one** (v 19) seems to leave Christians in a dilemma. If evil truly controls our world, it might seem tempting to abandon the world as hopelessly lost. The hyperbolic language in this section could unnecessarily move us to pessimism about the world.

But the larger biblical narrative demonstrates that God is at work to heal not only individuals but communities. God is earnestly at work to repair *in the world* what sin has broken. The world is not headed for ultimate destruction, but for restoration. Since this is true, surely Christians now should be co-laborers with God, working to bring healing to the world God created and loves. Jesus did, after all, pray, "Our Father . . . your kingdom come, your will be done on earth" (Matt 6:9-10).

Shaped by Christ or Shaping Our Own Idols?

The closing moment of the epistle (v 21) is not a carelessly offered afterthought or only a doxological custom. It represents the core issues of the entire letter.

In every age some people seek to *reshape Christ* into their preferred image by ignoring or distorting fundamental biblical claims by and about him. But the aim of 1 John, indeed of all Scripture, is that *Christ should shape us* into his image. First John presents Christ in clear terms as divine ("Word of life . . . life . . . eternal life," 1:1-2) and fully human ("come in the flesh," 4:2-3; 2 John 7). To make other of him, choosing only part of the written record, is to sell him, and ourselves, short. God has a transformed life in view for us as we embrace Christ for all that he is.

The demand for undivided devotion to Christ calls forth strongly. If Jesus is to be truly Lord, then all else must be either placed in a lower priority or renounced altogether. To do less is to live sub-Christian lives. To place God at the center of our life, and thus grant to Christ the divine and incarnate Son our supreme allegiance, and to live daily in harmony with the promptings of God's Spirit, is to live a life of Christian holiness. Holiness develops naturally for persons who have found the joy of willing and wanting only one thing, to know and do the will of God by an uncompromising devotion to Jesus Christ.

2 JOHN

INTRODUCTION

A. Authorship, Date, Provenance, Audience, Occasion, Purpose, Sociological/Cultural Issues, and Textual History

See discussion of these issues in the Introduction chapter of the commentary.

B. Literary Features

See the sidebar "Greco-Roman Letters" in Literary Features in the Introduction chapter. This brief personal letter includes the customary salutation from the writer ("the elder," v 1). The opening lines name the recipients ("the chosen lady and her children"). The author expresses a wish to "visit" (v 12) and ends with traditional "greetings" (v 13).

As in 1 John, a significant literary feature is the use of relational, especially family, language. The elder uses affectionate terms ("chosen lady," v 1; "dear lady," v 5; and "chosen sister," v 13). Believers are called "children" (vv 1, 4, 13). The divine characters mentioned include the "Father" (vv 3, 4, 9) and the "Son" (vv 3, 9). The absence of "brother" is a bit curious. It occurs thirteen times in 1 John and three times in 3 John. No personal names appear in 2 John, although the recipients seem well known to the elder, who remains unnamed.

C. Theological Themes

Numerous interpreters understand the phrase "chosen lady" (v 1) as a symbolic personification for the church (see Jones 2009, 251; Thomas 2004, 40; Painter 2002, 333; Culpepper 1998, 276; Strecker 1996, 220; Marshall 1978, 60). The OT sometimes refers to Israel with similar personified language. Jerusalem was compared to an abandoned child, left to die by the side of the road (Ezek 16:1-14). God's love for straying Israel parallels Hosea's marriage to his unfaithful wife. Paul saw husbands and wives as illustrations of Christ and the church (Eph 5:21-33). In Rev 21:2 the New Jerusalem is a "bride." There is ample precedent for symbolic language describing the people of God in female terms.

It is further possible that the "chosen lady" was a woman who provided the space for a house church. In Acts, Lydia hosts Paul and his associates (Acts 16:11-15). Priscilla and Aquila ministered to Apollos out of their home (Acts 18:24-26). John Wesley considered the Greek *kyria* ("lady") to be a proper name—Kyria (1983, n.p.), although no modern scholar embraces this view. Still, it is plausible that the elder wrote to an important female house-church host.

D. Hermeneutical Issues

Who is "the elder" (*presbyteros*, v 1; also 3 John 1)? With the article, "*the* elder" has no parallel in the NT. Anarthrous forms (with no article—"elder" or "elders") appear frequently. In the Gospels and the early part of Acts, "elders" refers to *Jewish leaders*. Midway through Acts, the term begins to refer to *leaders in churches* (Acts 14:23; 15:2, 4, 6, 22, 23; 16:4; 20:17; 21:18).

The latter elders were appointed to manage the affairs of the church (1 Tim 5:17; Titus 1:5) and lead in ministry (1 Tim 4:14; Jas 5:14; 1 Pet 5:1). There is no first-century evidence that elders in one church had jurisdiction over other congregations. The title later assumed this supervisory force (Bruce 1970, 144 n. 2 citing Irenaeus). But second-century church order should not be read back into a first-century text.

Any discussion of 2 John must address the issue of hospitality to traveling ministers. The theological and practical significance is large. Welcoming itinerant preachers with lodging and food made the hosts partners in their work (3 John 6). Conversely, hospitality was to be withheld from those espousing an aberrant theology (2 John 10-11; see the sidebar "Itinerant Teachers").

Major interpretive issues attach to "antichrist" (v 7). The elder's concern was not over a cosmic, larger-than-life future personification of evil. Antichrist activity was already evident *in his own time* (see the sidebar "Antichrist" at 1 John 2:18 and the commentary on 1 John 4:1, 3). These "antichrists" who taught contrary to the gospel traditions of John were alive and well on planet earth in first-century western Asia Minor.

COMMENTARY

VI. WELCOMES AND WARNINGS: 2 JOHN 1-13

A. Greetings and Relationships (1-3)

BEHIND THE TEXT

This letter combines family language (**chosen lady and her children,** v 1; and "the children of your chosen sister," v 13) with pastoral concern. While personal in tone, the letter obviously addresses a church. Some had left the fellowship (1 John 2:19). Their departure occasioned sharp warnings about remaining faithful to **the truth** (five times in vv 1-4; see the sidebar "Truth" at 1:6).

There were "many" (v 7) troubling opponents, apparently recruiting others for "wicked work" (v 11). Any such person was "the deceiver and the antichrist" (v 7). Their exact identity is unclear. But their primary offense was a faulty Christology, one that denied Jesus as having come "in the flesh" (v 7).

Some of the secessionists were itinerant preachers hoping for material support from the Johannine churches. The elder is adamant: "Do not take him into your house or welcome him" (v 10). Traveling teachers depended largely on others for lodging and meals. The *Didache* addresses this specifically.

Itinerant Teachers

Itinerant ministry largely defines the missionary journeys of the Apostle Paul. He and his co-workers traveled throughout the northern Mediterranean region. At times they received lodging and material support from Christian patrons. Concerns for safety and financial realities were factors in this practice. Staying in the homes of trusted friends reduced expenses and the risks associated with public establishments (see Acts 16:15; 18:2-3; and Phlm 22).

Providing food and lodging to traveling ministers was open to abuse. The elder demanded discernment about who was to be extended hospitality. Food, housing, and money should support legitimate Christian ministries, not encourage false teachers. If travelers stayed more than two or three days, or took more than bread from the home, or asked for money, they were to be regarded as false prophets (*Did.* 11; Koenig 1992, 299-301).

IN THE TEXT

■ **1** Who is this **elder**? No doubt his identity was known to the original recipients of the letter. But it is not so apparent to us. **The elder** (*presbyteros*) is a singular title, used only twice in the NT, here and 3 John 1. It may simply mean an older person (Rom 9:12; 1 Tim 5:2; 1 Pet 5:5). It also identifies Jewish Sanhedrin leaders (Matt 16:21; Acts 6:12) and local leaders in the churches (Acts 11:30; 20:17; 1 Tim 5:1, 17, 19; 1 Pet 5:1).

In 1 Peter, some Christian leaders are called "elders." The difference here is the exclusive sense, **the elder** (emphasis added), perhaps a claim of unique authority. No NT text reports a single, supervisory elder with power to insert himself into the affairs of another congregation. The term in 2 John and 3 John seems to imply a tradition-bearer, whose reputation and influence were significant (Brown 1982, 648-51).

The letter addresses **the chosen lady and her children.** Was the elder writing to a female recipient and her household? Why was she the object of his special spiritual concern? The term **lady** (*kyria*) is the feminine form of the word used in polite first-century Greco-Roman society to address a man as "sir" (*kyrios*, lit. **lord**).

Or was **the elder** using figurative language? If so, he addressed the church corporately as a personified female and used family imagery to describe the members of the church (Thomas 2004, 40; Strecker 1996, 220; Lieu 1991, 93; Brown 1982, 652; Boice 1979, 161; Marshall 1978, 60; Haas, DeJonge, and Swellengrebel 1972, 138; Brooke 1912, 167-70).

Or might both applications be in view? Bruce leans toward a corporate interpretation but leaves the matter open (1970, 137). Whether **chosen lady** refers to a church or an individual, or both, cannot be known with certainty (Earle 1984, 110).

The recipient of the letter is described as **chosen** (*eklektēi*) or "elect" (ESV, KJV, NKJV, NRSV). The language of election suggests the recipients were a church.

Election

Being elect indicates a covenantal relationship with God based on grace. One does not earn election. God takes the initiative. Election is the offer of intimacy with God. Israel understood its relationship to God as being an elect *nation:* "For you are a people holy to the Lord your God. The Lord your God has chosen you out of all the peoples on the face of the earth to be his people, his treasured possession" (Deut 7:6; see 14:2; Pss 105:6; 135:4; Isa 41:8-9; 44:1; 49:7).

Prominent *individuals* were "chosen" (e.g., David in Ps 89:3; Moses and Aaron in Ps 105:26). God designated kings of his choosing for Israel and Judah (1 Sam 10:24; 16:1; 1 Kgs 8:16). Even *places* like Jerusalem and the temple were divinely "chosen" (1 Kgs 8:44, 48; 11:13, 32; 2 Chr 6:6, 34, 38).

In the NT *Jesus* is God's chosen (Luke 9:35; 23:35; 1 Pet 1:20; 2:4, 6). The *disciples* are the chosen of Jesus (John 6:70; 13:18; 15:16, 19). In eschatological passages "the elect" appear often (Matt 24:22, 24, 31; Mark 13:20, 22, 27). Christians and churches are the elect of God (Eph 1:1; Col 3:12; 1 Thess 1:4; 1 Pet 1:1-2; 2:9; 5:13; Patrick 1992, 434-41; Shogren 1992, 434-44; Mendenhall 1962, 76-82).

The **lady,** understood as an individual, could have been an influential patroness, who hosted the house church. Three times in vv 4-5 the elder uses second person *singular* pronouns, suggesting he writes to an individual. In the balance of the letter, he employs second person *plural* verbs and pronouns to address his readers (ten times in vv 6, 8, 10, and 12).

The lady's faithful **children** (*tekna*, see vv 4, 13) are also addressed. The term occurs fourteen times in 1 John and once in 3 John. The **elder** shares the same Christian faith as the recipients of the letter and **all who know the truth.** The word **know** (*egnōkotes*, in the perfect tense) indicates a *past* event with *continuing* effect—***all who came to know truth in the past and still know it.***

■ **2** The **truth** (*aletheian*) was highly valued in Johannine circles (see the sidebar "Truth" at 1 John 1:6). The word occurs twenty-one times in the letters and twenty-four times in the Fourth Gospel. By comparison there are only eleven instances in all the Synoptic Gospels. Paul used the word freely (more than fifty times).

In 2 John **truth** is *the means by which* Christians love one another (v 1). It also refers to *content one knows*. The **truth** is personified—it **lives** in Christians. Characteristics of God, **grace, mercy and peace,** are **with us in truth** (v 3). Also, **truth** is relational and progressive, something we can "walk" in (v 4).

The present participle **lives (*remains*)** in us refers literally to *the presently residing in us truth.* A *formerly* resident truth would be inadequate. A stagnant, static "truth" also fails. Truth must *continue* in us, repeatedly "grasped anew as a gift" (Bultmann 1973, 108). The elder's reference to **the truth, which lives in us and will be with us forever** may echo teaching about the Spirit in the Fourth Gospel. There Jesus assures his followers that the Spirit "lives with you and will be in you" (John 14:17).

■ **3** The greeting is rich: **Grace** (*charis*), **mercy** (*eleos*), and **peace** (*eirēnē*) assemble prominent divine gifts. In all of Paul's letters "grace" and "peace" appear together. **Grace** and **peace** combine typical Hellenistic and Jewish greetings (Strecker 1996, 227). Elsewhere "mercy" also appears in two of Paul's Pastoral Letters (1 Tim 1:2; 2 Tim 1:2).

Grace, mercy and peace are qualities of God and God's intention for his people. **Grace** is a distinctive Christian nuance to the typical salutation of a Greco-Roman letter. The normal word for "greeting" (*charein*) was revised in Christian correspondence to "grace" (*charis*). **Mercy** (*eleos*) conveys biblical concepts of compassion and steadfast love. **Peace** (*eirēnē*, expressing the Hebrew *shalom*) is a traditional blessing for health and wholeness.

Familiar images appear. God is **Father. Jesus Christ** is **Son.** It is surprising that the Holy Spirit is not mentioned in 2 John, given the thematic links between 2 John and the Fourth Gospel (v 2 and John 14:17; v 5 and John 13:34-35; v 6 and John 14:23; and v 12 and John 15:11; 16:24). "Spirit" appears often in 1 John (3:24; 4:2, 6, 13; 5:6, 8).

But the elder's language may imply the presence of the Spirit. He writes of **truth . . . with us** (v 2) and of **grace, mercy and peace . . . with us.** This emphasis agrees with the role of the Spirit in the Fourth Gospel (14:17; 15:26; 16:13). So the Holy Spirit may be *quietly* present in 2 John. The letter does not present **truth** as simply *information* to be believed, but an abiding *presence* that transforms lives. The **truth** is *relational* and *dynamic*—it "lives in us" (v 2). As with the Spirit, the truth will be lived out, causing us to be "walking in the truth" (v 4; see Spirit in Theological Themes in the Introduction to 1 John).

The phrase **the Father's Son** (*tou huiou tou patros*) is uniquely worded but consistent with John's point in v 9 (Bruce 1970, 138). Painter calls the phrase distinctively Johannine (2002, 342), although the precise Greek construction appears nowhere else in the NT. The elder emphasizes the Father/Son relationship in language intended to counter opponents, who tried to separate the earthly Jesus from the heavenly Son of God (Haas, DeJonge, and Swellengrebel 1972, 141). In this way, John's salutation prepares for the warning in vv 7-11.

FROM THE TEXT

Life's Important Relationships

The author is **the elder** (v 1). His seniority probably referred to his age, maturity in the faith, and leadership status. Modern people undervalue a life lived well and the integrity of a long obedience in the same direction. As the elder neared the end of life, his eyes were fixed firmly on God, the church, and life's rich relationships. This is true power!

Women in the Life of the Church

The term **lady** (v 1, 5) conveys honor to females. If this **lady** was the shepherd of a house church, it affirms women's role in ministry. Adam Clarke suggested:

> The epistle was sent to some eminent Christian matron . . . who was probably *deaconess* of the Church [and] . . . likely had a Church at her house, or at whose house the apostles and traveling evangelists frequently preached, and were entertained. (Clarke n.d., 936)

Even if the elder was merely using feminine imagery as an analogy for the church, it dignifies the status of women. That the church is compared to a godly woman emphasizes the importance of the traditional feminine virtues of nurture, protection, and healing touch.

Children Are Valuable

The young in age or in faith must be high on the list of priorities for any church. The **children** (v 1) here may refer to actual "little ones" (Mark 10:14-16). The reference may also be to children in the faith, recent converts needing to be closely tied to **the truth** (vv 1, 2).

Prayer Is Intimate

The phrase **the Father's Son** (v 3) recalls Jesus' address to God as "Father" (in Mark 14:36, transliterating and translating the Aramaic *Abba*, as also in Rom 8:15 and Gal 4:6; Ashton 1992, 7-8). Likewise, the divine voice at both Jesus' baptism (Matt 3:17; Mark 1:11; Luke 3:22) and Transfiguration (Matt 17:5; Mark 9:7; Luke 9:35) called him "Son." As we pray, we enter an intimate conversation.

Truth Lives in Persons

Biblical faith is placed in **Father** and **Son**. As a result, God, the author of truth, lives in us. This faith enables a growing relationship based on an enlarging body of truth that is **with us forever** (v 2). God's truth continues to live within us as we continue to be obedient. The *Shema* (Deut 6:3) reminds us that true "hearing" requires faithful "heeding."

B. Joy Because of Obedience (4-6)

IN THE TEXT

■ **4** Letters, and those who delivered them, provided significant connection between separated Christians. Here, such communication evoked **great joy.** The phrase **has given me,** probably a divine passive (see the sidebar at 1 John 1:2), implies that God was the source of the elder's **joy.** The NT often identifies the experience of **joy** as having a divine origin (John 15:11; 17:13; Acts 13:52; 1 Thess 1:6).

That **some** were living in obedience to **the truth** may indicate that not all were (Burge 2002, 233; Haas, DeJonge, and Swellengrebel 1972, 142). The phrase at least indicates that some were wavering (Jones 2009, 256). The community's situation, including conflicts with Diotrephes (3 John 9-10), made it untenable to claim that "all your children" were "walking in truth" (Strecker 1996, 228). Bruce, however, contends that the phrase refers only to those whom the elder had met. It implies nothing about the obedience or lack thereof of others (1970, 139). But the elder's wording seems to express a pastoral concern that some may shy away from **the truth.**

Their **walking** (in the present tense) depicts an ongoing and relational experience of **truth.** To walk **in truth** or "in the light" (1 John 1:7) is to walk in the character of God. This imagery has OT precedents (Prov 4:18; Isa 2:5; for Qumran parallels see 1QS 3:20; 5:10; Vermes 1997, 101, 104). In the Johannine writings *peripateō* is used to refer to both literal and figurative walking (Ebel 1978, 943-45). Most often it symbolizes spiritual faithfulness (John 8:12; 12:35; 1 John 1:7; 2:6).

■ **5** The phrase **dear lady** addresses again "the chosen lady" (v 1). As before (v 1), it may address the church symbolically (Marshall 1978, 66).

Although **dear** has no warrant in the Greek, it reflects the respectful tone that *kyria* intends, much like the English "ma'am."

The command to love was **not a new** one. It recalls Jesus' words, "This is my command: love each other," in John 15:12 and 17. The elder varies the language by using **we** (twice in v 5 and again in v 6). This makes it clear that he situates himself among those who **love one another.**

The Fourth Gospel echoes in v 5 in the words **from the beginning.** At times in the letters, "beginning" recalls Gen 1:1, the origin of the cosmos. More often it refers to the early days of the gospel among the Johannine community (see on 1 John 1:1; 2:13, 14; and possibly 3:8). They had heard the command to love from John. That tradition continued to call for Christlike behavior, selfless **love** for **one another.**

■ **6** A paraphrase that captures the stress in **this is love** would be: ***this is what real love looks like. Real love*** means walking "according to His commandments" (NASB). It is the elder's express desire that his readers walk obediently. The verb translated **we walk** is in the subjunctive mood. This was John's purpose for writing, but the walking remained their decision. Discipleship is never forced.

The elder moves from the singular "command" in v 5 to the plural **commands** in v 6. Obeying the greatest commandment, to love God supremely and to love others as ourselves (Matt 22:36-40), inevitably leads to obeying the other **commands.** We develop a holy life by our choices *after* we have first settled the larger question of our love for God. Divine love flows into us, cleanses us, and leads us to increased conformity to God's will.

There is a cyclical aspect to God's love. The circle begins with God, whose love cannot remain passive but reaches out. This pursuing love sent Christ, who fully incarnated the Father's love. As that divine, incarnate love finds lodging within us, we are called into Christian community. In the faith community, and in all our relationships, we are enabled to embody God's love.

Transformed by divine love, we are unsatisfied simply to bask in its glow. Like the God who pursued us, we seek to serve others in tangible ways—**obedience to his commands.** All truly loving acts in the world have their origin in God, the sole source of all love. When we experience God's love, we find it natural to return it in praise to God.

Obeying God's commands is "walking in the truth" (v 4), **obedience,** and "love" (v 5). Such love is not vague sentiment; it is tied to ethics. Authentic **love** changes us. We think differently, experiencing a new mind (Rom 12:1-2) that revolutionizes our approach to truth and reshapes our worldview. Valuing truth in *concept* leads to truth in *action*.

As redeemed persons we *think* in new ways. We *feel* more deeply. We *choose* more wisely. Yet, the conditional nature of our spiritual relationship remains. The elder again uses a verb in the subjunctive mood—**you walk** (*peripatēte*). Walking in obedience was the elder's intent for his readers, but he knew that the way they walked depended on each person's daily choices.

FROM THE TEXT

Discipleship Is Daily

Jesus' call "follow me" to his first would-be disciples was an invitation to walk with him (Matt 4:19; Mark 1:17). Amos asked, "Do two walk together unless they have agreed to do so?" (3:3). Discipleship calls for putting one foot in front of the other again and again, without quitting. Discipleship requires keeping our eyes on Christ, going where he goes, not running ahead, not lagging behind, but endeavoring always to "keep in step with the Spirit" (Gal 5:25).

Discipleship Is Walking with Others

Jesus called diverse followers and expected them to walk in harmony. Matthew was a tax collector, an agent of Rome. Simon the Zealot, whose radical political leanings attached to his name, resented anyone associated with Rome. What fellowship challenges did those two have? Simon Peter, when he didn't know what to do or say, blurted out something, and plunged ahead. John seemed more willing to listen and reflect. Following Jesus didn't change their personalities, but Jesus expected them to nurture their mutual fellowship.

Our Grasp of Truth Grows

The **truth** (v 4) is not a body of knowledge swallowed whole at the beginning of the Christian journey. Granted, one must know something of the gospel to begin the journey. But the fullness of divine truth will only be known, ultimately, in God's presence in the kingdom to come (see 1 Cor 13:12). Still, the truth becomes more and more a reality in our lives as we walk in obedience to what we know.

C. Warnings to Enable Faithful Walking (7-11)

IN THE TEXT

■ **7** The elder warns of **deceivers** who are **antichrist**. These two labels identify one and the same group (Burge 1996, 233-34; Haas, DeJonge, and Swellengrebel 1972, 145). These opponents were **many**, indicating a high level of threat. These were not cosmic figures, but human adversaries (Strecker 1996, 237). Along with 1 Tim 4:1, this verse points out the demonic character of false doctrine (Böcher 1993, 100).

The reference in 1 John 2:18 to "many antichrists" offers a near parallel to v 7. What were the distinguishing marks of the **deceivers**? The word **deceivers** (*planoi*) may identify them as wanderers (Heb 11:38) from the truth (Jas 5:19). Jesus' enemies considered him and his disciples deceivers (John 7:12, 47; Matt 27:62-63).

As in 1 John 4:2, the **deceivers** in 2 John deny that Jesus has come **in the flesh**. Some interpreters suggested that this emphasizes Jesus' *continuing* humanity. The incarnation was not a blip on the screen of eternity. This implies a permanence to the incarnation (Marshall 1978, 70; Brooke 1912, 175). Jesus continues to be very God and very man. Jones objects that this view, which became orthodox in the ecumenical creeds, exceeds the present context (2009, 259).

Strecker contends for a future sense; the eschatological coming of Christ (1996, 234-36). But this is entirely absent from the context and contrary to the present tense of **coming** (Bultmann 1973, 112). The verse clearly parallels 1 John 4:2-3, which has no expressed concern for a second advent (Jones 2009, 258).

The concern here, as in 1 John 4:2, is to counter docetic Christology (Smith 1991, 144; Bruce 1970, 140-41), the gnostic denial of the incarnation (Jones 2009, 258). These words about the incarnation—**in the flesh** (*en sarki*)—echo the Fourth Gospel's emphatic declaration: "The Word became flesh [*sarx*] and lived for a while among us" (John 1:14).

The secessionists were the **deceivers** (the "antichrists" of 1 John 2:18-23; Smith 1991, 144) who had left the Johannine churches and were denying the incarnation. They considered spirit good and the body evil. They could not embrace a fully incarnate deity or one who truly died on the cross and rose bodily from the grave. They opted for a docetic Christology (from *dokeō*, "seem" or "appear"). They believed Christ only *appeared* to inhabit flesh, but did not really do so (see Theological Themes in Introduction). They were deceivers because they claimed his humanity was a deception. The elder viewed them as embracing a spirit opposed to a truth about Christ, thus they were "anti" (against) Christ.

The **deceivers** were secessionists. They had **gone out** of the Johannine community and departed from the faith. In 1 John 2:19 going out "from us" was evidence that "they" were never really part of the community, although they were once identified with the Johannine circle of churches.

These former members were engaged in missionary activity designed to attract the Johannine Christians to adopt their contrary and competing Christology (Thomas 2004, 45). Their exit recalls the departure of Judas after Satan entered him (John 13:27, 30; Brown 1984, 668).

They **have gone out into the world,** that is, into apostasy. In **the world** was the anti-Christ locale (1 John 2:15-19). Numerous people adopted this docetic, anti-incarnational view. Although the elder refers to **many** and **any such person,** he labels them corporately with a *singular* article—**the** deceiver (*ho planos*) and **the** antichrist (*ho antichristos*). The **antichrist** wasn't future; he was "already in the world" (1 John 4:3). Nor was he an embodiment of evil in a single person. Rather he was a "spirit" (1 John 4:3) that was manifest in any and every age that fails to recognize Jesus Christ as fully human.

■ **8** The elder warns—**Watch out** (lit. ***look out for yourselves***). The phrase expresses strong caution in NT apocalyptic passages (Eph 5:15; Col 2:8; Heb 10:25; Mark 13:5; Thomas 2004, 47).

The warning was intended to prevent the loss of what they **have worked for.** The loss was possible, but could be averted. The elder's language here does not seem to refer to the potential loss of salvation, but of reward. The subjunctive mood of the verb suggests an outcome yet to be determined. One **might be rewarded fully** (a unique expression in Johannine writings). But they might choose to walk in disobedience, choose apostasy, and suffer loss.

What is the ***reward*** (*misthos*)? In the LXX, *misthos* refers to the "portion" assigned to the Levites (Num 18:31) and priests (Mic 3:11) or to a worker's pay (Exod 2:9; Deut 15:18). In the Gospels (Matt 20:8; Luke 10:7; John 10:12) *misthos* is the wages of a day laborer. The word can mean repayment (Matt 5:12; 1 Cor 3:8).

The most likely parallel to 2 John 8 is John 4:36. There "wages" (*misthos*) refers figuratively to the "harvest" reward of a successful mission (Pesch 1991, 432). Does **rewarded fully** imply the possibility of a partial reward? Probably not. The elder simply urges full obedience in hyperbole.

The text fluctuates here from the second person plural, **you all watch out,** to the first person plural, **what *we* have worked for,** and back again to the second person, **you all might receive.** Later scribes sought to smooth out these tenses (similarly the NIV uses **you** in all three instances). But the manuscript evidence favors ***we*** in the second verb (so NASB and NRSV). The language serves both to *confront*—**you** often conveys this tone—as well as to *identify with* the readers—***we.***

■ **9** Was the one **who runs ahead** (*proagōn*), "outdistancing" orthodoxy, adding "advanced" teachings to the received traditions from Jesus (Marshall 1978, 73)? Did they consider themselves progressives? This is the sense of the NASB's "goes too far" in a purported "advance teaching" (Haas, DeJonge, and Swellengrebel 1972, 146; Bruce 1970, 141). They failed to keep "in step with the Spirit" (Gal 5:25; Earle 1984, 111).

The secessionists' separation from those they had formerly walked with shaped the self-understanding of the Johannine community. They had experienced this "with us or against us" mentality early by their expulsion from the synagogues (John 9:22). Later the departure of the secessionists from them reinforced this (Brown 1979, 56).

Along with the potential for lost reward (v 8) the elder warns that whoever **does not continue in the teaching of Christ does not have God. Anyone** who separated from the faith community would **lose what** he or she had "worked for" (v 8). None is exempt from the possibility of spiritual failure. To avoiding such loss one must **continue** (lit. *remaining*). The image is not passive but relational, drawing on the imagery of the vine and branches in John 15 (where forms of the same verb are used repeatedly). To continue, or abide, is to *intentionally* stay linked to the divine life (God/Christ) and to the like-minded (the church).

Some interpreters see in 2 John an increased interest in the received teaching. It is true that *didachē*, teaching, is not found in 1 John (but see John 7:16-17; 18:19; compare 1 Tim 2:15; 2 Tim 3:14). Such a changed emphasis *might* subtly shift the focus away from the *person* of Christ to *concepts about him* (Lieu 1991, 94). But the Gospel of John does not clearly separate the *person* of Jesus and *words about him*.

John 15 calls for disciples to remain *in Christ*. But the chapter also emphasizes remaining *in Jesus' words* (15:7, 10). Both the *person* of Jesus and careful *instruction* about him are integral to Christian faith. Lieu's distinction may be more apparent than real.

What does the elder mean by **the teaching of Christ**? It may mean the received traditions *from* Jesus himself. This takes **of** to mean what Christ himself taught (a subjective genitive). But the elder may refer to **the teaching of Christ** as the standard gospel message *about* Jesus (an objective genitive; Smith 1991, 145). Either interpretation is possible (Bruce 1970, 141-42). To learn from or about **Christ** is to experience or **have God,** that is, to have **both the Father and the Son** (see 1 John 2:23).

■ **10-11** Should an itinerant teacher with an aberrant Christology come seeking lodging in one of the Johannine churches, the elder insists: **do not take him into your house or welcome him.** This refusal of hospitality expands a Jewish practice typically directed toward Gentiles. Jews religiously avoided table fellowship with Gentiles (see Acts 10:28; Gal 2:11-13). It appears that the elder adapted Jew vs. Gentile practice to erect a protective barrier against those with a docetic Christology.

The prohibition was especially against a **welcome** into one's **house**. Since early churches met in homes, the "keep out" sign specifically refused the secessionists access to teach among the Johannine believers in such houses (Brown 1979, 676). The phrase **do not . . . welcome** is literally: ***do not speak to greet him.***

To welcome false teachers was to grant them theological affirmation. To give them material support would make them accomplices, sharing equal responsibility (*koinōnei*, **participate in**) for their **wicked work** (see 1 John's use of the same term to refer to Satan in 2:13, 14; 3:12; 5:18). Hosting false teachers was like inviting Satan to dinner!

FROM THE TEXT

Solo Faith Is Not Christian Faith

Running **ahead** (v 9) pictures someone separating from the group. Running alone spiritually disconnects us from the church. In the company of other Christians we are more likely to experience occasional correction that will help us journey well.

Hospitality Offered Is an Expression of Christian Grace

To open our homes offering food, lodging, and spiritual nurture is to extend the invitation of our welcoming God. It is extending a welcome laden with spiritual implications. Shared meals build shared lives.

Hospitality Withheld May Be an Expression of Christian Principle

At what point are issues so significant that we must withhold fellowship from others? The elder does not allow for compromise on Christology. The church must discern the false from the true. We must learn to be redemptive without compromising essential, core beliefs.

The Person of Jesus and the Texts That Tell of Him

Our allegiance is to the *person* of Jesus Christ. But this must be balanced with a devotion to, and command of, the *texts* that enable us to learn about him. We are far removed from the time of Jesus. So we must depend on texts, especially the Scriptures. But we can also learn from other helpful written witnesses to the development of the Christian faith, like the ecumenical creeds and the writings of the early church. We are able to participate in the faith of our fathers and mothers because they faithfully recorded their struggles and agreements, preserving them in writing. We are heirs of "the faith that was once for all entrusted to the saints" (Jude 3) through texts and those who preserved them.

But danger lies in relying on texts to the neglect of a vital, personal faith in Christ. Such a focus might create a disconnection between head and heart, whereas a truly biblical faith is holistic (see Deut 6:5; Matt 22:37; Mark 12:30; Luke 10:27).

The Antichrist

What are we to make of the modern fascination with the **antichrist** (v 7)? The term is rare in the Bible. John says, "Antichrist is coming," but quickly enlarges the concept, saying that *already in his time* there were "many antichrists" (1 John 2:18). The elder applies the label **antichrist** to *everyone in the first century who failed to affirm a fully incarnate Christ.*

The elder had no interest in a mythic, larger-than-life, end-of-the-age incarnation of evil. Modern Christians would do well to follow the elder's lead. We should ask how **antichrist** *spirits* manifest themselves in our world and refuse to forecast or identify an eschatological *person*. What matters is how evil is already among us. How has the spirit of antichrist invaded in our lives and systems; and what can we do about such evil now? (see the sidebar "Antichrist" at 1 John 2:18).

D. Future Plans (12-13)

IN THE TEXT

■ **12** The elder had yet **much to write**. Letters can exercise apostolic authority and pastoral concern. But he realized the limitations of **paper** (*chartou*, only here in the NT) **and ink** (*melanos*, lit. "black," elsewhere only in 3 John 13 and 2 Cor 3:3 in the NT; Earle 1984, 111). The elder hoped to meet his readers **face to face** (lit. *mouth to mouth to speak*). This imagery vividly pictures intimate personal conversation. The closing lines of 3 John 13 have identical words (see the commentary).

The LXX sometimes expresses the idea of personal meetings with "mouth" (*stoma*, translated as "face" in Gen 32:30; Num 12:8). Elsewhere, "face to face" in the NIV literally translates the Greek (Deut 5:4; 34:10; Judges 6:22). In one instance, "face to face" translates "eye to eye" (Num 14:14). In Exod 33:11 it translates "presence to presence."

Early Christian Letters as Tools for Ministry

Much of the NT employs aspects of the Greco-Roman letter genre. The NT letters enhanced Christian mission across miles of necessary separation.

They affirmed faithfulness by the churches and warned against error in belief or practice. Letters instructed believers (catechetical) or defended the faith against critics (apologetics). Written contacts might mediate a change of attitude and action in an individual (Philemon) or in a group of churches (Galatians). A letter conveyed one's ideas, and in a sense became the personal presence of the writer as his words were read. At least some considered Paul's letters more effective than his preaching (2 Cor 10:10).

It can be argued that twenty-one of the twenty-seven NT books are letters of some kind. The only exceptions are the four Gospels, Acts, and Revelation. But even Revelation is *packaged* as a letter (Rev 1:4-6; 22:21). Mention of lost letters appears in the NT. Paul *received* letters from the Corinthians—"now for the matters you wrote about" (1 Cor 7:1). The remnants of a communiqué to the churches surfaces in Acts as a letter imbedded in the narrative (15:23-29). Finally, there are the seven "letters" from the risen Christ to the churches in Rev 2—3 (adapted from Ehrman 2008, 186-88; Stowers 1992, 2:290-93; Seitz 1962, 113-15).

The elder writes to a community of believers. Twice in this verse he uses plural forms of **you**. Some manuscripts, probably due to the influence of the repeated **you**, read *"your"* **joy**, while others have **our joy**. The latter expresses a better sense of their mutuality. Their shared joy would eventually *become* **complete**. This suggests that joy must mature to achieve fully the purpose for which it was given. The theme of **joy** appears in all the letters (1 John 1:4; 2 John 4, 12; 3 John 3, 4). This **joy** likely was associated with the friendship of the elder and his churches. He rejoiced in their growing doctrinal clarity.

The letter ends with a hopeful tone. The outcome from the exchange of this letter, and the expected **face to face** visit must have had a positive result. Had the "chosen lady and her children" (v 1) not embraced the elder's views, the letter probably would not have survived.

The word for **complete** (*peplēromenē*, in the perfect tense) carries the sense of ***filled up***—their mutual **joy** was nearly overflowing. The tense indicates an event with a continuing effect: ***we receive joy and continue to live in that joy.*** Such consummate **joy** among Jesus and his followers is characteristic of the Johannine writings (John 3:29; 15:11; 16:24; 17:13; 1 John 1:4; Hübner 1993, 108).

The promise of **complete** joy may anticipate the messianic age (Strecker 1996, 250). Luke metaphorically links **joy** to the gift of God's Spirit: "the disciples were filled with joy and with the Holy Spirit" (Acts 13:52).

■ **13** The elder concludes 2 John as he began, with family language. A singular expression **sister** presents an image of the church as one living, interconnected whole. Believers are **children.** The church from which the elder writes is also **chosen** (see the sidebar at v 1). This communication was not just between the elder and a church. Rather, it was his attempt to connect at least two congregations *to each other.*

The personal closing greetings of 2 John are typical. The identity and location of the recipients, the "chosen lady and her children" (v 1), and the congregation represented in the final greeting—**the children of your chosen sister**—remain a mystery.

The degree of linkage between geographically distant churches during the late first century is hard to ascertain. The NT letters testify that important ties existed. There is occasional mention of intercongregational communication in Acts. Acts 15 reports an important meeting between delegates from Antioch and leaders in Jerusalem. Acts is largely the record of apostolic journeys to visit established churches or plant new ones. So "to write" and to "talk . . . face to face" grew the church in important ways, and maintained its sense of family.

FROM THE TEXT

Ministry Through Consecrated Homes

Many first-century Christian homes welcomed itinerant ministers and their messages. The elder reported his plans to **visit** and **talk . . . face to face** with believers in such a setting (v 12). This would have meant, at the least, a meal and short-term lodging. Paul expected to be received into Philemon's home (Phlm 22). Peter enjoyed the hospitality of Simon the Tanner in Joppa (Acts 10:6), then moved to Caesarea and remained for a time in the home of a Gentile convert (Acts 10:48). Christians in Jerusalem gathered in the home of Mary, mother of John Mark (Acts 12:12). In Philippi Paul and Silas found a ready hostess in Lydia, a recent convert (Acts 16:13-16, 40).

How can our homes be more Christian in their welcome? What needs to be removed or adjusted so as to create Christ-honoring space? Let us pray and plan to advance of the kingdom of God more effectively through the atmosphere of our households.

Ministry and Relationships Mingle in Our Theology

The concerns of 2 John developed within an elder-to-church relationship, as well as person-to-person, and church-to-church. Theology and healthy practice are formed in the company of others, not in isolation.

To belong to the church is to embrace the safety of shared faith. To isolate ourselves is to invite theological error and even eventual "antichrist" (v 7) practice. So, listening to the elder, we confess that we really do need each other. We need each other to enter faith, to maintain growing faith, and to advance to a perfected faith, a faith that reaches its goal.

Admittedly, **paper and ink** (v 12) have value, as do a host of electronic communication devices. These suffice in the interims of life necessarily apart. But the best and most significant means of fleshing out the mystery of the incarnation of Christ is through personal, face-to-face, intermingled lives.

This small but significant letter is often overlooked. One rarely hears sermons from 2 John. John Calvin wrote commentaries on the Gospel of John and 1 John, but not on either 2 John or 3 John. Luther lectured on 1 John, but not on 2 John or 3 John (Smith 1991, 146). John Wesley's comments on 2 John and 3 John are a sparse, few lines (Wesley 1983, n.p.). This letter deserves renewed interest in today's churches.

3 JOHN

INTRODUCTION

A. Authorship, Date, Provenance, Audience, Occasion, Purpose, Sociological/Cultural Issues, and Textual History

See the discussion of these issues in the Introduction to this commentary.

B. Literary Features

The letter we call 3 John is the shortest book in the NT. It is unique as the only NT writing that does not mention Jesus or Christ and the only Johannine writing to refer to "the church" (vv 6, 9, 10; Culpepper 1998, 278).

The letter includes traditional aspects of classical Greco-Roman letter-writing (see the sidebar "Greco-Roman Letters" in Literary Features in the Introduction to 1 John; see Thomas 2004, 16-17, for comparisons with similar nonbiblical letters). These include the sender ("the elder"), the recipient ("Gaius"), and words of warm greeting ("whom I love in the truth").

The body of the letter addresses the concerns and hopes of the elder. The letter ends with a traditional farewell ("peace to you") and final greetings ("the friends here send their greetings" and "Greet the friends there by name"). The letter's length is typical of ancient letters, about one page. An anticipated personal visit (v 14) may suggest why the letter is so brief. The situation is pressing (v 10) and a face-to-face meeting was needed both to confront Diotrephes and to lend support to Gaius (Jones 2009, 277).

C. Theological Themes

The letter highlights hospitality as a means of supporting itinerant Christian ministers (see the sidebar "Itinerant Teachers" at 2 John 1-3). It presumes that hospitality given or withheld was based on either theological or personal differences. When one received traveling ministers, providing them with food and shelter, this hospitality expressed support for their work. Refusal to welcome them was to reject their visitors' teachings (Varughese 2005, 336). Hospitality was not simply a social matter; it was a theological issue of considerable importance in early Christianity.

Another vital theological issue was how leadership was to be gained and perpetuated. When is a leader legitimate and when not? The elder had written "to the church" (v 9) seeking support for ministers whose work he appreciated. But a local leader, Diotrephes, perhaps the church's pastor, had spurned the elder's appeal. Furthermore, Diotrephes had put people "out of the church" (v 10) who had dared to provide hospitality to the elder's traveling representatives.

Though both the elder and Diotrephes seem to have moved in the same circle of Johannine churches (van der Watt 2007, 20), a significant disagreement over authority had emerged to set them at odds. Two rival groups of traveling missionaries were competing for control of the Johannine house churches in the region (so Jones 2009, 272, although the evidence is sparse).

How autonomous were local churches in the late first century? Were there supervisory ministers to provide oversight in a region? As the Christian faith moved further away in time from its apostolic beginnings, variations of expression in widely differing locales, cultures, and languages occurred. In many instances this led to increasing independence. The obvious tension in 3 John was probably not an isolated instance. Christians then and now struggle to understand and live out the faith in the midst of cultural and interpersonal differences.

D. Hermeneutical Issues

Interpretive challenges arise in the letter. One is the statement, "I pray that you may enjoy good health" (v 2). Some Christians have taken this as a divine promise of perpetual health for believing Christians. Others understand the phrase as merely a culturally conditioned and conventional word of greeting customary in ancient letters.

The reference to "the pagans" in v 7 begs for explanation and a more sensitive translation. Such labeling raises the defenses of people. It unnecessarily drives a wedge between those who would represent the Lord God and those who have not yet accepted God's offer of grace.

The letter also brings church discipline and power struggles among church leaders into view. What might 3 John have to say about church order? Is excommunication an appropriate form of ecclesial discipline today? What is meant by putting people "out of the church" (v 10)?

COMMENTARY

VII. SUPPORTING MINISTERS AND PAINFUL SEPARATIONS: 3 JOHN 1-14

A. Greetings and Relationships (1-4)

BEHIND THE TEXT

In 2 John the elder addressed a much-loved "sister" (v 1). Here, he writes to **beloved** Gaius. In both letters his love for the recipients is **in truth** (2 John 1; 3 John 1).

Third John follows many conventions of Greco-Roman letters. When the elder writes **I pray that you may enjoy good health** (v 2) he employs a common social greeting. In a Greco-Roman letter from Egypt a young man (Aurelius Dius) greeted his father in nearly identical words: "I pray that you enjoy good health" (Ehrman 2008, 187, translation of Oxyrhynchus Papyri 10, no. 1296; see other samples in Elwell and Yarbrough 1998, 194). The NT writers were people of their own time, and their letters reflect the style of personal correspondence of that day.

IN THE TEXT

■ 1 The author calls himself **the elder** (see the commentary on 2 John 1). Whereas 2 John utilizes the language of family, 3 John inclines toward terms of friendship. The elder calls Gaius my **dear friend** (lit. *the beloved*). In 3 John every instance of **dear friend** (vv 1, 2, 5, 11) translates a form of *agapētos*. The letter also uses the term "friends" (*philoi*, twice in v 14). Nevertheless, 3 John does include some familial language ("brother" in vv 3, 5, 10; and "children" in v 4).

Who is **Gaius**? This name, common in the Roman Empire, belonged to two or three others mentioned in the NT (see 1 Cor 1:14; Acts 19:29; 20:4; Rom 16:23; Brown 1982, 702). No convincing link can be demonstrated with any of these (Culpepper 1998, 279; Marshall 1978, 81-82). So here we have yet another Gaius (Smith 1991, 149).

The elder's affection for Gaius is clear: **I love** him **in the truth** (see the sidebar "Truth" at 1 John 1:6). The Greek words for **truth** (seven times), **love** (six times), and "witness" (five times) are the most frequent in this letter. They are also common in the Gospel of John (Thomas 2004, 20). Jesus' exhortation to "love one another" (John 13:34; 15:12, 17) became an important part of the Johannine vocabulary (1 John 3:11, 23; 4:7, 11, 12; 2 John 5). The Johannine community took love to be active. It was to become visible in what one did, not simply in what one felt. Godlike love acts in Christlike ways.

What is meant by the phrase **love in the truth** (echoing 2 John 1)? The love of God manifested in Christ drew the elder and Gaius into a relationship with God, the source of all **truth**. Having been drawn to God, they found themselves drawn closer to one another.

Johannine theology centers on a belief in and the practice of **truth**. Truth became an unyielding standard for the elder, a means by which he defined those who were in the faith he considered orthodox and those who were outside. The word appears eleven times in 1 John (1:6, 8; 2:4, 8, 20, 21; 3:18, 19; 4:6; 5:6); five times in 2 John (1, 2, 3, 4); and six times in 3 John (1, 3, 4, 8, 12). The term focuses on *content*—the truths that compose *the* truth. However, truth cannot be limited to a formal catechism of foundational beliefs. Here it was something of a slogan true believers employed to distinguish themselves from the secessionists (Lieu 1991, 95).

■ 2 The elder expressed interest in Gaius' **health** and **soul** (*psychē*, in the Johannine writings usually **life;** Smith 1991, 150; Bultmann 1973, 97). The NT often speaks of *psychē* as the essential person, understood in a holistic way (Schweizer 1974, 639, 642-44). The dualism of immaterial **souls** trapped in physical bodies has no NT support.

In the Gospel of John, *psychē* refers to one's life, not to spiritual existence. As the good shepherd, Jesus lays down his life (*psychē*) for the sheep (John 10:10, 15, 17). Peter brashly claimed to be willing to "lay down [his] life" (*psychēn*, John 13:37) for Jesus. In v 2 the elder *may* use *psychē* to refer to the spiritual condition of Gaius. But more likely he merely prayed for Gaius' health in *every* aspect of his life.

The health wish (**I pray**) appears in secular letters of the period (Thomas 2004, 22). The term can invoke a deity, and thus pray. But it can also simply express a sincere wish (Greeven 1964, 775-77).

The phrase **that all may go well with you** should not be taken as an implicit divine promise of physical health at all times for all God's people. Certainly it is not a basis for a "name-it-claim-it," "health and wealth," prosperity gospel (Thomas 2004, 22). It is merely a typical secular greeting. It employs the metaphor of being led along a good (*eu*) road or path (*hodos*, Earle 1984, 112; Marshall 1978, 83; Haas, DeJonge, and Swellengrebel 1972, 150). The passive infinitive does suggest that God is the source of all true success and health (Michaelis 1967, 109-14).

■ **3** Receiving word from Gaius had evoked **great joy** (*echarēn*, see 2 John 4) in the elder. The **joy** was first experienced upon the arrival of **some brothers,** who came as Gaius' representatives. This in itself likely pleased the elder. Further, the message that Gaius and those with him persistently **walk in the truth** (*peripateis*, in the present tense) occasioned more celebration. Their walking probably had in view both their adherence to the ethical truth of loving and the christological truth of believing (Jones 2009, 268; see 1 John 3:23).

We cannot know if the news of Gaius was carried to the elder orally or by letter. The text implies oral communication (*martyrountōn*, **testifying**). But ancient letters were customarily read aloud.

■ **4** The phrase **my children** identifies a close spiritual relationship between the elder and this community of faith. Perhaps Gaius and others had come to faith through the elder's ministry. Perhaps his mentoring of these young Christians had established a family-like emotional attachment between them.

The elder was extremely pleased—**no greater joy** (see v 3 and 2 John 4)—that his **children** were following the Christian path. To walk **in the truth** emphasizes both concepts to be believed and a lifestyle to be practiced. The present participle translated **are walking** conveys the image of an ongoing journey.

The elder apparently received the news at some distance. Perhaps travel and ministry responsibilities prevented his coming to Gaius and his church as frequently as he wished. Or age and infirmity may have hindered the old man's ability to travel. So he had to be satisfied with personal messengers and letters to keep him somewhat current. He was greatly encouraged by the news that told of their continuing in the path of **truth**.

FROM THE TEXT

The Gift of Friends

How much further would God's work in the world advance if we deepened our friendships with other believers? How much more effective would our witness be if we offered genuine friendship to those not yet in the faith? How did Gaius come to faith? Who nurtured his developing discipleship? To wonder about these questions is to stand gratefully before the sweep of divine grace that brings individuals to faith in Jesus Christ and into the churches.

The Gift of Prayer and Love

The elder prays for his friend and tells him so (v 2). Love is best known when it is expressed. Praying for others is an expression of love. Love for God makes us increasingly capable of loving others. When the source of truth is our focus, we are drawn closer to all who are likewise being drawn to God.

Health and Wealth?

Taken wrongly, v 2 could be used to assert that the only acceptable Christian norm is continuous physical health and material prosperity. But this contradicts the clear sense of Scripture, as well as the experience of godly people in every age. The only ones who have ever profited from the prosperity gospel are its unscrupulous, dishonest, or morally blind preachers.

How is one to reconcile a prosperity "gospel" with Paul's testimony in 2 Cor 6:4-10 and 2 Cor 11:23-29 where his faithfulness to Christ meant suffering and losses of every kind? What is one to make of Paul's remark that he left Trophimus at Miletus "sick" (2 Tim 4:20)? Did Paul or Trophimus lack the faith necessary for healing? What shall we do about Paul's "thorn in the flesh" (2 Cor 12:7-10)? How are we to deal honestly with those in any generation whose Christian life and walk is undeniable, but who struggle with physical infirmities, financial need, or wounded relationships through no fault of their own? What consolation can we offer

Christian mothers in impoverished corners of the world who still see half their babies die in infancy?

Real Joy

In what does **joy** consist? Many say, "In plenty of material goods." But these are easily lost and ultimately unsatisfying. What about fame? Fame is fleeting. Maybe power? But power can erode intimacy and fracture trust, if it is not carefully controlled. Pleasure? Pleasure is only truly satisfying if it can be enjoyed in the presence of a holy God and remembered without regret.

For the elder the greatest **joy** came in celebrating life in Christ with others. The elder's declaration that news of spiritual fidelity was his greatest joy should give us pause. Have we settled for lesser things, things that compete for the place of this **no greater joy** (v 4).

B. Ministry and Hospitality (5-8)

BEHIND THE TEXT

The absolute use of **the Name** (v 7) is intriguing. God placed his divine name in particular places—the tabernacle, the temple, the ark of the covenant, and in Jerusalem (Deut 12:21; 26:2; 2 Sam 6:2; 1 Kgs 3:2; 5:3, 5; 8:17, 20; 2 Kgs 21:4, 7). The phrase "my name," referring to God, occurs well over one hundred times in the Bible. The phrase is spoken by the earthly Jesus two dozen times in the Gospels in reference to himself. The resurrected Lord speaks of "my name" in Acts (9:15, 16) and Revelation (2:3, 13; 3:8).

The Greek term *kyrios*, used in the LXX for God, came to be used of Jesus by NT writers. The same sort of development seems to have occurred with "the name." This is the nearest the elder comes to naming Jesus in 3 John (Marshall 1978, 86 n. 10).

Christian missionaries seeking to make God's name known traveled widely, by faith, trusting for the prayers and material support of God's people. Receiving a traveling minister into one's home was an important means of support for their work (see the sidebar "Itinerant Teachers" in 2 John, Behind the Text).

IN THE TEXT

■ **5** The elder continues with warm, relational language—**Dear friend**. He commends Gaius' faithfulness for having served the **brothers**. Such a welcoming spirit transformed **strangers** (*zenos*, or "guests"; Bruce 1970, 149) into friends (Jones 2009, 269). Gaius *lived* faithfulness (lit. *faithful you are doing*).

The elder assumed a strong network of Christians who, although spread over a wide region, were committed to support one another. This faith network led to tangible acts. Gaius and others in his church had already treated the elder's messengers well (v 6). The letter encourages Gaius' continued generosity.

■ **6** This is the first instance of **church** (*ekklēsia*) in the Johannine writings. It appears again in vv 9-10 and twenty times in Revelation. Though limited in use, the term is part of the developing first-century Christian vocabulary (Brown 1982, 710).

Gaius and the church are urged to **send** the elder's representatives—"the brothers" (v 5)—**on their way.** This was a polite and indirect way of requesting aid (food, money, housing arrangements, traveling companions) for missionaries (Thomas 2004, 26; Haas, DeJonge, and Swellengrebel 1972, 152). This phrase, found only here in the NT, resembles Paul's wish expressed to the churches in Rome that they would "assist [him] on [his] journey" to Spain (Rom 15:24; see Acts 15:3; 1 Cor 16:6, 11; 2 Cor 1:16; Titus 3:13). **You will do well** is an idiomatic way of conveying a request or expressing thanks in advance (Marshall 1978, 85; Bruce 1970, 150).

The elder's standard for hospitality is **in a manner worthy of God** (see Col 1:10; 2 Thess 2:12). The theme echoes the teaching of Jesus: "Whatever you did for one of the least of these brothers of mine, you did for me" (Matt 25:40). The epistle to the Hebrews conveys a similar thought: "Do not forget to entertain strangers, for by so doing some people have entertained angels without knowing it" (13:2). While generosity can be abused, the call to honor those who honor God calls for erring on the side of generosity (Marshall 1978, 86).

The missionary enterprise in the first century was sustained in two important ways. Early Christian missionaries were often bivocational, like Paul—a "tent maker" (Acts 18:3). The advance of the gospel also depended on the generosity of ordinary Christians who provided food, shelter, encouragement, and money. Paul intended to visit the Christians in Rome—"after I have enjoyed your company for a while." He politely expressed his hope for hospitality and financial support for his mission to Spain from Christians in Rome, most of whom were strangers to him when he wrote (Rom 15:24).

Paul also wrote of several offerings coming to him from Philippi (Phil 4:16, 18). The Philippians, however, seem to be an exception among his churches. He writes that in "the early days" they alone had supported him in this way (Phil 4:15). So financial support was uneven, if Paul's case is representative.

A cluster of phrases in 3 John seem to reflect a developing structure in the Johannine churches, especially related to missionary activity. The phrases **send them on** and **worthy of God** (v 6) and **work together** (v 8), all imply a network of Christian workers. This arrangement is more characteristic of the Pauline tradition (Lieu 1991, 93). But there is sufficient overlap between Paul's travels and the geographical locations associated with John to understand these phrases as a helpful window into early church practice generally.

■ **7** The traveling preachers **went out,** perhaps a technical term for evangelistic activity (Jones 2009, 270), **for the sake of the Name.** Paul writes of "the name that is above every name" and that it is "the name of Jesus" that will someday cause all to bow and confess him as Lord (Phil 2:10). Acts 4:12 is similar: "Salvation is found in **no** one else, for there is **no other name** under heaven given to men by which we must be saved." The Jerusalem apostles rejoiced "because they had been counted worthy of suffering disgrace for the Name" (Acts 5:41). The absolute use of **the Name** is also found in Ignatius' letters to the Ephesians and Philadelphia (Brooke 1912, 185).

The phrase for the **sake of the Name** derives from numerous OT precedents. There the "name" is that of the Lord God (1 Sam 12:22; Pss 25:11; 31:3; 79:9; 109:21; Isa 45:4; 48:9; Jer 14:7, 21; Ezek 20:9, 14, 22, 44; 36:22). But in 3 John, **the Name** probably refers to Jesus (Jones 2009, 270; Painter 2002, 373; Marshall 1978, 86; Bultmann 1973, 99; Bruce 1970, 150).

In other Johannine passages, "the name" refers *primarily* to Jesus (John 1:12; 2:23; 3:18; 14:13, 26; 15:16, 21; 16:23, 26; 20:31; 1 John 2:12; 3:23; 5:13). *Occasionally* it is applied to the Father (John 10:25 by Jesus; in 12:13, by the crowd *about God* as they celebrate the coming of *Jesus* into Jerusalem).

Acts reflects a developing use of "the name" associated with Jesus (Acts 5:41; 9:16; 15:26; 21:13). Jesus speaks in a striking way in the Fourth Gospel—"Holy Father, protect them by the power of your name—the name *you gave me*" (John 17:11, emphasis added). Then he adds, "I protected them and kept them safe by that name *you gave me*" (John 17:12, emphasis added). For the biblical authors, one's "name" (*onoma*) and the person it represents are inseparable. So to speak in behalf of **the Name** was to speak with the understanding that Christ was present in the speaking (Strecker 1996, 259).

The elder reports **no help from the pagans** (*ethnikōn*). The NRSV translation has "non-believers." This may be the best option (Painter 2002, 370; Smith 1991, 152). Culpepper insists that the usual translation elsewhere in the NT, "Gentiles" (NASB), cannot be the meaning here. All three names in 3 John are typical Gentile names (1998, 280). The elder apparently used this term for non-Christians rather than as an ethnic distinction of Jews vs. Gentiles.

The elder's point would be that Christians should support Christian ministries and not expect unbelievers to do so (Smith 1991, 152). It is God's people who bear the responsibility for funding God's work. While generosity from not-yet-Christian people can be accepted (see Acts 10), the major appeal to generous giving to support missionary work is to people within Christian circles.

■ **8** The elder depicts **hospitality** as an expected expression of generous support of missionaries. This is clear from his insertion of the emphatic pronoun **we** (*hēmeis*; Bruce 1970, 151). His intent is clear: ***we indeed ourselves ought to receive such as these.*** Hospitality would include lodging, food, and money for the future travel of such missionaries (v 6).

When people like Gaius and those with him supported **such men,** the churches involved share their ministries: **we . . . work together for the truth.** Some Christians were planting the gospel in new geographical soil and among diverse people groups. Others provided a support system, the material means enabling itinerant evangelists and missionaries to be free to devote more time to preaching and teaching.

The germ of the missionary concept is in this passage. The work of God is worldwide and all Christ's followers are enlisted in this **work.** God employs people as ***workers*** **together** (*synergoi*). The verb *ginōmetha*, ***that we may become,*** suggests a decision to be made. The verb is preceded by *hina*, indicating purpose. The elder intended his writing to motivate the churches he addressed to become co-laborers with God and with each other.

The appearance of **the truth** is the fifth such instance in 3 John (with two more to come). The **truth** of Christ is the common bond of Christian heart-to-heart connections ("love in the truth," v 1). Truth calls for faithfulness (v 3) that is ongoing (see vv 3, 4). It testifies to a person's character (v 12), and flows out from the faithful (v 12). The elder calls his readers to **work together** in behalf of *the* **truth.**

FROM THE TEXT

Support for Those in Ministry

Generous support for evangelism and missions is thoroughly biblical and Christian. Unfortunately, a few ministers presume that being cared for in lavish ways is their due. This sense of entitlement leads to a wrong-spirited habit of taking advantage of the kindness of others. There is a vast difference between necessary support for daily needs (food, clothing, shelter) and using ministry for extravagant personal gain.

Sharing with Others in Ministry

The church is not defined by the pronoun "I," but rather by "we." Together we achieve results we could not individually. The work of God in the world advances as we live in community and in the truth (vv 3-4). The truth that flows from God impels us to engage in evangelism, telling the truth to those not yet convinced. The human hunger for truth may lead them to God.

C. Dangerous Division (9-10)

IN THE TEXT

■ 9 Strecker thinks the phrase **I wrote to the church** alludes to 2 John (1996, 253-54, 263). But the evidence is not compelling. Bruce, after discussing the possibilities, concludes that the reference is to a now lost letter (1970, 152; also Marshall 1978, 88).

Jones considers the Greek *ti* (**something**, left untranslated in some English versions) tantalizing, but not specific (2009, 271). The elder's previous letter had apparently not achieved its intended result.

The elder asserts that **Diotrephes . . . loves to be first,** and **will have nothing to do with us.** The Greek has simply *he does not receive us.* The same words in v 10 describe what **Diotrephes** does to the elder's representatives—"the brothers" (vv 5 and 10). The translation "does not acknowledge our authority" (NRSV) is not textually defensible (BDAG 2000, 370). Translation is best served by *does not receive* in both passages (Mitchell 1998, 317).

The elder wrote to **Gaius** because Diotrephes had refused hospitality to traveling ministers affiliated with the elder (v 10). Consequently, the elder accuses Diotrephes of placing himself above ministry, saying he **loves to be first.** The Greek word *philoprōteuōn* (from *phileō*, to love, and *prōtos*, first) appears nowhere else in the NT or in noncanonical Christian literature. It was perhaps coined by the elder to disparage Diotrephes (Bultmann 1973, 100).

In 1 Cor 5:9-13, Paul wrote of putting one "who calls himself a brother" out of the church because he had sinned and gave no evidence of repentance. If that kind of action is in view in 3 John, then the elder's group is being treated by Diotrephes as unrepentant sinners!

What would cause such a deep divide in a community bound together by love? It is tempting to insert the scenario of 2 John into 3 John. This reading might suggest that the elder and his group held an orthodox, incarnational Christology; and Diotrephes and his church were a docetic-leaning secessionist group (so Jones 2009, 272, 274). But the letter read alone gives no such suggestion (Thomas 2004, 18; Marshall 1978, 90). Lieu sees a war of words and name-calling, but finds no theological basis for the debate (1991, 92). Here, an interpreter's assumptions about the origin of the three works plays a powerful influence in how one reads them (see the Introduction to 1 John).

Painter cites the similar "wicked work" language of 2 John 11 and the evil **gossiping** words of 3 John 10 and the views of Diotrephes as evidence that he was one of the false teachers (2002, 364-65, 375). But if Diotrephes was aligned with a false Christology, the elder fails to label him as a deceiver or worse (Culpepper 1998, 281; Smith 1991, 154).

Third John may be evidence of some kind of power struggle between two church leaders in the Johannine churches (van der Watt 2007, 20-21). Bultmann repeats Harnack's suggestion (1897) that the conflict was over congregational organization (1973, 100).

■ **10** The elder writes **if I come,** using the subjunctive mood. Although his prospective visit remained in the uncertain future, he seems to state something he fully expected to happen (Haas, DeJonge, and Swellengrebel 1972, 154). In 1 John 2:28, "when he appears" similarly refers to the certainty of Christ's future appearing. Only its timing was uncertain. So the elder promises that perhaps ***when*** he does accomplish a visit he **will call attention to,** or show in its true light (Brooke 1912, 189), the malicious words being spoken falsely about him.

Does the elder imply a public face-off, a dispute before the congregation, was in the offing? The elder seems to assume that he should have some influence over Diotrephes. Or at least he contends for such influence (compare Gal 2:11-14).

The elder lodges several charges against Diotrephes. He has spoken evil of the elder and his followers. He has been **gossiping maliciously,** spreading false charges against him (Earle 1984, 113). Further, Diotrephes has refused hospitality to the elder's representatives—**the brothers.** This demonstrates an ironic reversal of 2 John 10-11. There the elder prescribes a refusal of hospitality to the representatives of the secessionists. In 3 John, the elder and his trusted associates are on the receiving end of the practice! This ecclesiastical tactic was used by various parties to their own purposes (Bruce 1970, 154). But as Brown reminds us, in a quite dualistic-minded community like the Johannine circles, such sharp lines of difference were to be expected (1982, 747).

The resistance from Diotrephes, however, went beyond refusing to receive those approved by the elder. Any who offered hospitality to the elder's group he put **out of the church.** The verb *ekballō*, **puts . . . out,** means throw out or away. It describes what Jesus did to demons (Matt 8:16; Mark 1:34) and to the moneychangers in the temple (Matt 21:12). It describes how the "Spirit sent [*ekballei*] [Jesus] out into the desert" (Mark 1:12). In a dramatic scene after Jesus' synagogue sermon in his hometown, the people of Nazareth "drove him out [*exebalon*] of the town" (Luke 4:29).

The word obviously has strong force. It calls for a formal action. Clarke (n.d., 942) used the term "excommunicated." But it may have been more informal pressure by Diotrephes that stirred up the congregation and isolated certain members (Haas, DeJonge, and Swellengrebel 1972, 156). If Diotrephes hosted the house church, his actions can be thought of as local discipline and not an overarching ecclesiastical decision (Painter 2002, 376-77).

Regardless, the word in this context suggests an expulsion of some sort of those who were providing hospitality to the elder's representatives (Brooke 1912, 190-91). An illustration of a similar practice appears in the Gospel where the man born blind but healed by Jesus was thrown out (*exebalon*) as a result of confessing his faith in Christ (John 9:34). There, the former blind man was thrown out of the synagogue by the Jewish leaders (9:22, 34).

Although Diotrephes was a person of some authority, his position seems not to have prevailed. The survival and canonization of this little letter suggests that the elder's appeal was successful (Bruce 1970, 153). Otherwise the NT may have included letters written by Diotrephes!

FROM THE TEXT

Position-Seeking Is Contrary to Christ's Spirit

How can a Christian love **to be first** (v 9) when Jesus said, "If anyone wants to be first, he must be the very last, and the servant of all" (Mark

9:35)? But the people of God are not immune to the allure of power, even if within the petty "kingdom" of a small local church. Those who would follow after, and be shaped by, Jesus, would do well to recall his testimony, "I am among you as one who serves" (Luke 22:27).

Good Christian people involved in ministry for Jesus' sake will sometimes differ, even deeply. Acts reports "sharp disagreement" between Paul and Barnabas over John Mark's role in early Christian ministry (Acts 15:36-40).

Seeking Power Can Undermine Relationships

Whenever position and power become primary considerations in the life of a church, relationships are wounded and sometimes broken. The interconnectedness of the body of Christ (1 Cor 12:27) means that both suffering and honor for one person becomes the experience of the whole body (1 Cor 12:26). Position-seeking that wounds calls for confession, repentance, and forgiveness.

The Malicious Use of the Tongue Causes Deep Rifts in Relationships

When position and power are threatened, mean-spirited words can erupt. How better to defend ourselves than by castigating another? How better to improve our position than by degrading that of others? But how unchristlike! Deep harm can come from words spoken more out of self-interest than as reasoned, prayerful responses that aim for the health of the church (see Jas 3:1-12).

D. Healing Words and Hope (11-14)

IN THE TEXT

■ 11 The elder cautions his readers, **do not imitate what is evil.** He likely referred to what Diotrephes was doing. He urged his readers, rather, to model themselves after **what is good.** The language here is similar to Paul's (see Eph 5:1; 1 Thess 1:6; 2 Thess 2:14). While the English word "mimic" derives from the Greek word here, "model after another" is preferable.

Doing what is **good** here echoes 1 John 2:29, where doing "what is right" gives evidence that one has been born of God. The idea surfaces in a negative sense in 1 John 3:10—"anyone who does not do what is right is not a child of God." For the elder there was no such thing as a faith that left one's ethics untouched. Children of God will give evidence of this in their daily choices for the good and against evil.

From God

The phrase "from God" (*ek tou theou*) is prominent in the Johannine literature. It suggests that one's origin is from God (Jones 2009, 275). In 1 John 4:2-7 the phrase appears seven times. The words are associated with testing spirits in 1 John 4:1-3. The phrase affirms that Johannine Christians are from God, his "dear children" (4:4); and that "love comes from God" (4:7). Anyone not doing "what is right" is not from God (3:10).

None of the Synoptic Gospels uses the phrase. The Gospel of John, by contrast, has eleven occurrences. Most are on the lips of Jesus (6:46; 7:17; 8:40, 42; 13:3; 16:27, 30). Paul used the phrase extensively with a wide array of applications. In most instances, the phrase refers to divine qualities (like comfort, holiness, power, righteousness, wisdom) or to the divine presence in the person of the Holy Spirit (1 Cor 2:12; 6:19).

In this wide usage across the NT, the major interest in "from God" is to the origin of Christ (and his followers). But it also characterizes their purpose and destiny. Being "from God" can be the basis of a future reward (2 John 8) and specifically of the hope of Christ's coming (2 John 7). But God's truth and presence is already manifest in believers. Thus, being "from God" is both already and not yet (Strecker 1996, 266).

The elder claims that his opponents, Diotrephes and his followers, have **not seen God**. This is a clear reversal to the positive in 1 John 1:1, 3—"we have seen." The opponents are not faithful witnesses to Christ, but "a stranger to him" (Wesley 1983, n.p.).

The close biblical juxtaposition of **good** and **evil** begins as early as "the tree of the knowledge of good and evil" in Gen 2:9. The pair of polar opposites appears over thirty times in the OT and over twenty times in the NT. But the only other occurrence of this **good** and **evil** couplet in the Johannine literature is in the Fourth Gospel. There, Jesus speaks of future resurrection and judgment: "All who are in their graves will . . . come out—those who have done **good** will rise to live, and those who have done **evil** will rise to be condemned" (John 5:29).

■ **12** **Demetrius** was obviously one in whom the elder had confidence. He describes him as **well spoken of by everyone** (see on v 3). The words are obviously hyperbolic, since Diotrephes' group clearly did not share this view. The phrase, containing a perfect passive participle, suggests a life proven over time (Jones 2009, 276).

The elder writes that **even . . . the truth itself** testifies to the character of Demetrius. This personification of **truth** (see John 8:32; 2 John 2) and the linking of "Spirit" and "truth" in the Johannine writings (John 14:17;

16:13; 1 John 5:6) suggests that this may be a quiet description of the Holy Spirit (Brooke 1912, 192-93).

It is one thing to measure up well against the expectations of others. But to measure up well against the objective standard that speaks of the highest kind of character is noteworthy. The elder writes, **we also speak well of** Demetrius. By using **we,** the elder speaks for himself and all those allied with him. Three witnesses vouch for Demetrius—the Johannine community, the truth itself, and the elder. This accords with the Torah requirement of Deut 19:15 (Thomas 2004, 33).

Who was this **Demetrius,** besides the probable courier of the letter (Jones 2009, 276; Burge 2009, 422; Marshall 1978, 93)? The name occurs twice in the Bible, here and in Acts 19. We should resist the temptation to link them. The Demetrius in Acts (19:24, 38) was a working adult when Paul was in Ephesus no later than the mid-50s. He would have been an old man by the time 3 John was written in the 90s. It is unlikely that the same person was a traveling minister in his declining years.

The elder's preference for certain words shows up in this sentence. He uses forms of *martyria* (**witness** or **testimony**) three times, and *alētheia* (**truth**) twice (see the sidebar "Truth" at 1 John 1:6). The assertion **our testimony is true** recalls John 19:35 and 21:24. Words declaring the truth of one's testimony seem to have become standard among the Johannine churches (Smith 1991, 158).

■ **13** The elder acknowledges that his letter leaves much unsaid: **I have much to write** (see John 20:30). The farewell remarks in the letter are similar to those in 2 John 12, although specific words vary. Some of the variety is due to the fact that 2 John is written to a church ("the chosen lady and her children," 2 John 1), whereas 3 John is directed to an individual ("my dear friend Gaius," 3 John 1). As in 2 John, the elder speaks of his reluctance to write at length, preferring to see his recipient in person (v 14). The elder writes with a **pen,** literally ***a reed*** sharpened to a point for use as a writing instrument.

■ **14** The elder, as all the other authors of NT documents, appreciated the value of the written word. But the elder also knew the power of a personal visit. One's presence usually communicates more than a faceless document. So the elder desired to see Gaius in person (on **face to face,** see the commentary on 2 John 12). Literally, he refers to speaking mouth to mouth, a culturally appropriate metaphor for personal conversation. The elder anticipates that their meeting may be **soon,** shortly after the arrival of the letter (Bruce 1970, 156).

The elder closes his letter with a benediction. This is v 15 in the Greek text (so NRSV), but the NIV and NASB combine it with v 14. This is a grace-filled Hebraic benediction: **peace to you.** Paul typically combined the Hebraic benediction of peace (*shalom*) and a modified Greek greeting of "grace" (*charis,* a variation of the standard *charein,* to greet). The author of 3 John, however, refers only to **peace.**

While this was a standard convention of letter writing of the time, it stands in some tension with the obviously strained relationship between himself and Diotrephes. Perhaps the elder offers the word as not only a customary social exchange, but as something more—a prayer for reconciliation among the churches. In a letter concerning strife in the church, this Hebraic greeting is striking. Perhaps, peace was forever cemented into Christian vocabulary by its use by the risen Christ (John 20:19, 21, 26). The elder must have prayed it would have a calming effect in his churches (Boice 1979, 173).

The letter closes with traditional greetings, both from **the friends here** with the elder and to **the friends there** with Gaius. The elder urged his readers to greet their fellow believers **by name,** but does not list them. Occasionally, other NT letters greet specified individuals by name (Rom 16:1-15; Col 4:15; 2 Tim 4:19). Several other NT letters conclude with a similar more general greeting to all. The language of **friends** may suggest the greetings were directed to all those who agreed with the elder (Marshall 1978, 94-95). This implies a circle of friends to which Gaius belongs, but who may not acknowledge the authority of Diotrephes (Bultmann 1973, 103).

This short letter depicts the elder as an outsider, facing opposition from other Christians. Still, he has the authority of his personal standing among the churches and seeks to exercise it. That 3 John became a part of the NT suggests that the elder's understanding of Johannine Christianity in the region prevailed as the orthodox view.

FROM THE TEXT

Labeling Others

While terms such as "evil" and "good" flow freely in the Johannine letters, name-calling is seldom a persuasive argument for the rightness of one's position. Labeling another as "evil" or "godless" has more potential for breaking relationships than for restoring them. Might Diotrephes have been more easily reconciled to the others in the community if the elder had not maligned him as loving **to be first** (v 9)? The public affirmation of

Demetrius surely encouraged him to do even better in the future. Perhaps, the lesson for us is to assume that other Christians act out of the best of intentions and to be slow to condemn. This compels us to give the elder the advantage of the doubt, even if we must hesitate to follow his example in characterizing our opponents.

Choices Reflect the Orienting Center of Our Life

Who and what we commit to define us. Choices lead to habits, and habits form our character. When our lives are totally surrendered to the lordship of Christ, the evidence flows naturally from within us. To live at peace with one another requires that we all live in an intimate, loving relationship with God, the source of love and of all that is good and true. **Peace to you** (v 14).

www.ingramcontent.com/pod-product-compliance
Lightning Source LLC
Chambersburg PA
CBHW070804230426
43665CB00017B/2476